Souvenir Programs

OF TWELVE CLASSIC MOVIES
1927-1941

edited by

MILES KREUGER

DOVER PUBLICATIONS, INC., NEW YORK

Published in Canada by General Publishing Company, Ltd., 30 Lesmill Road, Don Mills, Toronto, Ontario.
Published in the United Kingdom by Constable and Company, Ltd., 10 Orange Street, London WC 2.

Souvenir Programs of Twelve Classic Movies, 1927-1941, first published by Dover Publications, Inc., in 1977, is a new selection of original programs from the collection of the Institute of the American Musical, Inc. (Miles Kreuger, President). See the individual booklets for dates, printers, distributors and publishers.

International Standard Book Number: 0-486-23423-1
Library of Congress Catalog Card Number: 76-20162

Manufactured in the United States of America
Dover Publications, Inc.
180 Varick Street
New York, N.Y. 10014

Foreword

All the films represented in this collection of souvenir programs are today regarded as screen classics or at least films of considerable historic importance. Yet the eminence of the pictures themselves was purely speculative when the publicity departments of the various studios assigned their staff writers and designers to prepare these programs. Lacking the support of eventual critical and public acclaim, the writers were armed with only the basic facts about the films (casts, production staffs, etc.) and their own intuition about what might or might not be important or interesting about each work.

Because of the nonscholarly approach of their authors, the programs contain marvelous pieces of information that have often been bypassed in the more intellectual body of criticism that has developed around each film. Regarding even a masterpiece like Orson Welles's *Citizen Kane,* on which hundreds of essays, articles, and books have been written, it is not common knowledge that Welles wears 37 different costumes in the picture, or that the giant fireplace at Xanadu measures 25 feet in width and 18 feet in depth, or that Welles's brilliant makeup is largely the work of Maurice Seiderman.

Of somewhat greater historical interest is a description of the precise action that takes place in the original opening reel of *Lost Horizon,* which was allegedly destroyed by director Frank Capra following an early preview. We learn that, unlike most pictures, *Grand Hotel* was shot virtually in the sequence in which its scenes appear in the final print. We learn that Carl Laemmle, Jr., producer of *All Quiet on the Western Front,* first offered the leading role to the book's author, Erich Maria Remarque, and when he turned it down discovered Lew Ayres, who was at that time a musician in the dance band at the Cocoanut Grove.

We even discover that Charlie Chaplin filmed his dual roles in *The Great Dictator* at different speeds. To retain the silent-movie aura for the barber character, the camera turned at only 16 frames a second, while the dictator was shot at 25 frames a second.

When projected at normal speeds, the barber's movements would naturally be speeded up to suggest the jerkiness of silent-movie action.

These souvenir programs also contain minutely detailed production histories of *Captains Courageous, The Good Earth, Lost Horizon, Gone with the Wind,* and other pictures, in addition to cast and production-staff data on all the movies.

For the first half of this century, almost all souvenir programs for Broadway shows and later for Hollywood movies were priced at 25 cents. While this may seem inexpensive by comparison to today's prices, one must remember how meager salaries were for most Americans, and that during the Depression a quarter could buy a modest meal in many adequate restaurants.

Although infrequently seen today, early souvenir programs, many of them published by the late Al Greenstone, were issued for almost every major motion picture released from the mid-1920's until the paper shortage of World War Two. We have selected for this volume 12 major films, including four Oscar winners for best picture of the year: *The Broadway Melody* (1929), *All Quiet on the Western Front* (1930), *Grand Hotel* (1932), and *Gone with the Wind* (1939).

This is not film history being analyzed in retrospect. These are reproductions of the actual programs that were held in the hands of first-nighters attending the world premiere of *Gone with the Wind* on December 15, 1939, at Loew's Grand, Atlanta, or *Grand Hotel* on April 12, 1932, at the Astor. At the next Chaplin festival, be sure to bring along this book and pretend you are watching *The Great Dictator* at its dual premiere engagements at the Astor and Capitol on Broadway, or simply turn on your television set when one of the other pictures is broadcast and have your own, private first night. All it takes is a little imagination.

Miles Kreuger

December 2, 1975
New York City

Contents

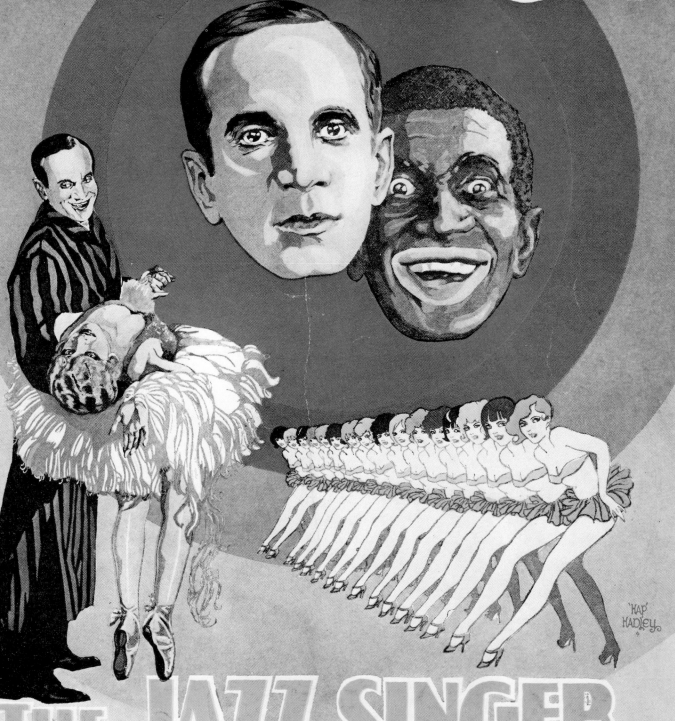

THE WORLD'S GREATEST ENTERTAINER

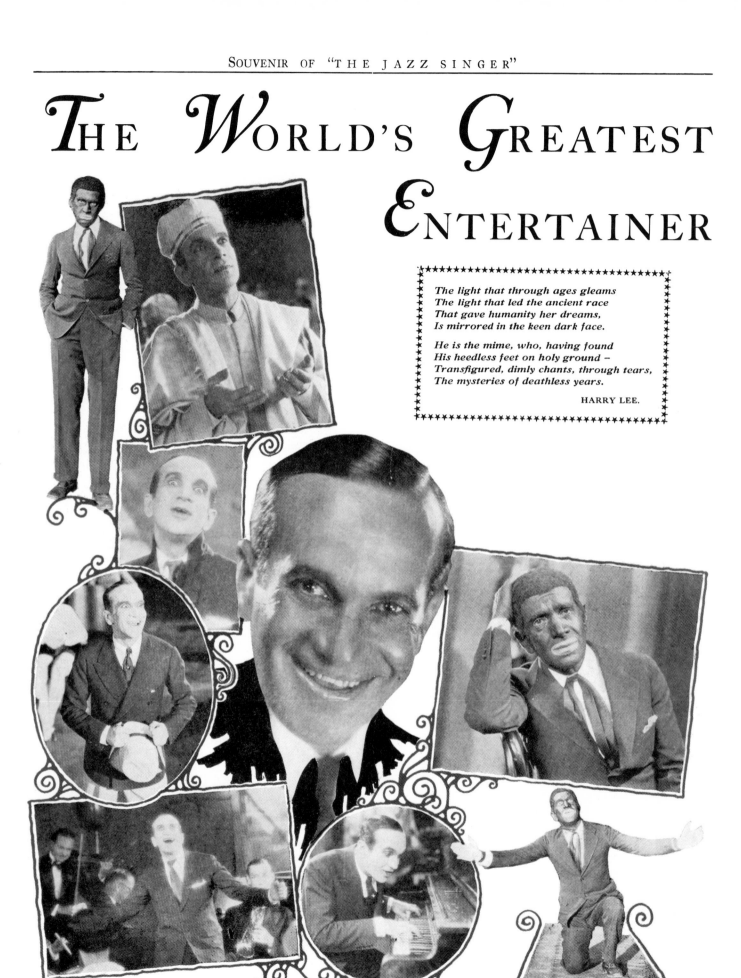

WARNER BROS.
SUPREME TRIUMPH

AL JOLSON

in

"The Jazz Singer"

Characters	*Players*
JAKIE RABINOWITZ later JACK ROBIN	AL JOLSON
Mary Dale	May McAvoy
Cantor Rabinowitz	Warner Oland
Sara Rabinowitz	Eugenie Besserer
Cantor Josef Rosenblatt	By Himself
Moisha Yudelson	Otto Lederer
Jakie (13 years old)	Bobbie Gordon
Harry Lee	Richard Tucker
Levi	Nat Carr
Buster Billings	William Demarest
Dillings	Anders Randolf
Doctor	Will Walling

Concert Number by Cantor Josef Rosenblatt

Based upon the play by Samson Raphaelson as produced on the spoken stage by Lewis and Gordon and Sam H. Harris

Director	ALAN CROSLAND
Scenario	Alfred A. Cohn
Assistant Director	Gordon Hollingshead
Cameraman	Hal Mohr
General Press Representative	A. P. Waxman

*Vitaphone Synchronization Arranged
And Conducted By Louis Silvers.*

ENTIRE PRODUCTION AND VITAPHONE SYNCHRONIZATION
PRODUCED BY WARNER BROS. STUDIOS, HOLLYWOOD, CAL.

3

The Story

TONIGHT Jakie left the house ratner warily. Hereafter he must be very careful. How was he to know that his father would object so violently to the career he had chosen? It had all come out the night before when Jakie had broken the Synagogue window and his father had finished his reprimand with:

"You ought to be ashamed, Jakie. A fine Cantor you are going to be, smashing synagogue windows."

"I don't want to be a Cantor—I want to sing in a theayter!" Jakie had replied

Jakie knew he had said enough. He listened to his father going into the details of his family history. He was a Cantor, and the family of Rabinowitzes had been cantors for five generations back—and Jakie must be a Cantor too. Jakie had learned long ago not to interrupt his father at a time like this. When it was all over, Jakie understood more than ever how careful he would have to be.

And tonight when he left the house, he wondered if anyone suspected. Muller's Cafe had never seemed so far away. After intricate windings and many crossings through the Ghetto, he finally arrived at a low crude building and slipped through the swinging door marked "Family Entrance." He walked quickly past the bar, called to the piano player just below stage, and stepped upon the platform.

He was at ease now. Jakie was always at ease on a platform. He could sing for hours and manage to forget his audience completely. It was curious to see the business personality Jakie assumed after he finished each song. Coins were flying from every direction, and Jakie picked up each one. Then the piano player struck up a jazz number, and the boy began to sing in his best darkey manner. Just when he started the chorus, he heard the door hinges creak, and saw his father coming up the aisle. Jakie turned ashen white. He stopped singing when the Cantor jumped up on the platform, and dragged him down by the collar. Now Jakie's face was red. He was ashamed before all these people who had been so kind to him. He could never never go back there again.

At home Cantor Rabinowitz explained to his wife.

"I will teach him he shall never again use his voice for such low songs. He will be a Cantor."

He seized Jakie by the shoulder and raised his hand to strike him, but Sara stopped his arm.

"It will do no good, Papa — and anyway Jakie must get ready for Shule. It is nearly Yom Kippur."

The Cantor pushed her aside, still determined to do his duty by Jakie who was now looking up at him with renewed courage.

"If you whip me again, Papa, I'll run away."

Jakie's rebellion only made matters worse. A few minutes later Sara put her hands over her ears in order not to hear Jakie's cries from the bedroom. And she wept because she knew Jakie. He had meant what he said about leaving home.

Three thousand miles away from the Ghetto in a little restaurant called "Coffee Dan's" Jack Robin, who used to be known as Jakie Rabinowitz ten years ago, and a friend of his were eating bacon and eggs with an appetite that showed they had not been having three meals a day. When they had finished their food, Jack's friend Buster stepped over to the manager, talked to him a few minutes, and then came back with the news that Jack had a job for the evening.

Jack Robin sang his best that night. It was a new place — and there might be opportunities waiting for him. But perhaps the real reason was that while he was singing, he noticed two blue eyes looking up at him from below — and a charming face smiling her approval.

Everyone knew Mary Dale by sight—that is, everyone in vaudeville. Buster introduced them.

"I think your voice would get you a long ways," she said. "You sing jazz, but its different — there's a tear in it."

Jack looked at her gratefully. He had had such a hard time even though his jazz was "different" that a few words like Mary's — especially coming from her — were stimulating.

"—and if you come over to the Orpheum tomorrow I'd like to introduce you to the manager."

* * *

BACK in the Ghetto Cantor Rabinowitz sat at the table in the living room of the Rabinowitz home, listening to a frail very homely youngster singing. The Cantor interrupted him.

"You must sing it with a sigh, Moey, — like you are crying out to your God."

Moey tried again, but he was stopped once more. The Cantor shook his head.

"I wish I had my Jakie here — he could show you how to sing it." Moey looked up at him curiously.

"He ran away, didn't he?"

OF "THE JAZZ SINGER"

"I have no boy," the Cantor corrected.

"But, insisted Moey," Mike Lefkowitz says your boy is a singer in a theayter out West."

"That is all for today — come back tomorrow."

Sara wept silently. She alone knew how much Papa was hurting himself, but she was sure that even if he wanted to relent, he would not allow himself to do it now. And day after day she sat and listened to him instructing the other boys while both of them thought only of Jakie. Jakie must be a big man now! His last letter had told of his success in vaudeville, — and a prospective trip to New York to play the lead in a musical comedy. Maybe he would come soon — their Jakie.

The next night when Cantor Rabinowitz was at his Sunday school class Mama sat by the window knitting. Suddenly a man stood in the doorway. The man was holding out his arms to her and was calling her "Mama."

It was a wonderful reunion. Jack Robin had to tell her everything, especially about Mary Dale who had gone to New York to work in a musical comedy — and now suddenly he too had been called here — like Mary Dale. And Mama, Mary Dale was a lovely girl — and he wanted her to meet Mary. But Mary wasn't Jewish—would that make any difference? And would Mama like to hear him play and sing one of his famous jazz tunes?

Perhaps if he hadn't played, things might have been different — but when Cantor Rabinowitz walked in and heard the sinful music, he was pale with anger.

"I taught you to sing to God — but you sing to the devil!" he almost shouted.

"Oh Papa," Jack remonstrated, "now that I'm back—"

"Now that you're back, you're no different. First you sing on the sidewalks — then in beer halls — and now in theayters!"

Jack kissed his mother and left. There was nothing at home for him after all these years. He turned back to the Cantor.

"Some day maybe you'll understand things like Mama does—"

Jack had gone home even before inquiring about the job at the theatre. Now he must hurry over — if only to forget about what had happened at home. He had always wondered who had recommended him — perhaps he could find out from the manager.

But there was nothing to find out, when he saw Mary Dale. It was she who had suggested that they send for him as soon as she came East even before she could write to Jack Robin.

At dinner Jack tried to thank Mary.

"I can never — if I live to be a million — show you how much I appreciate everything — and Mary, I've wanted so to hear from you. I don't know why it should be so hard to say, but I'm crazy about you."

Mary answered very promptly.

"I'm crazy about you too."

He looked disturbed for a moment — and then said.

"You don't know what I mean. I mean that I love you — that I want to marry you."

"That is what I thought you meant."

If Jack ever was ambitious, he was ambitious now — to live up to the opinion Mary had of him — to be worthy of her. At dress rehearsal he realized more than ever that it was his last chance to perfect his singing. Tonight he would have to be at his best — regardless of anything — forgetful of everything. He was applying the burnt cork to his face when a boy announced that there was a lady to see him. Jack continued with his making up and waited for the lady.

He hadn't even thought about who the lady would be, but he would have expected his mother least of all.

"Jakie," she sobbed "Papa is dying, and there is no one to sing Kol Nidre tonight. God will ask him — and he will have to tell him — his only son is singing in a theaytre instead—"

It was a hard struggle for Jack Robin. The opening night had meant everything to him. Meanwhile he was being called for rehearsal. Mrs. Rabinowitz watched through the wings and thought: "It's the same Jakie — with the cry in his voice, just like he used to sing in the synagogue."

An hour later Jack arrived at his home in time to see the doctor. He pressed the doctor's hand and whispered something to him.

The doctor shook his head. When he walked out, Mary and the producer, Harry Lee, walked in. Jack Robin would have to appear tonight, Lee insisted. It would mean a tremendous loss — the backer had threatened to withdraw his money.

But Jack Robin had suddenly become Jakie Rabinowitz. There was a tear in his eye when he looked at Mary, pleading with her with his eyes to understand. While Lee was urging him, Sara was weeping silently.

"You got to sing in synagogue tonight, Jakie. There is nobody to sing Kol Nidre — and Papa — he wants you should sing. You got to do it for Papa."

Mary gave Jack an understanding look, and urged her to drop the matter.

Sara and Mary sat by the Cantor's bedside, while through the open window they could hear the sobbing voice of Jakie singing Kol Nidre in the synagogue. The Cantor smiled and pressed Sara's hand. Now he could die at peace with his God.

He closed his eyes, and Sara and Mary knew that it was the end. At least, it was a happy end.

They alone knew that it was Jakie's last time in the Synagogue.

A short while later Mama and Mrs. Jack Robin sat in the front row of a crowded theatre listening to a beloved black face comedian singing "I'd walk a million miles for one of your smiles, my Mammy." Sara turned to Mary.

"That's my Jakie — with the same cry in his voice — like when he sang in the synagogue. He makes everybody laugh and everybody cry."

AL JOLSON'S OWN STORY:

*I*N the story of America's accomplishments the Jewish race has written many chapters. Particularly in the field of art has its gifts to the nation been rich. It is perhaps in the American theatre that they have been the most lavish of all.

Humble Jewish homes ordered by the precepts of orthodoxy have nourished the talents of boys who were later to become international celebrities—great playwrights, great musicians, great actors.

Behind the career of each a picturesque tale of achievement might have invited the inspiration of a story-teller. But none was so colorful as the one suggested by the rise of the small son of a Jewish Cantor whom the world now knows as America's greatest comedian, Al Jolson.

Samson Raphaelson, the playwright, recognized the possibility of building from it a great human drama, a drama of conflicting ideals, a drama of the old generation's rigid orthodoxy and the young generation's restless yearning for change. The result was the play, "The Jazz Singer," in the story of which it is easy to see the analogy to Jolson's own life.

The child who was later to become the world's greatest entertainer was born in a drab street in St. Petersburg, Russia, and was named Asa Yoelson. His father who had carried on the tradition of five generations of cantors, came to the United States when Asa was very small and settled in Washington, D. C. His paternal heart cherished the hope that the boy would succeed him some day at the synagogue where he was commissioned to sing. It was with trepidation, therefore, that the venerable old man found manifesting in his son a leaning toward the ragtime songs of the street which he personally believed sinful and corrupting. Moreover, Asa even dared on occasion to assert that some day he was going on the stage.

Protestations from the scandalized parent were vain. There was no keeping Al Jolson, as he now began to call himself, from appearing before the public. When very young he gave an extremely creditable performance in Israel Zangwill's play, "Children of the Ghetto." Fascinated by this taste of professional life, he refused to go back to school and joined a circus as a ballyhoo man.

Shortly after the Spanish War he found himself back in the neighborhood of home hired to sing in a cafe. One night the performance was abruptly ended when the elder Yoelson strode indignantly in and forced his son to leave the stage. Later he resumed his incipient career with Al Reeve's burlesque show. Spreading the doctrine of his calling, he next induced his brother to join him, and in company with a third boy, they appeared in vaudeville as Jolson, Palmer and Jolson. The recognition they won, however, was meagre; and after a few seasons Jolson struck out for himself in a "single." Still in white face, he continued to meet with indifferent success.

The turning tide was a chance conversation one night with an old darky. The man was a southern negro who assisted the comedian when he dressed. Jolson was extremely fond of him and appreciative of his loyalty through the lean days of his vaudeville tours. In Washington Al had acquired a sympathetic interest in negro life and had learned to mimic the accent of the race.

One night when the two were preparing for a performance in a small theatre in Brooklyn, the actor confided to his old dresser his misgivings as to the merits of his act.

"How am I going to get them to laugh more?" he mused.

THE JAZZ SINGER IN REAL LIFE

THE darky shook his head knowingly. "Boss, if yo' skin am black they always laugh."

The idea struck Jolson as plausible and he decided to try it. He got some burnt cork, blacked up and rehearsed before the negro. When he finished he heard a chuckle followed by the verdict.

"Mistah Jolson, yo, is just as funny as me."

Jolson in blackface was an overnight hit. His act was a wow. His salary was raised and his route extended as far west as the circuit had houses. This was in 1909. For the next two years success came consistently.

In 1911 he believed it was time to strike out into new fields. A renewal of his vaudeville contract was waived and he joined Dockstader's Minstrels. Another turning point came when he appeared with them one night with J. J. Shubert in the audience.

Shubert listened to Jolson sing a solo number. He was interested. He heard another and he became eager, sure that he had found a comedy genius. The coincidence was an unusually happy one because the Shuberts were that season preparing to open their great Winter Garden and real talent was scarce.

The hour of opportunity for the Cantor's son had struck. His first Winter Garden productions were "Bow Sing" and "La Belle Paree." Thereafter he appeared in any number of Winter Garden programs with ever increasing popularity. In an amazingly short time his fame as the mammy singer with a sob in his voice became world wide. Dozens of imitators have risen and have fallen. The public will have none of them. They have recognized Jolson's unique talents and they have proclaimed him peerless.

His Winter Garden shows have been the means of his introducing songs that have spread their popularity around the earth. These shows include "The Whirl of Society," "The Review of Reviews," "Vera Violetta" and "The Honeymoon Express" in which he was co-starred with Gaby Deslys.

By 1914 he was deemed so popular that revues were written around him. "Dancin' Around" was the first. This was followed by "Robinson Crusoe, Jr." and "Sinbad." When "Bombo" was produced a few seasons ago Jolson was firmly entrenched as America's black-face favorite and a playhouse, Jolson's Fifty-Ninth Street Theatre, was named for him.

Jolson has been received by Presidents and Senators, Kings and Dictators, including Mussolini. He has been lavishly entertained by social and political celebrities and by the leaders of the show world. He has been met in all parts of Europe and the Orient. He has had theatres, night clubs, jazz orchestras, cigars and babies named in his honor. In short, he has friends all over the world.

For ten years motion picture producers tried to entice him to the camera with fabulous salary offers. They failed. It remained for Warner Bros. to accomplish the signing of a contract that brings him at last before the millions who make up the film-going public. The great, vital story of "The Jazz Singer" was the decisive factor in attracting Jolson to a motion picture debut.

Jolson's genius stands alone. This production more than any other can emphasize its scope. Not only does it give full play to Al Jolson, the comedian, but to Al Jolson, the dramatic actor. For like Chaplin, Al Jolson is more than a maker of fun. He is a master not only of laughter but of pathos — of the smile that is whimsical because very near it there is a sob.

Al Jolson in "The Jazz Singer" is a milestone in film history because it marks the great actor's first screen appearance. There is added significance in the fact that the story itself is one of the most appealing human dramas ever told. It is appropriate indeed that Jolson, the world's favorite jazz singer, should play its title role.

The Making of

THE JAZZ SINGER," starring Al Jolson, the world's most popular musical comedy artist, is considered by Warner Brothers to be their supreme triumph. It is indeed a stupendous achievement, and, incidentally, a superb example of the germination of an idea, the oak from the acorn.

The acorn was a short story by Samson Raphaelson which appeared several years ago in one of the popular magazines. It was called "The Day of Atonement" and recounted the adventures of the son of a Cantor who ran away from his home in the Ghetto, became a Broadway idol, and returned on the eve of the Day of Atonement, to sing Kol Nidre in the synagogue, in answer to the pleadings of his dying father. The little story might have been forgotten but for the genius of Mr. Raphaelson who remade it into "The Jazz Singer," the drama which held Manhattan spellbound for almost two years, followed by even greater success on the road. But that was not to be the end. Arline de Haas wrote a brilliant novelization of the play, which ran serially in hundreds of newspapers over the country, and which was published in book form, running into a score of editions. And now the screening of "The Jazz Singer."

One of the most unique features of "The Jazz Singer" is the fact that it nearly parallels the actual life of Al Jolson, envoy extraordinary of blackface, minister plenipotentiary of the mammy-song. Jolson, then, was the man of all men, to play the star part in the screen version which Warner Bros.

Left: Alan Crosland, the Director

contemplated. They were aware that the most munificent offers of the most august of movie magnates had been met by the comedian's positive refusal to appear in pictures. Undaunted, Warner Bros. stormed the Jolson stronghold. The impossible was accomplished. Jolson went to Hollywood. Warner Bros. insured him for half a million dollars.

No effort or expense has been spared in making the presentation of "The Jazz Singer" authentic. The New York Winter Garden, scene of so many Jolson triumphs, the State Theatre in Chicago, and the Orchard Street synagogue, in the vicinity of which the childhood of the jazz singer was passed, all play a large part in the story. A complete theatre modeled after the Metropolitan show-place, with huge stage, boxes and orchestra pit, was built, as well as a replica of the stage of the Chicago playhouse. Since the production was to be synchronized for Vitaphone it was necessary to erect immense sound-proof stages and sets, in order to shut out from the recording rooms any discordant note, during the reproduction of action and vocal or instrumental numbers.

For certain of the spectacular New York sequences the Winter Garden itself was secured through the courtesy of the Shuberts. Cordons of police were necessary to control the crowds during the shooting of the scenes that showed a New York first night opening.

Orchard Street, the very heart of the New York Ghetto, was photographed without the knowledge of its inhabitants. Director Alan Crosland came from Hollywood with a large retinue, descended upon the street with its motley crowd of foreigners, its pushcart-lined curbs, its teeming stream of vivid life, and took hundreds of feet of film, showing the people moving through their daily routine, without their being in the least aware that they were motion picture actors. Many touches of realism were caught in this manner, which would otherwise have been lost in the mad rush for acting honors.

The picture-making procedure was as follows: Warner Oland, who plays the featured part of Cantor Rabinowitz, father of the jazz singer, sat at a table of a second story restaurant, from the window of which the director trained his camera on the street. When the action was ready to be shot, Oland, descended to the street, losing himself in the throng, as just another patriarchal Jew. Soon the denizens of Orchard Street saw an old man grab a boy

Darryl Francis Zanuck, Al Jolson and Jack Warner.

Alan Crosland directing Al Jolson, in The Winter Garden Scene

"THE JAZZ SINGER"

of fourteen out of a gutter and lead him by the ear to a hallway. Many of those who passed had enacted like roles with their own children, but the short journey was not made without the irate objection of several onlookers, to whom the theatrical character of the proceeding, was with difficulty explained.

But even then the Orchard Street sequences were not complete. There remained the moving shots. For these, Mr. Crosland hid his cameras in the back of an old moving van, which was covered behind by a burlap drop. Through a slit in the burlap, the eye of the camera photographed the business of the Ghetto, moving slowly down Orchard Street, to the clicking of the hidden camera. Every scene was repeated three times for safety, yet Orchard Street was none the wiser. More than a month was spent in filming the New York sequences.

The interior of the Synagogue, a replica of the ancient one on Orchard Street, was built on the West Coast lot, and here the stirring scenes of the hero's childhood, and his return when grown to young manhood, to sing Kol Nidre, on the eve of the Day of Atonement, in response to the petitions of his dying father, were enacted. For these scenes, the aid of Cantor Josef Rosenblatt, sweetest singer of modern Israel, was enlisted. The ancient rites are performed with deeply moving sincerity and reverence. The faithful portrayal of Jewish home life is largely due to the unobtrusive assistance of Mr. Benjamin Warner, father of the producers, and ardent admirer of "The Jazz Singer."

One of the most picturesque locales of this most picturesque of productions is "Coffee Dan's," the San Francisco after-theatre rendezvous of the people of the stage and screen. It is here that the jazz singer meets the beautiful vaudeville star who is to give him his opportunity for fame. It is one of the immemorial customs of Coffee Dan's to furnish each guest with a small mallet. Thunderous table-rappings greet each arrival. The genial master of ceremonies, as the spirit moves him, wends his way to the orchestra platform, calling upon this or that celebrity, or perhaps on some obscure vaudevillian to do a "turn." Mallet work, cat calls and wise cracks, rend the air as the performer climbs the stage. If he is well "knocked" he has pleased the crowd, and may fall heir to a good contract.

Prolonged research preceded the four months required for the actual making of "The Jazz Singer." Nothing was hurried, nothing haphazzard. While perfection was being approximated in mechanical details even greater care was being exercised in the choice of the cast. May McAvoy, the airy and diminutive, was the unanimous selection as the dainty toe-dancer who was to bring both the genius and the love of the jazz singer into flower. Warner Oland, one of the greatest character actors of the generation, gives the most brilliant characterization of his career as Cantor Rabinowitz, the orthodox father. Eugenie Besserer is the personification of universal motherhood. Bobby Gordon might be any boy anywhere and Otto Lederer and Nat Carr give comedy creations of subtle reality. Richard Tucker is superb as the worldly wise man. And there are the golden voices of Cantor Rosenblatt and Al Jolson!

"The Jazz Singer" is epoch-making. It is without doubt the biggest stride since the birth of the industry. It is the first story to be done with Vitaphone sequences —and glorious sequences they are, ranging from the ancient soul-stirring Songs of Israel to the latest Broadway Jazz. The production is unique. There is but one "Jazz Singer" — one Al Jolson!

Above: Shooting night scenes at the Winter Garden.

The Winter Garden in New York prepared for use as a movie set.   *May McAvoy teaches Jolson the art of movie makeup.*

WHO'S WHO IN THE CAST

MAY McAVOY

May McAvoy, the Mary Dale of "The Jazz Singer," belongs to the younger set of motion picture stars and is extremely popular with screen enthusiasts in all parts of the world. Miss McAvoy is petite, blue-eyed and charming. The actress was born in New York City and is a graduate of Wadleigh High School. She made her first screen hit in "Sentimental Tommy," which caused her cleverness to gain immediate recognition. Then came her success in "The Enchanted Cottage," to be followed by her hit in Warner Bros.' production of "Lady Windermere's Fan." In the production of "Ben Hur," Miss McAvoy scored as Esther. Another of her big hits was registered in "The Passionate Quest." As one of Warner Bros., stars Miss McAvoy has added to her fame by her work in "Matinee Ladies," "Irish Hearts" and "Slightly Used," she being particularly delightful in the light comedy scenes in the latter picture.

ALAN CROSLAND

Alan Crosland, the director of Al Jolson in "The Jazz Singer," has had a varied career. A New Yorker by birth, he started out as an actor, appearing with Annie Russell's company. Later he became a newspaper reporter, a step that led him into motion pictures, where he won fame with the Edison company as the youngest director in the field. The World War found him overseas in the photographic service of the army. Motion pictures again claimed him on his return. Among the stars directed by Mr. Crosland are Olive Thomas, Elaine Hammerstein, Eugene O'Brien, Alma Rubens, Robert Mantell, Alice Brady in three pictures, and Lionel Barrymore in two pictures. In his direction of "Bobbed Hair" for Warner Bros. Mr. Crosland established a reputation that has grown steadily since then by his direction of John Barrymore in "Don Juan;" Mr. Barrymore and Dolores Costello in "When A Man Loves;" Miss Costello in "Old San Francisco," and now in Warner Bros.' supreme triumph, Al Jolson in "The Jazz Singer."

WARNER OLAND

Warner Oland, was a well known legitimate actor before entering the motion picture field. He not only supported many of the big stars, but became a recognized star in his own right. For three years Mr. Oland was dramatic director at Williams College, and is credited with having started the little theatre movement in this country. Mr. Oland has been in motion pictures steadily since 1916. He is noted for his versatility. His work in "Don Juan," "When A Man Loves" and "Old San Francisco" stamp him as one of the best "heavies" on the screen. The actor's portrait of the old cantor in "The Jazz Singer" is regarded as a gem. Mr. Oland was born in Sweden and is married to Edith Shearn, famous portrait painter and playwright. This talented actor is responsible for introducing the works of August Strindberg to American playgoers and is remembered as one of the stalwart protagonists of the campaign which helped to popularize Henrik Ibsen in this country.

OTTO LEDERER

Among the things of which Otto Lederer is proud are the fact that he acted in the support of Richard Mansfield, was the first character "lead" in the original production of "Abie's Irish Rose," played Warfield's role in "The Music Master," and the further fact that he had opportunity of appearing as Moisha Yudelson in the support of Al Jolson in "The Jazz Singer." Mr. Lederer was graduated from the University of Prague, the city of his birth, being awarded a dramatic scholarship. His

stage debut was made in "Wilhelm Tell" in which he played the son of Tell. The actor's screen work has been impressive and his ambition is to become a practical director of motion pictures.

EUGENIE BESSERER

There is an artistic stamp to the performance of Eugenie Besserer as the mother in "The Jazz Singer" that makes the characterization memorable. It is obvious that the actress has brought many talents to the screen. Born in Marseilles, France, Miss Besserer came to this country at an early age. She made her stage debut with Maurice Barrymore, father of John Barrymore, the noted actor. For a considerable time she appeared in the support of famous stage stars. In 1910 Miss Besserer made her screen debut in "The Padre." One of her outstanding successes was scored in the Barrymore-Costello presentation of "When A Man Loves." Miss Besserer is the holder of the woman's championship for fencing.

Alan Crosland, director of "The Jazz Singer"

RICHARD TUCKER

Richard Tucker, born in Brooklyn and educated on Staten Island, made his stage debut "carrying a spear" in the original production of "Ben Hur." Then came a season with Nat Goodwin, which was followed by stock company experiences in various cities. Mr. Tucker made his screen debut in "The Southerners." His most important roles have been in Warner Bros.' productions of "Beau Brummel," "Matinee Ladies," with May McAvoy; "Dearie," with Irene Rich; "The Bush Leaguer," with Monte Blue, and now with Al Jolson in "The Jazz Singer." In the latter production, the actor has the role of Harry Lee.

BOBBY GORDON

An energetic youngster is Bobby Gordon in "The Jazz Singer" and an equally energetic lad is he in real life. He first appeared in pictures in "Penrod and Sam" and made such a hit that he was engaged for a series of 68 comedies. He seems to have come into the world with "camera sense." The youth played an important part in Warner Bros. production of "What Every Girl Should Know." Young Bobby was born in Pittsburgh, is prominent in all sports of the Los Angeles schools and intends to study law when he graduates from college.

NAT CARR

It is said of Nat Carr that he is known where ever there is a theatre. Born in Winnipeg, Canada, educated in San Francisco, he began his stage career in vaudeville. Until he became a screen actor Mr. Carr divided his time between musical comedy and the music halls winning popularity in both. To his credit are a number of outstanding motion picture successes, one of them having been scored in "Millionaires" and another in the support of George Jessel in "private Izzy Murphy," both Warner Bros.' productions. The actor's portrayal of Levi in "The Jazz Singer" shows his artistic capabilities.

GORDON HOLLINGSHEAD

Gordon Hollingshead, the assistant director, surely deserves credit for his work in "The Jazz Singer." John Barrymore paid him the following tribute, after working with him:

"He has the dexterity of Houdini, the plausibility of Talleyrand, the patience of St. Agnes, and the stoicism of John L. Sullivan."

OTTO LEDERER

RICHARD TUCKER

BOBBIE GORDON

EUGENIE BESSERER

WARNER OLAND

MAY McAVOY

WARNER OLAND

ANDERS RANDOLF

AUDREY FERRIS

NAT CARR

MYRNA LOY

WILLIAM DEMAREST

HOW I CAME TO WRITE "THE JAZZ SINGER"

By SAMSON RAPHAELSON

WHEN I was a Junior at the University of Illinois, it became very necessary that I should impress a certain young lady. I had a date with her for a certain evening. I wanted to show her the best time to be had in the town of Champaign, Illinois. I borrowed ten dollars and bought two tickets for the one-night performance of Al Jolson in 'Robinson Crusoe' Jr."

I had never seen Jolson before. I had heard of him. I shall never forget the first five minutes of Jolson—his velocity, the amazing fluidity with which he shifted from a tremendous absorption in his audience to a tremendous obsorption in his song. I still remember the song, "Where the Black-Eyed Susans Grow." When he finished, I turned to the girl beside me, dazed with memories of my childhood on the East Side — memories of the Pike Street Synagogue.

I said to the girl, "My God, this isn't a jazz singer. This is a Cantor!"

This grotesque figure in blackface, kneeling at the end of a runway which projected him into the heart of his audience, flinging out his white-gloved hands, was embracing that audience with a prayer—an evangelical moan—a tortured, imperious call that hurtled through the house like a swift electrical lariat with a twist that swept the audience right to the edge of that runway. The words didn't matter, the melody didn't matter. It was the emotion — the emotions of a Cantor.

I said to my friend, "There's a story in this — a dramatic story."

I went backstage after the performance and I talked to Jolson. He was very busy, but I shall never forget the feeling I had about what a "damn decent guy" he was. I was a youngster deeply stirred by something which undoubtedly stirred him as much as it did me. He sensed that. In those days he had already become the world's greatest entertainer," and a lot of stirred youngsters must have tired to say nothing in particular to him. He behaved as if I were the first. He told me a little of his background.

But I had already guessed it. I knew there was the spirit of Cantors in him, the blood of Cantors in him.

Five years later in California I wrote the story, I called it "The Day of Atonement." My stories at that time were being published in various magazines. I was a professional writer. I knew most of the editors and they knew me. I said to myself, the first editor that sees this will jump at it. For I felt that it was easily the best story I had ever written. The story turned down by five magazines, Sewell Haggard, editor of Everybody's, bought it. When it appeared I got letters, from my other editors saying, "Why don't you send us stuff like that?" Solomon should have added to a certain remark, "And the ways of an editor with an author."

Mr. Haggard, when he accepted the story, wrote me: "For goodness' sake, don't sell the movie rights on this. You have the makings of a play. Write the play first."

Three years ago I wrote the play. I felt about it as I did about the story. I sent it to Sam H. Harris, who turned it down. I couldn't believe it and wouldn't believe it. I went to his office with genuine concern for Mr. Harris' welfare, fretted him into a state where he handed me over to Al Lewis. Mr. Lewis pointed out certain things in the play which could not be done on any stage. He suggested that if I rewrote it he might be interested. I rewrote it and read it to him. When I finished, there were tears in his eyes. He said, "I'm sorry, but I can't produce this play." I said, "Then why were you crying — because it broke your heart to turn me down?"

I really think Mr. Lewis accepted this play because I wore him out.

If anyone had told me ten years ago, when I first saw Jolson, that he would be in a movie of a play inspired by my seeing

---

PREFACE TO "THE JAZZ SINGER"
By Samson Raphaelson

HE who wishes to picture today's America must do it kaleidoscopically; he must show you a vivid contrast of surfaces, raucous, sentimental, egotistical, vulgar, ineffably busy — surfaces whirling in a dance which sometimes is a dance to Aphrodite and more frequently a dance to Jehovah.

In seeking a symbol of the vital chaos of America's soul, I find no more adequate one than jazz. Here you have the rhythm of frenzy staggering against a symphonic background — a background composed of lewdness, heart's delight, soul-racked madness, monumental boldness, exquisite humility, but principally prayer.

I hear jazz, and I am given a vision of cathedrals and temples collapsing and, silhouetted against the setting sun, a solitary figure, a lost soul, dancing grotesquely on the ruins... Thus do I see the jazz singer.

JAZZ is prayer. It is too passionate to be anything else. It is prayer distorted, sick, unconcious of its destination. The singer of jazz is what Matthew Arnold said of the Jew, "lost between two worlds, one dead, the other powerless to be born." In this, my first play, I have tried to crystallize the ironic truth that one of the Americas of 1927 — that one which packs to overflowing our cabarets, musical revues, and dance halls — is praying with a fervor as intense as that of the America which goes sedately to church and synagogue. The jazz American is different from the dancing dervish, from the Zulu medicine man, from the negro evangelist only in that he doesn't know he is praying.

I have used a Jewish youth as my protagonist because the Jews are determining the nature and scope of jazz more than any other race — more than the negroes, from whom they have taken jazz and given it a new color and meaning. Jazz is Irving Berlin, Al Jolson, George Gershwin, Sophie Tucker. These are Jews with their roots in the synagogue. And these are expressing in evangelical terms the nature of our chaos today.

You find the soul of a people in the songs they sing. You find the meaning of the songs in the soul of the minstrels who create and interpret them. In "The Jazz Singer" I have attempted an exploration of the soul of one of these minstrels.

him, it would have sounded like a bit of fairy tale to me. At the time this article is being written the motion picture of "The Jazz Singer" has not yet arrived. Jolson, who was so damn decent to me in Champaign, Illinois, in 1916 — Jolson, who came up to me in Stamford after the opening of "The Jazz Singer" two years ago and said, "Boy, if there's anything I can do to make this show a success, just say the word. If it flops, I'll put my own money into it to keep it alive." — Jolson, electric, palpitating, the most American figure in the world today — Jolson's going to be in it. And I'm as eager to see it as if the movie was based on his play, not mine.

CRITICAL IMPRESSIONS of AL JOLSON

GEORGE JEAN NATHAN in "THE AMERICAN MERCURY"

The power of Jolson over an audience I have seldom seen equalled. There are actors who, backed up by great dramatists, can clutch an audience in the hollow of their hands and squeeze out its emotions as they choose. There are singers who, backed up by great composers, can do the same. And there are performers of divers sorts who, aided by external means of one kind or another, can do the same. But I know of none like this Jolson— or, at best, very few—who, with lines of a pre-war vintage and melodies of the cheapest tin-piano variety, can lay hold of an audience the moment he comes on the stage and never let go for a second thereafter. Possessed of an immensely electrical personality, a rare sense of comedy, considerable histrionic ability, a most unusual musical show versatility in the way of song and dance, and, above all, a gift for delivering lines to the full of their effect, he so far out-distances his rivals that they seem like the wrong ends of so many opera-glasses.

ROBERT BENCHLEY in "LIFE"

A while ago we intimated that some one (we forget who just now) might take Al Jolson's place. We were just crazy, that's all. We doubt whether anyone could ever take his place. Certainly no human being. We can't imagine what we were thinking of to have said such a thing.

When Jolson enters, it is as if an electric current had been run along the wires under the seats where the hats are stuck. The house comes to tumultuous attention. He speaks, rolls his eyes, compresses his lips, and it is all over. You are a life member of the Al Jolson Association. He trembles his under lip, and your hearts break with a loud snap. He sings, and you totter out to send a night letter to your mother. Such a giving-off vitality, personality, charm, and whatever all those words are!

ALAN DALE in "NEW YORK AMERICAN"

They call him "the world's greatest entertainer." It doesn't seem exaggerated. There he stood in that stupendous auditorium, telling stories, laughing, kidding, dominant, authoritative, magnetic and irrepressible, whilst the audience howled, yelled, and screamed. The audience was as interesting as the show. It was one hundred per cent engrosed, and one sees that so seldom nowadays. And Jolson did everything.

There is no other comedian in the world that I've ever seen— anywhere—who can compare with this priceless actor.

HEYWOOD BROUN in "THE NEW YORK WORLD"

With his glow and his gayety and his immensely infectious vitality unbated, the master minstrel of them all came back to town last evening and all's right with the Winter Garden.

He has come back refreshed, straining at the leash, magnificent, capable of rocking the Winter Garden with an ancient laughter and flooding it with the rue and the tenderness of an ancient art. This is the testimony of one who never admired or relished him half so much before.

Jolson can take a song and make it do things its composers did not dream were in it; he can tell a story with a guile and a zest that no one can surpass. And, then suddenly filling his voice with a tide of unshed tears, he can play a scene as to remind you that he is one of the true actors of his day and generation in the theatre.

ALEXANDER WOOLCOTT, in the "N. Y. EVENING SUN"

There is no other performer who holds such an absolute dictatorship over his audience. There is something magical in this power.

O. O. McINTYRE in "LOS ANGELES EXAMINER"

Jolson has the same magnetic qualities that lifted Mansfield, Duse, Tree and Jefferson to the heights.

"N. Y. EVENING POST"

Jolson takes an average Broadway musical show and breathes upon it. He croons over to it. He surges fantastically through it. He recites a piece about being a weakling, his mouth twitching with the pathos of it and his eyes challenging you to laugh and you do. And weep. He tells a joke, and the laughter makes him sad. He sings spirituals with his jubilee singers, dances in overalls and battered straw hat, and seems to be all over the place all of the time.

There is very little equipment in the language to say anything about Jolson. If you say he is a matser entertainer it suggests, somehow, a man pulling a rabbit out of a tall hat or extracting providentially broken eggs from his socks. If you say he can sing, it is inferentially a comparison with other singers, and if it is said that he can dance it is in the assumption that others can too.

Jolson has nothing to do with these others. He is as solitary upon the heights of an art he has made peculiarly his own as Chaplin is upon his. Or Chaliapin. Or Raquel Meller.

"WARNER BROS. *Present*"

WHEREVER there is a motion picture theatre there is a place set aside for announcements of the program of the day and the days to come. Frequently the movie fan sees a line that arrests his attention. It brings a glow to his face. It is a line prefacing an announcement and it reads:

Warner Bros. Present.

Time was when this line brought no thrill of expectation. That was years ago when Warner Bros. were little known outside the motion picture industry. What happened since then sounds like romance, and would be taken as such if it were not for the concrete facts which accompany a story that might be called: "The Making of A Name."

'PA" WARNER

The story of Warner Bros. opens in Poland in 1885 when Benjamin Warner, chafing under conditions which prevented his children from getting an education, made his way to the land wherein all men are free and equal. Landing in Baltimore, he opened a shop and a few months later sent for his wife and youngsters.

The elder Warner found it no easy matter to feed a family of six, but the youngsters exhibited a sense of responsibility not only to themselves, but to their parents. School sessions over, they hustled for work.

One day news came of a boom in Bluefield, West Virginia. Benjamin Warner went to investigate it, leaving the shop in charge of ten-year-old Harry M. with admonitions that he look after his three brothers, Albert, Sam, and Jack.

After ten years spent in the Monumental City the family moved to Youngstown, Ohio, where Harry and Albert stuck over a shop a sign reading: "Bicycles Repaired." Occasionally Sam would help, but the thing he loved was the theatre. When he got a job at a summer park outside Sandusky, Ohio, Sam was elated.

Motion pictures were coming along at this time and those exhibited at the Sandusky park intrigued Sam. He talked Albert into going in with him on the purchase of "The Great Train Robbery," a two reel classic of its times, and began exhibiting it in that famous country known as "the sticks." The tour was not a success, but oh, what a lot it taught those boys!

Going into Newcastle, Penn., Sam and Albert leased a house contracting for two changes of bill a week. The initial payment was all right, but when told they had to deposit two hundred dollars as a guarantee of good faith, they paled. They did not have it. But Harry came to their rescue,

sold his bicycle shop and found himself also in the movie business.

From this point on one would imagine the young men had easy sailing. Far from it. Having opened an exchange they set about establishing a chain of houses for which they would guarantee to supply the pictures. This was the first plan for a booking exchange. When the whole thing was ready, a combination of the picture producers was instrumental in wiping out their plan and also every dollar they had. It was a terrible blow. The brothers saw that if they were to succeed they would have to produce their own pictures. Harry was to do the financing. It was not long before motion picture exhibitors were showing films that bore the introductory line: "Warner Bros. Present."

A resume of the record of Warner Bros. since that time is illustrative of what can be accomplished by brains, perseverance, and honest business dealings. These men had the will to succeed and refused to allow any little tricks of fate to retard them. Since Warner Bros. produced Ambassador Gerard's "My Four Years in Germany," they have done many big things, including the introduction of John Barrymore as a star in "Beau Brummel," to be followed by "The Sea Beast," "Don Juan," and "When A Man Loves." The Warners introduced Dolores Costello as a star, in "Old San Francisco" for which the public has applauded them. Syd Chaplin's greatest screen successes have been scored under the banner of Warner Bros. Among the other stars identified with the Warner name are Monte Blue, Irene Rich, May McAvoy, Conrad Nagel, Louise Fazenda, Clyde Cook, Warner Oland, and last but not least, that tremendously popular screen figure, Rin-Tin-Tin, the wonder dog of the ages.

It was Harry M. Warner who virtually developed Vitaphone, which is the biggest thing in connection with motion pictures since the birth of pictures themselves. Surely an enviable record. And now comes their supreme triumph, Al Jolson, the greatest comedian of the times, in "The Jazz Singer."

As it was found fitting to open this sketch with reference to Benjamin Warner, it should be fitting to close it with further reference. What became of him as his boys grew to manhood? That he should have gone into motion pictures seems only natural, and for years he proudly guided the destiny of a cosy theatre in Niles, Ohio. It was only the other day that he agreed to retire. Then with his wife he went to Hollywood. Unobtrusively he moved through the Warner Bros. Studios during the filming of "The Jazz Singer." Once there arose some question of the authenticity of a Ghetto scene. He quietly settled it and from that moment his presence was felt and his advice welcomed. From this point, Mr. Warner practically became a technical director of the picture and much of the charm of the home and Ghetto scenes is due to his suggestions. Always eager to listen to their father, the Warners are more eager to do so to-day than ever, so while the public only knows of four Warners there are in reality five, including the quiet figure that takes so much interest in every thing bearing the announcement: —Warner Bros. Present.

H.M. WARNER

ALBERT WARNER

S.L. WARNER

J.L. WARNER

Novelization of the "Jazz Singer" by Arline de Haas.
Based on the play by Samson Raphaelson.

Printed by The Gordon Press, Inc., N. Y.

Reprinted through courtesy of "Vanity Fair"
and the artist, William Auerbach-Levy.

Anita
Page

The Quality Talking Picture

NOT a talking picture scene of any kind was "shot" at the Metro-Goldwyn-Mayer studios until months of painstaking preparation under expert supervision made it apparent that everything was in readiness to produce dialogue films technically and artistically as good as the best silent dramas. The futility of a "haste-makes-waste" policy was recognized at the start, and the groundwork was laid with the utmost care and attention to detail.

The two great sound-proof stages at Culver City are the largest to be found at any studio, and completely outfitted for the production of any type of sound film, from a one-reel monologue to a musical comedy demanding spectacular effects. Each stage is 100 by 125 feet, surrounded by eight-inch concrete walls. When the two-ton doors of the stages are closed by machinery, the interiors are hermetically sealed, ventilation being supplied through sound-filters. These stages were designed by Professor Verne O. Knudson of the University of California, and each contains six sound-proof camera booths, housing, in addition to the camera equipment, motors synchronized with the recording instruments in the two-story building abutting on the tall windowless stages.

Representing, as they do, an investment of millions of dollars and presaging a new and unlimited field of development for the motion picture, these talking film facilities are under the management of the best electrical engineers—men who, for the most part, have followed through the attempts to develop a practical talking picture from the time of the earliest "flickers."

"The Broadway Melody," M-G-M's first all-talking film, a unique combination of musical comedy and dramatic technique, was the first picture to tax the full resources of the big sound stages, which had previously been used only for short subjects and experimental work. Other all-talking films which have just been completed here include "The Trial of Mary Dugan," with Norma Shearer, and "The Voice of the City," an original screen play both written and directed by Willard Mack. Among the other all-dialogue films projected for the near future are "The Last of Mrs. Cheyney," and "A Free Soul," adaptations of two popular Broadway plays; "Rosalie," the musical comedy success; "Dynamite," a Cecil B. De Mille production; "College Days," a new sort of campus story to be directed by Sam Wood; and "White Collars," which William C. deMille will make.

Noted stage players who have recently been signed by M-G-M to appear in talking pictures include Basil Rathbone, Elliott Nugent, Charles Bickford, Kay Johnson, Mary Eaton, Oscar Shaw, Lowell Sherman, Louise Groody, Ruth Chatterton, Raymond Hackett and Charles King, musical comedy star, who has the featured male lead in "The Broadway Melody." In addition, every star and virtually every featured player on the Culver City lot has already demonstrated an ability to meet vocal requirements for talking films, many of the players amazing the producers by the recording quality of their supposedly "untrained" voices.

Metro-Goldwyn-Mayer's Eastern sound studio in New York City, planned with the same care as the one in California, is located at 127th Street and Second Avenue. Here, under the supervision of Major Edward Bowes and Louis K. Sidney, from three to six Metro Movietone acts are being turned out weekly, starring such performers as Vincent Lopez, Van and Schenck, Raymond Hitchcock and George Dewey Washington.

Charles
King

The Cast

QUEENIE . . . . *ANITA PAGE*

HANK . . . . *BESSIE LOVE*

EDDIE . . . . *CHARLES KING*

UNCLE BERNIE . . . . *JED PROUTY*

JOCK . . . . *KENNETH THOMSON*

STAGE MANAGER . . . . . *EDWARD DILLON*

BLONDE . . . . *MARY DORAN*

ZANFIELD . . . . *EDDIE KANE*

BABE HATRICK . . . *J. EMMETT BECK*

STEW . . . . *MARSHALL RUTH*

TURPE . . . . *DREW DEMAREST*

AUTHOR: EDMUND GOULDING

DIRECTOR: HARRY BEAUMONT

CONTINUITY: SARAH Y. MASON

LYRICS: ARTHUR FREED

MUSIC: NACIO HERB BROWN

DIALOGUE: NORMAN HOUSTON and JAMES GLEASON

HISTORY: An original screen story by Edmund Goulding

Bessie
Love

The Story

of

"THE BROADWAY MELODY"

A million lights they flicker there,
A million hearts beat quicker there—
No skies of grey on the great White Way,
That's the Broadway Melody.

AT THE instigation of her sweetheart, Eddie Kerns, a composer who has "crashed" Mazda Alley in less than two years' time, "Hank" Mahoney and her sister "Queenie" arrive in New York seeking positions in Zanfield's new revue, for which Eddie has written the music. The two girls have played small-town vaudeville as the Mahoney Sisters, and both expect that "Hank" will marry the successful Eddie as soon as they reach Manhattan.

Eddie meets them at the train and is startled to discover that "Queenie," whom he knew as a little freckle-faced cut-up, is no longer either little or freckled, and that there is more of a thrill in kissing her than in embracing her sister.

The girls' act is accepted intact for the Zan-

field production, but cut out after the dress rehearsal. "Queenie," however, attracts the attention of Jock Warriner, one of the backers of the show, and is featured in one of the numbers, while "Hank" is demoted to the chorus.

Eddie and "Queenie" realize now that they are in love with each other. "Hank" appears to have no idea of the new romance that is progressing almost under her nose, and "Queenie" is determined that she will not interfere in her sister's love affair. She encourages Jock's attentions, hoping that this will turn Eddie back to "Hank."

When "Queenie's" birthday arrives, she ignores the modest little party her sister has arranged, and goes instead to a glittering entertainment staged by Jock at a sumptuous night club. She doesn't get home until daylight, and then she exhibits an expensive bracelet and babbles somewhat thickly to her sister about a Rolls Royce she is going to have

and an apartment, with everything that goes
with it.

"Hank" argues, pleads, cajoles, and so does
Eddie, but in vain. It is not until "Queenie"
goes with Jock to a housewarming at his new
apartment that "Hank" finds out, from the
manner in which Eddie talks, that he is really
in love with her sister. Then, heroically con-
cealing her own wound, she begs Eddie to go
to the rescue of the girl he loves. Eddie,
ashamed of his own behavior toward "Hank,"
hesitates, but she pretends that she has never
cared for him and has merely been "string-

"Queenie" Speaks Her Piece

A Pledge of Love

ing" him for whatever help she could obtain
in her career.

Eddie trails "Queenie" and her wealthy
escort to the latter's apartment. He confronts
Jock, in his private den, just as "Queenie" is
beginning to get distinctly worried about her
situation. Jock, furious at the intrusion, summons some of his whoopee-making friends,
and Eddie is thrown downstairs. For
"Queenie," this is the decisive factor; rushing to the side of the man she loves, she pours
out all her love for him and swears she will
never leave his side again.

Eddie and "Queenie" are married and go
to live in a pretty bungalow "Hank" selects
for them in Long Island. Although the

happy couple urge "Hank" to remain with
them, she makes a decision in keeping with
her previous unselfish conduct and refuses,
strengthened by the thought that her sister's
happiness is assured. Finding another partner
for the Mahoney Sisters act, she obtains
thirty weeks' booking out in the provinces,
where Broadway is only a vaguely exciting
legend. The show must go on.

The Vaudeville Booking Office

Undressed Kids

372-8

*Handing
Them a Good
Line*

Ever
Since Helen
of Troy . . .

"Queenie" Joins the Chorus

Eddie, "Hank" and "Queenie"

TWO of the three principals in "The Broadway Melody," Charles King and Anita Page, were unknown to most screen fans a year ago, while the third featured player, Bessie Love, makes her talking picture debut in the present picture.

Charles King, who plays Eddie, is a Manhattanite by birth, and has lived in New York all his life except when serving in the navy or trouping out in the provinces. His wife is a first cousin of George M. Cohan, and they have a beautiful home at Great Neck, Long Island—which may be bad news for the more susceptible of the flappers.

Given his first chance outside of vaudeville by George M. Cohan, King appeared first in "The Yankee Prince," fulfilled a special engagement at the Tivoli in London, and after eighteen months of submarine dodging, played in the Ziegfeld "Follies," "Good Morning, Judge," "The Little Millionaire," with Al Jolson in "The Honeymoon Express," and in several other popular musicals. Later he scored a great hit in "Hit the Deck," and was playing in Philadelphia in "Present Arms" when Louis K. Sidney, M-G-M executive, arranged an interview with Louis B. Mayer and a screen test. After the first "rushes" of "The Broadway Melody" were inspected, King's rich baritone voice was thought to be ideal for talking and singing pictures, and he was signed to a long-term contract. His first action then was to wire to his wife to come to Hollywood.

King is a great animal lover. His Long Island home is famous for its polo ponies and dogs, and his best-liked house pet is an English bulldog. He admits his favorite week-end diversion now is to run down to Tia Juana for the races.

Anita Page, who plays "Queenie" in "The Broadway Melody," owns up to eighteen birthdays and is also a newcomer to the films. After appearing in only a couple of photoplays she was selected as a Wampas Baby Star and her future is believed to be a brilliant one.

Officials of the company still chuckle over the story of her initial visit to the M-G-M studio, where an interview had been arranged for her by her energetic mother. It was one morning last spring, and it looked like rain. Anita had a cold, her hair wasn't curled and she was inclined to be fretful after the long bus ride. Sam Wood, director, and John Lancaster, casting director, suggested a screen test.

"I don't want to—I want to go home!" pouted the girl. The two directors had never heard of a girl who

"Hank" and "Queenie"

wouldn't jump at the chance for a screen test and they were astonished. At the same time a casual interest on their part was transformed into a positive insistence on a test. The independent young visitor was photographed that day and within a week had been given the leading feminine role in William Haines' "Telling the World."

As soon as this film was completed the young actress was given a long-term contract, while enthusiastic moguls evidenced a desire to make her work overtime. She appeared successively opposite Lon Chaney in "While the City Sleeps," with Joan Crawford in "Our Dancing Daughters," and opposite Ramon Novarro in "The Flying Fleet." Then she was given her most important part in "The Broadway Melody."

Born in Flushing, Long Island, Miss Page attended a New York high school, then joined a small free-lance movie unit which was a financial failure. Finally she persuaded her mother to chaperon her to Hollywood, where, like pre-cinema Caesar, she saw and conquered.

Bessie Love, seen as Anita Page's older sister, "Hank," supplies a shining example of a girl who combined unusual perseverance and resourcefulness with natural talent to win a place on the top rung of the movie ladder.

A little more than a year ago, Miss Love, a D. W. Griffith alumna, decided that it was time to do something about her career other than accept so-and-so roles in so-and-so-pictures. The talking films were just beginning to win a hearing. The actress had an idea, and with unusual foresight she followed it through. For a long time she had been very popular at house parties as a dancer and ukelele tickler, but had never tried to cultivate her voice. She started taking lessons and made remarkable progress.

Leaving pictures she accepted a season's vaudeville contract. Her song-and-dance act proved a sensation, and was the direct means of giving her a chance to do an equally successful Movietone short. Harry Beaumont saw it and told M-G-M executives that he had found the ideal girl to play with Anita Page in "The Broadway Melody." After the first song numbers had been seen Miss Love was signed to a five-year contract and the dialogue and music writers were told to get busy and provide some other good roles for her.

Miss Love appears indefatigable. During a recent "vacation" visit to New York she relaxed from the strain of a twelve to eighteen-hour studio day by taking singing and dancing lessons for four hours daily, shopping and trying on gowns for three hours.

Harry
Beaumont

New Melodies for Broadway

"Broadway Melody"

"You Were Meant For Me"

"THE Broadway Melody" stands out as the first motion picture presenting, as an integral part of the story, a series of new dance songs.

"You Were Meant for Me," "Broadway Melody" and the other song hits of the new picture were created especially for the production by Nacio Herb Brown and Arthur Freed, the melody-making companions who were responsible for the entire musical score of the photoplay.

The music for "The Broadway Melody" was composed with the principals and the story well in mind all the time. In essence the new talking film becomes a combination of musical comedy spectacle and rhythm with a "straight" dramatic story of New York back-stage life. The production may thus be termed the first original musical comedy composed for the screen, while at the same time it promises to create an entirely new vogue in film fare.

It is obvious that there is a world of dif-

ference between songs and a musical theme which are an essential part of a screen story and a group of song numbers which are interpolated after the picture has been completed.

The work of Brown and Freed has been praised by Tin Pan Alley experts as by far the best this pair, who did "The Doll Dance," "The Boy Friend" and "Moonlit Waters," have ever turned out. Brown is the composer of the music for "The Broadway Melody," while Arthur Freed supplied the lyrics. Both have just signed new long-term contracts with Metro-Goldwyn-Mayer.

"Those boys will be as famous in the field of sound movies, before they get through, as Gilbert and Sullivan were in light opera." This was the comment, a short time ago, of another Hollywood musician.

The song numbers of the new picture are being released simultaneously with its Broadway premiere and seem likely to be near the top of the musical best sellers before the 1929 crop of wild strawberries has blossomed.

More Song Hits

"Tin Pan Alley" is rapidly moving into Hollywood. Noted songwriters and composers are spending much of their time now providing musical scores and novelty numbers for talking pictures.

At the Metro-Goldwyn-Mayer studio Gus Edwards, who wrote "School Days," Fred Fisher, author of "Dardanella," Billy Rose, whose best known piece is "Me and My Shadow," Nacio Herb Brown and Arthur Freed are working under long-term contracts. In the production of "The Broadway Melody" Brown and Freed were "teamed" to prepare the musical score.

"Thematic songs and numbers in sound pictures will be popularized exactly as are the song hits in shows," declared Brown recently. "Song composers throughout the country are beginning to realize the tremendous scope of the talking picture field. The influx of song writers has just begun, and I believe it is only a matter of time until the popular music centre will be Hollywood rather than New York.

"I suppose the general public doesn't realize that only about eight per cent of the songs published ever become hits, in other words, sell in advance of 400,000 copies.

"The sound film, coupled with radio, will unquestionably give a wider publicity range to good popular songs than ever before in history."

The Mysterious Bracelet

A Clinch Without a Referee

Ambitious Anita

When Anita Page, featured in "The Broadway Melody," passed her voice test with flying colors, instead of resting on her oars she went ahead immediately with plans to iron out any small flaws that might exist.

"The voice test was nearly as much of a thrill as my first day in pictures," asserted Miss Page. "I was so excited that I scarcely remember what I did first. I remember mother and I went down to the university, where I enrolled in a class for voice culture.

"Every night after work I would go to school for two hours, studying the enunciation of difficult words, voice modulation and so on. They have a special apparatus called the 'voice dissector' at the University of Southern California, and this has been a great help to many persons starting talking picture work. In a jiffy you can pick out any small faults and start correcting them. At home I went through my dialogue script with mother, dad and my small brother and we had great fun."

Two in a Row

Sarah Y. Mason, who is just one more example of the rising tide of femininity in motion picture circles, prepared the continuity, or working script, of the last picture to play at the Astor Theatre, "Alias Jimmy Valentine," as well as the present film, "The Broadway Melody."

Choosing a Chorus

In going through the long lines of girls from which were "weeded out" the sixty members of "The Broadway Melody" chorus, an effort was made to select a number of varied types. Director Beaumont and his assistant, George Cunningham, had a rigid list of requirements to which all the girls selected must conform, yet at the same time they were looking for photographic individuality. The result was that many were called before even a few were chosen.

Among the girls in the line are Diana Verne, dancer in "Chu Chin Chow" and "Artists and Models"; Alice Pitman, captain of the Tiller Sunshine Girls; Alice Weaver, a Broadway featured dancer; also the Angeles Sisters, and many show girls and dancers who have scintillated with the Follies, Vanities or George White's Scandals.

The average height of the girls is five feet two inches and their average weight 110 pounds. Blondes are distinctly in the majority and about one-third of the sirens of syncopation have long hair. No inexperienced applicants even had a chance of "getting by." Incidentally, nine of the girls, or about 15 per cent., claim college diplomas—a development that might have amazed the leg-of-mutton epoch, when brains in jumpers were undreamed-of commodities.

A Backstage Confab

Salient Facts About

The first all-talking picture from Metro-Goldwyn-Mayer.

Harry Beaumont, the director, made "Our Dancing Daughters," "Main Street," and "Beau Brummel."

Everyone concerned with "The Broadway Melody" is an expert in his own line.

Blonde beauties and bewildering brunettes—sixty—count them!—in the chorus.

Radio listeners who remember the Biltmore Trio will have a chance to hear them in this film.

One of the most costly revue scenes ever staged is used as a setting.

Arthur Freed and Nacio Herb Brown did the lyrics and music—and will remain with M-G-M indefinitely.

Did you see the perfect reproduction of a certain New York night club?

Whistling statisticians say the song hits will be repeated 930,465,880 times by July 1.

Anita Page, Bessie Love, Charles King and their director all signed long-term contracts after this film.

Yellow Canyon, or Mazda Alley, otherwise known as Broadway, was never dramatized so poignantly before.

Main Stem characters by real Main Stem writers is the secret of the play's great humaneness.

Edmund Goulding, who wrote the story, and Jimmy Gleason, dialogue writer, know show life upside down.

Laurence Stallings says the film world will now be paging Miss Love and loving Miss Page.

One thousand girls were looked over in picking "The Broadway Melody" beauty brigade.

Dance connoisseurs may now try out the "Tampa Step"—designed for this film.

Younger generation plays reach their climax with this singing-dancing-talking musical drama.

A Breach—But No Breeches

A Spy in No Man's Land?

*The
Solicitous
Sister*

Too Much Static

No Explanations Required

Webster Didn't Know It All

Fun-loving picture fans who attend "The Broadway Melody" may derive some of their principal enjoyment listening to the principals employ a *patois* used in the "best" theatrical circles.

This vocabulary has a raciness, an audacity, a sardonic humor, that make the phrases "hit home." Does someone make a fantastic suggestion? "Your arm is swelling!" "Cut 'em deep and let 'em bleed" is less sanguinary than it sounds. It is merely an exhortation to a group of chorus girls to work hard to put over a number.

To "inhale poison" is to drink bad liquor. "The lingerie" is a generic name for the fair sex. "Pump" is the cardiac and "smeller" the olfactory organ. A good provider, as most persons know, is a "sugar daddy," and an opulent elderly lady is a "classy mamma." To be sophisticated is to know one's "goulash." A meager stipend is "coffee and cake jack." A joy-ride in a high-priced motor car is invariably referred to as a "buggy ride." Tiffany diamonds are "cracked ice."

The expression "five yards" is monetary rather than textile; it is half as much as a "grand," which is one thousand dollars. When someone says "she needs the do-re-me pretty bad" he does not mean that she is acutely lacking in her musical education, but merely that she could use some extra cash. "How about getting hitched up?" is not a polite invitation to a horse, but an eloquent way of asking a girl to marry.

It is not necessary to use a glossary when seeing "The Broadway Melody," although you will hear many of these phrases in the picture which is believed to have zestfully caught the argot, glamor and humor of New York's "Main Street" better than any other photoplay.

Between the Acts

Whoopee Wizard Not So Wild

If you lined up all the directors in Hollywood, probably the last one you would pick out as the man who turned out "Our Dancing Daughters" and "The Broadway Melody" would be Harry Beaumont.

After this director had produced in succession two such jazz-tinctured pictures, one of the coast journalists dubbed him "the screen's wizard of whoopee."

The paradoxical part of it is that Beaumont is one of the most thoroughly domesticated individuals who ever handled a megaphone. The proud father of twins, he doesn't go to cafes and parties, and hasn't the slightest interest in saxophone salons where they serve nightcaps with the morning milk.

He doesn't wear balloon trousers with flask-size hip pockets and the rear end of his automobile isn't fitted out with a "jazzbird" horn. He can't dance the Black Bottom or Charleston and wouldn't if he could.

And yet Beaumont has demonstrated an almost uncanny ability to catch the spirit of modern youth by the coattails and hurl it on the screen, with a perfect accompaniment of popping champagne corks, silk-stockinged legs and all the other flamboyant effects. "Our Dancing Daughters" broke house records everywhere and "The Broadway Melody" has everyone on the M-G-M lot smiling like the Scotchman who won a cow in a raffle.

"If a lot of kids having fun is 'naughty,'" declared Beaumont recently, "then I guess my screen philosophy is all wrong. What the public wants, and needs, in my belief, is to get away from drabness. We have to face too much of it every day. When you go out for entertainment you want life, color, pep—something with zip to it to make you wish that you were young again and at the same time glad you are past the age of folly!"

The Jack of Spades

"Now, My Dears —"

Undress Styles

If ponderosity of chorine clothing were to be accepted as an accurate index of decorous thoughts in the on-looker, the Tired Business Man of two decades ago must have been sixty times more Platonic-minded than the T. B. M. of 1929.

Fifteen pounds was the average weight of the garments worn by the billowy and buxom chorus girl of the gay nineties and the years following the turn of the century. The regular working costume of a dancing maid in our uninhibited era causes a pressure of just about four ounces on the scales.

Whatever the inference to be derived from this comparison, it is a certainty the "Floradora Sextette" and similar musical comedy troupes gave contemporary monitors of morality little opportunity to cry for reform. It would take a singularly vigorous imagination to find traces of indecent exposure in a fifteen-pound silken ballast.

In those days the chorus girl draped her frequently undisciplined figure in a full-length skirt extending at least four inches below the knee. This was made of heavy taffeta, banded with a velvet waist, the flowing skirt creating a counterfeit bustle about the hips. Bright colors and flower designs never seen by the hearthside added a touch of daring.

Undergarments—which may properly be discussed by the unashamed historian—consisted of six underskirts of heavy China silk, with "accordion" pleats. These were usually of varied colors, and the high spot of the evening was reached when some pert damsel kicked just a bit too high, producing a rainbow effect. A corset was imperative, as were voluminous silken bloomers, unending cotton stockings, and high-top black shoes with spool heels.

The cost of such a mummy-like outfit was seldom more than $25. The four-ounce costume costs close to $100. But this is another story.

After the Show

Trials of Vaudeville

Living in sparsely furnished plaster-porous rooms, doing washing in the handbowl, cooking eggs or coffee on an inverted electric flatiron or open gas jet, and putting on a "front" when their pockets contain nary a penny—such are the expedients of the small-time vaudevillians, some of whom appear in "The Broadway Melody."

The genus vaudevillian is a member of a little world apart from the rest of creation. His joys and sorrows, his "smart cracks" that hide tragedy in many instances, and his incessant groping for the Ultima Thule of vaudeville—a "spot" on the bill at the Palace in New York—are all inferred from the party scene in "Hank's" apartment where she entertains some of her former vaudeville friends.

The average small-time vaudeville entertainer—and from the ranks of these eventually rise the "big timers" —often gets his start in some lodge show or amateur theatrical affair. His friends tell him his act is good, and he starts off on the road of starvation that may (if he's lucky) lead him to "big time" fame. Al Jolson, greatest of headliners in the varieties, once was a cigar clerk, and Will M. Cressy once a printer's devil. Charles Wither's act, "For Pity's Sake," resounded round the world; but he was once a stereotyper on a Kansas City newspaper.

They come from many sources, and, once in vaudeville, are assimilated by the little world within a world. They get its ideas and ideals, absorb its traditions and actually come to look like vaudevillians, a distinct type apart from the rest of the world.

The vaudevillian's greatest aim in life is to "put up a front." He may be broke, and out of a job (which he calls resting), but he always tries to look prosperous. He shines his own shoes, but cultivates perfect poise.

Sisters—

Will Disagree!

A Keyhole Revue

Noiseless Dresses

Since the "talkies" have entered the motion picture field the costume designers have had to add to their list of "do's" and "dont's" special care in the selection of silks that do not rustle; any noise on the set detracts the attention from the voices of the stars and interferes with their proper recording.

Many interesting experiments were tried out by David Cox, Metro-Goldwyn-Mayer costume designer, during the making of the all-talking synchronized picture, "The Broadway Melody," which has as its central locale the stage of a New York theatre.

One dance number depicts a group of girls in abbreviated costumes of silver cloth with lavish embroidery trimmings of beads and sequins. In rehearsing the number it was found that the swish of the beads while the dancers were in motion reverberated through the recording machines, partly drowning out the music. By experimenting Mr. Cox found that the beads were more pliable when strung on rubber bands, so the fringe trimmings were all re-strung on elastic.

In another scene the girls appeared in taffeta dresses with metallic fringes, but this material was taboo, as the rustle of the edges recorded unfavorably. The dresses had to be discarded and new ones substituted.

Costume experts at the studio believe that "The Broadway Melody" and other talking pictures may have an important influence on feminine styles for 1929 and 1930. With gowns of soft clinging materials being used almost exclusively on sound stages, the theory is that women will demand the same styles in the shops.

Evolution in Sound

Making talking pictures fifteen years ago and making them today is as different a procedure as taking off in an old glider, then stepping into a modern de luxe air cruiser. Harry Beaumont chuckles reminiscently as he recalls the little Edison "talkies" of 1913 and contrasts them with his new musical extravaganza, "The Broadway Melody."

"The talking picture idea, of course, is not new," declared Beaumont. "The principle in the early experimental days was the same as at present, except that the tools we had were very crude. We reproduced a bit jaggily through a phonograph horn and a big cylinder, while now synchronization of the wax disc record is perfect, and we can also implant the sound directly on the edge of the film.

"It wasn't only because of their technical imperfections, however, that the one-reel sound pictures of those days didn't get by. The public was just getting used to the new art of silent drama, and had shown an interest in the movies as a novelty that was entirely different in technique from the spoken word.

"At the present time I believe we have reached a point where an entirely new creation is being perfected —a form of entertainment combining some of the best elements of stage and screen, but distinct from either. I look upon real human interest stories with a natural musical setting as the most fertile field for progress here."

The new screen development presents many difficulties even to the veteran director, according to Beaumont.

"The direction of talking pictures demands much closer attention to detail than the silent film," he said. "A sound picture is virtually 'made' before its scenes are photographed, for every sequence must be rehearsed until it is perfect before the filming.

"The recording of various sounds simultaneously is one of many kinky problems. In one scene in 'The Broadway Melody' in which Miss Love does a tap dance, plays the ukelele and sings, we spent three hours on rehearsal alone. The 'mikes' must catch all sounds evenly."

Jimmy Gleason, author of the stage success, "The Shannons of Broadway," and co-author of the dialogue for "The Broadway Melody," seems as much pleased as are Bessie Love and Charles King over the completed script.

"Jack Fell Down . . ." But Jill Came After.

A Metro-*Goldwyn*-Mayer PICTURE

MAURICE CHEVALIER

"THE LOVE PARADE"

AN ERNST LUBITSCH PRODUCTION

with JEANETTE MacDONALD LUPINO LANE LILLIAN ROTH

A Paramount NEW SHOW WORLD Picture

25¢

MAURICE CHEVALIER

Adolph Zukor and Jesse L. Lasky

present

MAURICE CHEVALIER

in an

ERNST LUBITSCH

production

"THE LOVE PARADE"

with

JEANETTE MacDONALD

LUPINO LANE and LILLIAN ROTH

By Ernest Vajda *and* Guy Bolton

From the famous stage play, "The Prince Consort"
by Leon Xanrof and Jules Chancel

Music by Victor Schertzinger. *Lyrics by* Clifford Grey.

B. P. Schulberg, *General Manager, West Coast Productions*

A Paramount Picture

ERNST LUBITSCH

THE CAST

Count Alfred . . . . Maurice Chevalier

Queen Louise . . . . Jeanette MacDonald

Jacques . . . . Lupino Lane

Lulu . . . . Lillian Roth

The Master of Ceremonies . . . . . Edgar Norton

The Prime Minister . . . . Lionel Belmore

The Foreign Minister . . . . . . Albert Roccardi

The Admiral . . . . Carlton Stockdale

The Minister of War . . . . Eugene Pallette

The Afghan Ambassador . . . . . Russell Powell

The Cabinet Ministers . . . {
Anton Vaverka
Albert de Winton
William von Hardenburg

The Ladies in Waiting . . . . . . {
Margaret Fealy
Virginia Bruce
Josephine Hall
Rosalind Charles
Helene Friend

JEANETTE MACDONALD

The March of the Grenadiers.

THE STORY

*J*ACQUES, a gentleman's gentleman, is setting the table in in the home of his master, Count Alfred, attached to the Sylvanian embassy in Paris.

In another room, Paulette, a Parisienne, is furiously berating Alfred, charging that he is deceiving her with other women. Alfred, although he looks as though he is guilty on all counts, is stoutly defending himself. Paulette draws a tiny jewelled pistol on Alfred. He gently takes the pistol from her and lays it on the table.

A few moments later, Paulette's infuriated husband forces his way into the bedroom where Paulette and Alfred are wrangling, sizes up the situation, sees the gun, takes it and fires at Paulette. She falls at his feet.

The husband fires the gun at Alfred, who, to his own and the husband's surprise, remains unhurt by the shot. Paulette, realizing that she is not shot, for the gun contains only blanks, arises. The husband, happy to have Paulette alive at any cost, is full of love and tenderness. But Paulette is furious with him, because she has lost so delectable a morsel as Alfred.

After Paulette and her husband are gone, Alfred's joy is short lived, for he is almost immediately visited by the Sylvanian ambassador, who tells him that his shameless escapades have become unbearable. He must report in person immediately to the Queen of Sylvania.

And so, that night Alfred starts packing for his exile.

In Sylvania, things are not going smoothly. To the discomfiture of her subjects, Queen Louise, although she is young and beautiful, is having trouble getting married. There is a law in Sylvania that the husband of the Queen does not become

King. He becomes Prince Consort. As Prince Consort, he has no hand in the affairs of the realm. He is merely a lay figure with no legal rights or privileges, to be dominated by the Queen at her will.

The Queen has become very sensitive on the subject of marriage, for she feels that any man should be happy to be her slave, her Prince Consort.

On the morning that Alfred is speeding back to Sylvania by plane, the Queen is being awakened to the sounds of the Wedding March, played by the Imperial Band. In her fury, Louise demands that at peril of life and limb, the Band must never again play that tune.

Alfred is first on the list to see the Queen. He tells her that he is Count Alfred, ordered home for an audience with the Queen. In her irritation she barely notices him.

While Alfred is waiting for her to collect herself, his eye falls on a document headed

CONFIDENTIAL REPORT SCANDALOUS
AFFAIRS OF COUNT ALFRED IN PARIS—

A moment later he sees the Queen take the paper and start to read. As she reads, she becomes more and more interested. From her expression, Alfred knows that not one detail has been omitted. When she finishes, she walks up to Alfred, who is standing at attention, looks him up and down as though she were thinking of some dire punishment. Then suddenly leaves the room.

Alfred cannot imagine where she has gone, but the truth is that she has gone to powder her nose. When she returns, her voice is very severe and she tells him that she will have to punish him.

(Continued on Page 9)

LUPINO LANE   LILLIAN ROTH

THE STORY OF "THE LOVE PARADE" (*Continued from page 7*)

At once the lover, he insinuatingly suggests that the Queen sentence him to stay at the palace always, attached to her

The Queen is furious at his impudence, but is already so intrigued with him that she commands that he dine with her at eight o'clock that night in white uniform.

At eight o'clock that night, Jacques is standing outside the palace. He suddenly catches sight of Lulu, attendant to the Queen's dog. He goes over and picks up an acquaintance with her. He tells her that he is watching out for the Queen's husband. Lulu laughingly tells him that the Queen has no husband. Jacques confidentially says that before Alfred leaves the palace that night, the Queen will be crazy about him. Lulu obviously finds Jacques something new and intriguing in men.

Meanwhile, in the Queen's dining room, Alfred and Louise are getting on famously. An orchestra is playing a dreamy waltz. The Queen's eyes are misty with love, and Alfred obviously finds her the acme of the beautiful women he has known.

And as she sings her willing answer to his love song, they seal their engagement with a kiss.

The wedding of Alfred, raised to the status of a Prince by a command of the Queen, and Queen Louise is an affair of beauty and grandeur. It is almost upset, however, when Alfred, surprised by part of the marriage ceremony which makes him promise to fulfill the Queen's wish, to execute her every command and to be an obedient and docile husband, hesitates to say "I do". But, reassured by a warm smile from the Queen, he forgets his misgivings and all is well.

But the Ambassador of Afghanistan, who has his own ideas about a man who is willing to take the wife's part in the marriage relationship, has noticed Alfred's hesitation. And it is important that the minister of Afghanistan shall realize how happy this marriage is to be. There is an important loan at stake.

It is several months later. Alfred has had time to get bored and fed up with his position as Prince Consort. He has no duties, no rights, no privileges. He cannot even have his breakfast until the Queen, finished with her morning parades and duties in which he has no part, arrives to eat with him. No servant in the house will obey him. He is practically the Queen's slave to order about as she will.

Then comes the night of the advertised royal appearance at the opera. The Queen, without consulting Alfred, has gone ahead and made all arrangements for their joint appearance.

The Queen warns the Master of Ceremonies to tell Alfred that he must be in best of humor at the affair. If the Prince does not smile, it will mean disaster, since Sylvania is in a bad way financially, and unfortunately the Afghan Ambassador is to be at the opera.

At this point, Alfred comes in. He is in much better humor, for he has worked out a practical solution of the country's financial difficulties. But the Prime Minister says haughtily that he is not permitted to receive suggestions from the Prince Consort in affairs of State. And so he refuses to even read Alfred's document. Alfred angrily leaves.

At seven o'clock that night, Alfred has not even started to dress. It is the talk of all the servants. The women of the palace are all on the Queen's side, the men on Alfred's.

Downstairs, the Queen is furious. She sends for Alfred, saying that if he (*Continued on Page 12*)

"Not a scandal with one woman, Your Majesty — with several!"

The Queen bathes.

"Count Alfred, you should be thoroughly ashamed of yourself. Dine with me this evening at eight".

THE ROYAL WEDDING

PERHAPS the most dazzlingly spectacular scene yet witnessed and heard in a talking motion picture is the marriage ceremony of Queen Louise (Jeanette MacDonald) and Count Alfred (Maurice Chevalier) in "The Love Parade".

It is the glamorous climax of the swift courtship of the beautiful Queen by the dashing and incorrigible Count. It takes place in the luxurious throne room of the palace in Sylvania. The flower and beauty of the kingdom in their shimmering gowns are there. The court ladies in marvelous costumes, the Ministers and the Ambassadorial Suite in brilliant uniforms, the stalwart Grenadier Guards in dress attire, make a picture never to be forgotten.

And, of course, the central interest focusses upon the royal pair—the Queen in a bridal gown such as adorn only Queens and the handsome Alfred resplendent in crimson and gold.

Director Ernst Lubitsch has outdone himself in this scene and motion picture audiences the world over will talk about it.

THE STORY

(*Continued from Page 9*)

refuses to come voluntarily, she will send soldiers for him When Alfred appears, he is dressed for traveling. To the Queen's surprise, he says that he is going to Paris. The Queen tries threats, pleas, uses her charms on him, but he is adamant.

After Alfred is gone, we see how much Alfred really means to her. The Queen breaks down, but she is determined at all costs to be the sole ruler.

So we find the Queen arriving alone at the opera. The audience is astonished and there is much murmuring over Alfred's absence. To her distress, she sees the Afghan Ambassador, his expression sarcastic and ironical. Suddenly she notices that the conversation in the audience has stopped and everyone in the audience rises, looking up toward the royal box.

Astonished, she sees Alfred in his uniform and medals smiling happily. He kisses the Queen's hand, which is the signal for much applause. The Queen sees how popular Alfred is with the people.

The Queen is jealous and annoyed. She turns on Alfred tells him that he needn't have come at all. He starts to leave but she asks him to stay.

"Beg me to stay", says Alfred, and the Queen is forced to beg him to stay.

"You wanted to humiliate me. That's why you came!" says the Queen.

"I came," explains Alfred, "because after all, I didn't want to ruin the woman I once loved. But tomorrow morning I'm leaving for Paris. and as soon as this loan is signed, I shall file papers for divorce."

The Queen is nonplussed, and, to her horror, she notices that Alfred has his opera glasses trained on some pretty and very unclothed dancers on the stage. Her jealousy is aroused, but, noticing the new look, of respect on the face of the Afghan Ambassador, Louise realizes that she must go through with colors flying.

Later that night, Louise is in her own room, look-

ing her most entrancing, waiting for Alfred to come to her When he does not come, she telephones to his room to find out what he is doing. He says he is packing, and he refuses her offer to help.

A few moments later he comes to the Queen's bedroom to get his pajamas which the Queen, thinking that things are now all right, has brought into her room. Without a word he takes the pajamas and goes back to his own room. The Queen follows and locks the door.

Alfred is annoyed. "So you are using force again, Madam," he says.

But Louise will not be put off. She tells him that she is going to Paris with him; he can never get rid of her. Then, he retorts, there is little reason for him to go. He might just as well stay here.

Louise agrees. Alfred says that he must find some way to punish Louise. She suggests that he take over the command, not only of the Council of State, not only of the General Staff, not only of the Army and Navy, but also at home. In other words, he is to become King, while she will be the feminine side of the household. That is all that Alfred wants, for he loves Louise, and so the future promises well in Royal circles of Sylvania.

$11.00 A SEAT

THE elite of New York City gladly paid $11.00 a seat to witness the glamorous world premiere of "The Love Parade" at the Criterion Theatre, on Broadway. The wise theatre goer will regard that statement with a whole salt cellar full of salt. He knows that at the usual premiere where advanced prices are advertised the percentage of the audience that comes in on complimentary tickets exceeds those who have bought tickets. This was not true at the "The Love Parade" premiere. Every seat was actually sold at $11.00. So great was the advance fame of the picture that New York's finest eagerly paid.

No longer Queen—but a loving and suppliant wife.

Four little maids at court. The Queen's Ladies in Waiting.

(Below) The Queen marries.

Below) Jacques, the valet, attempts to make friends with the Royal Guard.

(Above) "Why is it so difficult to find a husband for me? Am I not as beautiful as other women?

SEE SYLVANIA FIRST!

Progress reaches the kingdom -- or rather queendom -- of Sylvania.

Jacques and his Lulu

MAURICE CHEVALIER
The Big Happiness Boy from Paris

IN the course of a single motion picture, "Innocents of Paris", Maurice Chevalier has become an idol of the American screen public. His first production had a record run of eighteen fervent weeks in San Francisco. It established its star in the front rank of film favorites throughout the country.

Chevalier has long been well and enthusiasticly known to millions of theatre goers throughout the world. He first leaped into fame in 1913 as the magnetic dancing partner of Mistinguett, she of "the million dollar legs", at the Folies Bergere in Paris. The following year came the great war and Maurice went to the front. He was seriously wounded by shrapnel and taken prisoner. After more than two years of incarceration he made his escape and returned to the French capital, incapacitated for further military service.

His long illness and imprisonment had robbed him of his confidence. He made a trial reappearance at the Casino Montparnasse, one of the smaller Parisian theatres. His success encouraged him. After a few more neighborhood engagements he returned to the Folies with Mistinguett.

His first appearance in an operetta-revue was in "Gobette of Paris" at the Femina. Soon his inimitable rendition of the Chevalier type of song, his personality, his sparkling sense of humor and his superb powers as actor and mimic made him the idol of all Paris. To the post-war French public he was the personification of France leaping triumphant from the ruins of war. Even his characteristic costume of jaunty tuxedo and straw hat tilted rakishly over one ear emphasized this spirit.

Soon the rest of the world demanded their share of this talented artist. He made his debut on the English speaking stage in a revue with Elsie Janis. He appeared in Buenos Aires and won the hearts of the South American throngs as easily as he had charmed France and England.

Then came talking pictures and a momentous visit of Jesse L. Lasky, first vice president in charge of production for Paramount, to Paris. Instantly Mr. Lasky recognized the marvelous opportunity the new medium of entertainment offered to Chevalier, then playing in his native France. A bit sceptical at first, Chevalier consented to come to Hollywood.

In the interval between the completion of his first talking, singing screen production, "Innocents of Paris", Chevalier filled an engagement on the Ziegfeld Roof in New York. Never did a star receive such a reception from critics and public. Each night it was necessary to remove Chevalier's piano from the floor before the wildly applauding audiences would cease demanding encores.

"Innocents of Paris" was a tremendous personal triumph for Chevalier. He caught the fancy of the American screen public with amazing speed. Now comes "The Love Parade". It takes no box office wizard to predict that the French idol's hold upon the cinema millions will be clinched forever by this truly brilliant achievement.

The flashing entertainment jewel that is Maurice Chevalier is now seen in its perfect setting.

MAURICE IN MANY MOODS. The amazing versatility of Chevalier is not the least of his host of charms.

ERNST LUBITSCH

The Man Who Made "The Love Parade"

Director and star talk it over.

IN a recent poll conducted among newspaper critics by Film Daily, a leading motion picture publication, to determine the screen's foremost director, Ernst Lubitsch was chosen by an overwhelming majority. Over two hundred leading critics cast their votes for him. This tribute to Lubitsch will undoubtedly be seconded by millions of film fans. His place in the cinema world is high and unquestioned.

One of the secrets of Lubitsch's success is undoubtedly his thorough training in his profession. His early experience in the theatre was secured in perhaps the most instructive and exacting school in the world, that of Max Reinhardt in Germany. Under Reinhardt's direction he began his stage career at the age of twenty. He appeared in all sorts of plays, serious and light, straight drama and musical comedy. His chief fame as an actor was won as a comedian.

Lubitsch's comic talents displayed on the Berlin stage brought him to the attention of the UFA organization, the foremost producers of motion pictures in Germany. He transferred his make-up box to their studios and starred in one and two-reel comedies on the screen. Then he became interested in the directing side. Starting with the production of short comedies, he was gradually given more important assignments. He directed Pola Negri in "Carmen" and others of her major successes abroad. He produced "The Loves of Pharaoh". American producers became conscious of Lubitsch's high competence. He was lured to this country at about the same time that Miss Negri arrived.

Practically every Lubitsch picture produced in Hollywood has been a major success. Included among them are "The Marriage Circle", "Forbidden Paradise", "The Patriot", "Lady Windermere's Fan" and "The Student Prince".

Lubitsch's superb talent is based upon technical perfection plus a vaulting imagination and a humorously sophisticated outlook on life which he gets over on the screen. No director is more thoroughly familiar with such fundamental details as lighting, construction of settings, the organization of a smooth-flowing continuity and the potentialities of a picture camera than the Great Ernst. He is meticulously care-taking. He re-hearsed the major players in "The Love Parade" for weeks before he permitted a camera to be turned on them. Himself a musician, he memorized the entire score of the picture before he started directing it.

Critics rave about "the inimitable Lubitsch touch". There is an atmosphere about a Lubitsch picture that you find nowhere else. His players live their parts. They are flesh-and-blood, civilized people. They do nothing that does not seem utterly natural. They have a slyly humorous outlook on life. If they are indiscreet -- and they very frequently are -- they are delicately so. They sin with polish and a smile. They are supremely, gorgeously alive!

Combine the talents of a Lubitsch with the sparkling personalities of such splendid players as Chevalier and Jeanette Mac-Donald and the others, and you can understand the amazing perfection of "The Love Parade"!

Photographing the gorgeous wedding procession in "The Love Parade". Note cameras on wheels and Lubitsch sitting in front of them.

Directing two scenes simultaneously. On the right, Chevalier and Miss MacDonald; on the left, Lupino Lane and Lillian Roth. Lubitsch seated at the bottom of the white line, which indicates division of two scenes.

(Right) A fateful meeting in the boudoir of the Queen.

(Above) The kiss that rocked a kingdom.

An old friend in a new setting -- Ben Turpin.

Her Majesty awakens.

The Queen reviews the Royal Grenadiers.

Beautiful women add sparkle and zest to "The Love Parade"

JEANETTE MacDONALD

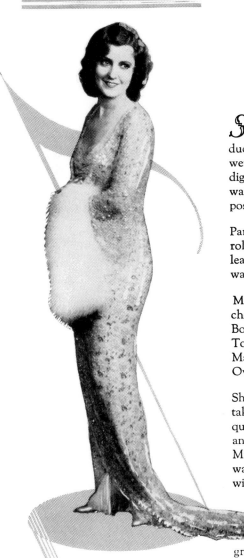

SHE must be beautiful. She must possess an exceptionally fine soprano voice that is microphonically perfect. (And even the best of soprano voices may not reproduce well on the audible screen.) She must be able to wear gorgeous clothes as if she were born to them. She must be an excellent actress. She must have the bearing and dignity of a Queen, and in the next moment she must display the full-blooded warmth of a woman lost in the ecstacies of a great love. And, in addition, she must possess a lively sense of humor.

Paramount looked high and low for such a woman. They wanted her to play the role of "Queen Louise" in "The Love Parade". Tests were made of practically every leading woman on the musical comedy and operetta stage. Then Jeanette MacDonald was lured before a camera -- and the search was triumphantly ended!

Miss MacDonald, a Philadelphia girl of Scottish descent, made her stage debut in the chorus of a Ned Wayburn revue. She understudied the prima donna in "The Night Boat", a successful Broadway musical comedy in which Jack Oakie and Ernest Torrence were comedians. In successive seasons she was featured or starred in "The Magic Ring" with Mitzi, "Tip Toes", "Irene", "Tangerine", "Sunny Days", "Bubbling Over", "Yes, Yes, Yvette", "Angela" and "Boom Boom".

She has red-gold hair and sea-green eyes. Though famous for her singing voice, she takes a private singing instructress with her wherever she goes, to check upon the quality of her work. Her favorite food is milk. Her ambition is to play gamin roles, and her first two parts in motion pictures are both Queens. For, so outstanding was Miss MacDonald's performance as "Queen Louise" in "The Love Parade" that she was at once signed by Paramount to play the Queen in "The Vagabond King" with Dennis King. Later she put her name upon a long-term Paramount contract.

Much of the same magnetic personality and gay, refreshing view-point that is Maurice Chevalier's is also Jeanette MacDonald's. No more fitting choice could have been made for a leading woman for the great French star. No feminine heart in the audience will rebel when the handsome Maurice lays his heart at the well-shod feet of the fair Jeanette in "The Love Parade".

THE prime essential of a great motion picture is a good story. Realizing this, Paramount employed the best literary brains available on "The Love Parade".

Though the picture is based upon the famous stage play, "The Prince Consort", by Leon Xanrof and Jules Chancel, the final story is practically an original by Ernest Vajda and Guy Bolton.

Vajda is the well known Hungarian playwright who at one time had four successful plays running simultaneously in New York. The plays were "The Harem", produced by David Belasco; "Grounds for Divorce", produced by the Charles Frohman Company; "Fata Morgana", a Theater Guild hit; and "The Little Angel", produced by Brock Pemberton. Previously Vajda had written Budapest's prize operetta, "The Carnival Marriage", with music by Poldini, which is revived each year in the Hungarian capital.

Since 1927, Vajda has been in Hollywood under contract to Paramount and has written some of the most successful picture stories of all times.

Guy Bolton has written or collaborated on forty seven musical shows. His principal collaborator has been P. G. Wodehouse. Their successes include "Have a Heart", "Oh,

Boy"! "Leave It to Jane", "The Riviera Girl", "Miss 1927", "See You Later", "Oh, Lady, Lady", "The Girl Behind the Gun", "Ask Dad" and "Sitting Pretty". Others in which Bolton has had a hand are "The Five O'Clock Girl", "Rio Rita", "Lady, Be Good", "Polly Preferred", "Sally", "Miss Springtime" and "Very Good Eddie".

"LOVE PARADERS" IN CONFERENCE

Reading left to right: Victor Voyda, Clifford Grey, Ernest Vajda, Victor Schertzinger, Guy Bolton, Maurice Chevalier and Ernst Lubitsch.

LUPINO LANE

A Frenchman is starred in "The Love Parade". A German directed. The leading woman is an American of Scottish descent. The story is by an Hungarian. The cast includes an Italian, a Welshman, a Czecho-Slovakian, a daughter of Spain, and a Canadian.

The chief comedian, Lupino Lane, adds to the gayety of nations by being an Englishman.

Lane comes of an illustrious family of London music hall artists. No variety show bill in England would be considered complete unless there was a Lane on it. Lupino gained fame in his native land before coming to this country He had the comedy role in many famous Broadway musical successes. Several years ago he journeyed to Hollywood to try his luck in pictures.

Contrary to the fate of most European comedians on the American screen, he was at once successful. Humor is notoriously provincial in scope; that is why a great laugh-getter is seldom a hit when transplanted to another clime. Charlie Chaplin and Lane are exceptional examples of English musical hall stars who have scored even greater triumphs in America.

Lupino Lane is more than a comedian. He is an acrobat and he possesses an excellent singing and talking voice. Moreover, he is a good actor even when his lines are serious. His performance as "Jacques", the all-wise valet, is one of the high spots in "The Love Parade".

LILLIAN ROTH

*T*HE Broadway musical comedy and vaudeville stage has lost another star to Hollywood!

When Lillian Roth, Boston born, New York bred, was five years old, she was appearing before the motion picture camera at a studio in Fort Lee, New Jersey.

When she became a young lady of ten years of age, Lillian toured a vaudeville circuit with her younger sister, Ann, doing dramatic impersonations of Ethel Barrymore, Ruth Chatterton, John Barrymore and others.

At fifteen, she first attempted to sing professionally and won a part in the Shubert's production of "Artists and Models" by her successful rendition of a touching ballad called "Red Hot Mama".

A few years later and she was a sensation as a blues singer in New York night clubs, the Ziegfeld Follies, in Earl Carroll's Vanities, in Delmar's Revels and as a vaudeville headliner over the Orpheum Circuit.

When Jesse L. Lasky went to Ziegfeld's Midnight Frolic one evening to hear Maurice Chevalier, Lillian Roth was on the same bill. The result was her appearance in two singing short features at Paramount's Long Island studio. So successful were these that she was signed to a contract and sent to Hollywood to play the role of "Lulu", the gamin maid, in "The Love Parade".

---

*C*ONTRIBUTING to the success of "The Love Parade" is the fact that all of the smaller parts, even the bits, were assigned to the best character actors in Hollywood.

For instance, one of the Queen's Ministers will be recognized as Eugene Pallette, the comedy detective of "The Greene Murder Case" and "The Canary Murder Case". E. H. Calvert, the straight-backed "District Attorney" in those same two famous successes, is here seen as the "Sylvanian Ambassador" to France. The divorced eyes of Ben Turpin are glimpsed for the first time in a talking picture in a bit in "The Love Parade". The fiery French lady caught by her husband in a rendezvous with Chevalier in the first sequence in the picture is Yola D'Avril, one of the real beauties of Hollywood.

Edgar Norton, "Master of Ceremonies" at "Queen Louise's" court, has been seen in

Of white satin, seven yards long, two feet wide, embellished with rhinestones, pearls and sequins is "Queen Louise's" bridal gown.

many Paramount pictures, particularly as valet to Adolphe Menjou.

The quartet of beautiful young women who portray the "Ladies in Waiting" to "Queen Louise" illustrate the type of juvenile actress now coming to the fore in Hollywood—girls who are not only stunning looking but who also possess good singing and speaking voices. Incidentally, one of them, Rosalind Charles, was up to the time of her appearance in "The Love Parade" a stenographer in the story department of Paramount's Hollywood studio. Victor Schertzinger, who wrote the music for the picture, heard her singing over her work and, struck with her voice, had a test made of it.

Practically every actor in the cast of "The Love Parade" has enjoyed feature billing in other productions. And, by the way, Russell Powell, who succeeds in looking the fierce "Afghan Ambassador" to the life, is very much an American!

THE MUSIC

THE LILTING MELODIES of "The Love Parade" are one of its fascinating charms.

"PARIS, STAY THE SAME". Sung by the magnetic Maurice as he bids good bye to his French lady loves.

"DREAM LOVER". Jeanette MacDonald describes in song the man of her midnight imaginings.

"LET'S BE COMMON". Lupino Lane and Lillian Roth have musical ideas of love — and tell them.

"NOBODY'S USING IT NOW". Chevalier here sings the type of sly, roguish air for which he is famous.

"ANYTHING TO PLEASE THE QUEEN". Maurice makes a daring, melodious promise that he finds hard to keep.

"GOSSIP". Lupino and Lillian retail in song the palace scandal to the eager kitchen staff.

"MARCH OF THE GRENADIERS". Queen Jeanette and her 'guards make the welkin ring with a rousing martial air.

VICTOR SCHERTZINGER, who wrote the music for "The Love Parade" is motion picture director as well as composer. Among his picture hits are Richard Dix's "Redskin". His most successful previous song is "Marcheta", one of the famous best popular sellers of all times.

CLIFFORD GREY, who did the lyrics, performed the same job, for Chevalier's first stage musical comedy in English, "Hello, America". He is also the lyricist for Ziegfeld's "Sally" and "The Three Musketeers". Also for "Hit the Deck".

This book sold only in theatres showing "The Love Parade". It may be purchased in quantity from Al Greenstone, 1547 Broadway, N. Y.   Printed by the Gordon Press, Inc. N. Y.

Souvenir Program

25¢

ALL QUIET ON THE WESTERN FRONT

A UNIVERSAL PICTURE

Carl Laemmle

Carl Laemmle, president of Universal Pictures, is the only one of the motion picture pioneers who is still actively in control of the company which he started. He presents "All Quiet on the Western Front" in the twenty-fifth year of his film leadership, as the outstanding achievement of his long and meritorious service to the screen public.

Carl Laemmle, Jr.

At twenty-two, Carl Laemmle, Jr., as the producer of "All Quiet on the Western Front," brings to the screen Erich Maria Remarque's supreme story of youth in war. Every detail of the massive production, which took months in the making, passed under the watchful eye of this young and brilliant creator of great pictures.

Lewis Milestone

As the director of "All Quiet on the Western Front," into whose hands was committed the greatest directorial assignment in film history, Lewis Milestone was given one order: "Tell the story as Remarque wrote it." How triumphantly he succeeded, the picture itself reveals.

Erich Maria Remarque, author of "All Quiet on the Western Front," the sensational novel-- the best seller of the past ten years. He is now writing the sequel to "All Quiet," which Universal will also bring to the screen as a super-production.

One of "The Iron Youth"

Foreword

"All Quiet on the Western Front"—the book and the picture—is not the story of one war, but of all wars. Not the story of one army, but of all armies. Not the story of the youth of one nation, but of all nations.

When he wrote his masterpiece, Remarque wrote it in that spirit.

When he entrusted its screen transcription to me, I agreed that his book would be picturized in the same spirit.

We have kept faith with him. There is nothing in the picture that is not in the book.

We believe we have transposed the greatness of the book to the screen. All the resources of our organization have been called into play to achieve this result.

We have kept faith with the public, too. The millions who have read Remarque's book will find it on the screen as he wrote it; will find the amazing and sensational narrative that has received world acclaim—

The immortal story of all war seen through the eyes of all youth. The picture tells the story!

Carl Laemmle

"Her mouth speaks words I do not understand. Nor do I fully understand her eyes; they seem to say more than we anticipated when we came here."

(From the Book)

63

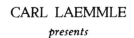

CARL LAEMMLE

presents

"All Quiet On The Western Front"

A UNIVERSAL PICTURE
From the novel by ERICH MARIA REMARQUE

Produced by CARL LAEMMLE, Jr.
Directed by LEWIS MILESTONE

Dialogue by Maxwell Anderson and George Abbott
Adaptation by Maxwell Anderson
Screen story by George Abbott
Cameraman Arthur Edeson

The Cast

CHARACTERS	PLAYERS
Katczinsky	LOUIS WOLHEIM
Paul Baumer	LEWIS AYRES
Himmelstoss	JOHN WRAY
Gerard Duval	RAYMOND GRIFFITH
Tjaden	GEORGE "SLIM" SUMMERVILLE
Muller	RUSSELL GLEASON
Albert	WILLIAM BAKEWELL
Leer	SCOTT KOLK
Behm	WALTER BROWNE ROGERS
Kemmerich	BEN ALEXANDER
Peter	OWEN DAVIS, JR.
Mrs. Baumer	BERYL MERCER
Mr. Baumer	EDWIN MAXWELL
Detering	HAROLD GOODWIN
Miss Baumer	MARION CLAYTON
Westhus	RICHARD ALEXANDER
Lieut. Bertinck	PAT COLLINS
Suzanne	YOLA D'AVRIL
Kantorek	ARNOLD LUCY
Ginger	BILL IRVING
French Girls	RENEE DAMONDE / POUPEE ANDRIOT
Herr Meyer	EDMUND BREESE
Hammacher	HEINIE CONKLIN
Sister Libertine	BERTHA MANN
Wachter	BODIL ROSING
Poster Girl	JOAN MARSH

Time	1914-1918
Locale	GERMANY AND FRANCE

Western Electric Sound System
C. ROY HUNTER, *Recording Engineer*

Produced in its entirety at
Universal City, Calif.

RUSSELL GLEASON
("*Muller*")

HAROLD GOODWIN
("*Detering*")

LOUIS WOLHEIM
("*Katczinsky*")

WALTER BROWNE ROGERS
("*Behm*")

George "Slim" Summerville
("*Tjaden*")

Lewis Ayres
("*Paul Baumer*")

Owen Davis, Jr.
("*Peter*")

Yola D'Avril
("*Suzanne*")

Scott Kolk
("*Leer*")

Ben Alexander
("*Kemmerich*")

John Wray
("*Himmelstoss*")

William Bakewell
("*Albert*")

The Story of "All Qui

SEVEN German schoolboys, all under 20, troop off to war in 1914 with the fire and patriotism of youth. They are trained under a brutal drill-master, their former postman. This is their first disillusionment—to find that this martinet is all powerful. The young soldiers—Paul Baumer, Albert, Kemmerich, Muller, Behm, Peter, Leer—are put through long drills, including crawling in the mud. Humiliations increase.

They are taken to a railway station where they see the wounded being received and rushed to hospitals. Military planes drone overhead. . . . This is war . . . a grim-visaged spectre . . . no pomp, no panoply.

Next, they go nearer the front. Back of the lines they meet Katczinsky —known as Kat—a veteran. They learn from him that food is one of war's big problems. He teaches them that the ability to get food is greater than the ability to read books.

They move into the actual firing lines. Under Kat's leadership, they lay barbed wire. It is a terrible experience. All about them, men fall dead and wounded. But they survive . . . yet a little while.

Now they go into battle. A town is stormed and taken. Its village streets are shelled. The Germans enter and take possession.

At this point there is an interlude. . . . War is not all death and terror. Some of the lads meet three French girls on the edge of a canal. An acquaintance is formed and the boys arrange to meet the girls that night. It is moonlight and the three soldiers, with their boots filled with bread and sausage held above their heads, swim across the canal and enter the girls' home. Paul Baumer, most of his illusions gone, still is able to believe

the Western Front"

himself in love. . . . It is the soldier's respite, his brief moment of escape from the terrors of the battlefield.

They go back to the front lines. Kemmerich, whose soft leather boots were the envy of his comrades, is the first to fall. The others will not believe that death has touched their ranks. Then Behm goes. Himmelstoss, the tyrant, fails at the moment of danger in the sight of the boys, now veterans, but a little later redeems himself by going bravely to his death.

The war wears on into years. Hardened soldiers now, the survivors of the little group who marched so gaily away from their schoolroom, have stormed over miles of shell torn country. In a shellhole, while guns thunder and star shells burst, Paul encounters one of the enemy and wounds him mortally. Frantic, he pleads with the Frenchman not to die—searches his pockets, finds the pictures of his wife and children. It is the first man Paul has killed, and the terror of it drives him to the point of madness.

In the dug out, the boys discuss their experiences and what they would do if the war was over. Paul, slightly wounded, complains bitterly of the futility of their life and how their ideals have been destroyed. But others relieve the tension by humorous remarks.

One by one the "Iron Youth" are killed. Paul finds himself one of a generation lost forever to the world. He goes home on leave. All is changed. He is a stranger in his home town. His mother, now an invalid, and his sister—they have suffered, too.

He returns to the firing lines from which he never returns, although on the day he falls, the army report simply states: "All Quiet on the Western Front."

How and Why Eri
"All Quiet on th

"I WROTE it to free myself from something. That something was my mem
of the war, my thoughts and those of my companions. It was only afte
had completed it that I thought of trying to sell it."

Thus Erich Maria Remarque put, in his own simple way, the reason for
writing of "All Quiet on the Western Front," the best-selling book of the gene
tion.

Remarque was born 32 years ago in Northwestern Germany. With a c
of youngsters of eighteen or thereabouts, he a
his brother enlisted in the infantry, moved by
exhortations of their teacher. Both were wound
but lived through the war, unlike Paul in the st
who is killed just before the armistice on a
so devoid of incident that the army report
confined to the statement: "All Quiet on
Western Front."

When he returned from the war, Remar
became, in succession, a teacher, an organist
motor-car dealer, a draughtsman, and a newspa
man.

One night he came home from his work
the Berlin illustrated weekly, by which he
employed, and began to write. He was writ

What They Said About the Book

*"With this book the American public may manage
to learn that war is the same in all armies."*
—HEYWOOD BROUN.

"It's wonderful."
—H. G. WELLS.

*"It was worth waiting ten years after the war to
get the war written in perspective, truthfully, power-
fully, beautifully."*
—WILLIAM ALLEN WHITE.

*"Let this book into every home that has suffered no
loss in the War, and to every home that had to
sacrifice any of its kindred, for these are the words of
the dead, the testament of all the fallen, addressed to
the living of all nations."*

—WALTER VON MOLO,
President of the German Academy of Letters.

aria Remarque Wrote
estern Front"

o free himself from the war. He told his story simply, without heroics—just let the facts peak for themselves. He finished the book in six weeks. It wrote itself, says Remarque.

His book went begging for more than a year after he completed it.

"The first publisher to whom I offered it kept it a long time," Remarque explains. Then I offered it to the Vossische Zeitung to run as a serial. They hesitated. Finally, they decided to take a chance."

What happened made history in the publishing world. "All Quiet" has far out-stripped in sales the best sellers of the past ten years. It has been translated into fifteen languages. The sales in Germany climbed to the 950,000 mark; in England to more than 300,000 and, in the United States, where it is still breaking records, the sales ran quickly to 335,000 in a few months.

Carl Laemmle, President of Universal Pictures, went to Germany and purchased the picture rights from Remarque. Then Mr. Laemmle urged the young author to come to America and himself play "Paul Baumer" in the great picturization which Universal was then planning.

"But I am not an actor," said Remarque. "I would rather do other things. I am going to write another book."

Universal will make a picture from that book, too.

Thus Remarque, who lived the life of "Paul Baumer" at the front, wrote "All Quiet on the Western Front," the sensational novel.

What They Said About the Book

"It is certainly a remarkable book."
—Frank B. Kellogg,
Former Secretary of State.

"A gorgeous and epical paean to the indomitable spirit of youth. Unquestionably the best story of the World War so far published."
—H. L. Mencken.

"It possesses characteristics of genius beyond any nationalism."
—London Times.

"The quiet honesty of its tone, its complete human candor . . . make it supreme."
—Christopher Morley.

Filming the Great Book

A GREAT military camp was built by Universal on the historic 930-acre Irvine Ranch in Southern California for the filming of the battle scenes in "All Quiet on the Western Front."

Twenty acres were made into a perfect replica of a part of the Western Front. The shell holes pock-marking No-Man's Land were real, made by blasts of dynamite and filled with muddy rain water.

A complete system of trenches was constructed under the supervision of army officers who had gone through the Great War.

There were 2,000 soldiers, all of them ex-service men—Americans, Germans, Russians, French, Italians, English. They lived under strict military regulations. In the picture, all wore the one uniform—the green gray of Germany.

More than 20,000 pounds of black powder and six tons of dynamite were used to give the effect of shell fire and mine explosions. Six thousand bombs were planted and exploded.

Twelve flame-throwers were used. Twenty German howitzers, captured by the A.E.F. and now trophies at American Legion posts, were fired in the bombardment scenes.

A canal, half a mile long, was dug for one of the dramatic scenes in the picture.

A French village covering ten acres was especially constructed and then blown to pieces in the bombardment.

At Universal City one of the largest exterior sets ever built represented the German training barracks.

(Above)

In the yard of the great German training barracks as shown in "All Quiet on the Western Front."

A giant crane, weighing 280 tons, carrying cameras and sound equipment, was used to give absolute realism in sight and sound to the making of the great scenes.

As Remarque Wrote It

Direction of the battle scenes for "All Quiet on the Western Front," involving two thousand men scattered over half a mile of location, was one of the biggest problems that confronted Director Milestone. With the aid of six assistant directors, the big scenes were rehearsed by the help of telephones, sirens, whistles and pistol shots.

In making these scenes several former army sergeants were employed. These men had charge of squads and companies of soldiers. Many of the scenes were rehearsed more than a dozen times before they were "shot." Actual army regulations were in force in making these scenes and when actually photographed by cameras concealed from all angles, they were carried out with remarkable precision. There was little megaphone work. The "shots" were carefully timed by stop watches in the hands of men of long experience.

Men employed as soldiers in the picture found their own diversions. They gathered in groups and related past war experiences. There existed at all times a splendid spirit of friendship among the nationals of many nations.

The making of the picture was a tonic in human fellowship. Barriers of language and race were swept away in filming this vast panorama of war as reflected in the vivid pages of Remarque's "All Quiet on the Western Front."

Ready for the march to the front. Showing a part of the 2,000 ex-service men of many nations who donned German uniforms for the making of "All Quiet on the Western Front." In the background, one of the many villages constructed for the picture.

Exact reproductions of German hospital trains, operated on actual rails, were built at the Universal Studios from scale drawings prepared by technicians.

Youth T

"ALL QUIET ON THE WESTERN FRONT"—the book and the picture—is a story of youth . . . *the great story of youth.*

Youth in the picture . . . and youth in the making of the picture.

Remarque believed his "generation was lost" . . . "The generation of men who, even though they may have escaped its shells, were destroyed by the war" . . . Then he added: "The generation that has grown up after us will be strange to us and push us aside."

But the generation that grew up after Remarque and his schoolboy soldiers in "All Quiet" did not push them aside.

Instead, they seem to have understood most of all. It was the generation that grew up after him that made the picture.

mphant!

Carl Laemmle, Jr., who produced the picture, is 22 years old. Lewis Ayres, who has the role of "Paul Baumer," Remarque's autobiographical character, is 20. The other six boys who play "Paul's" six comrades—Russell Gleason, William Bakewell, Scott Kolk, Walter Browne Rogers, Ben Alexander, and Owen Davis, Jr., range in age from 19 to 22. When Remarque went from school to war these boys were in the grammar school grades. Young Laemmle was then six years old. Lewis Milestone, who directed the picture, is but 33 years of age. Remarque was 30 when he wrote "All Quiet." Milestone, too, served in the war.

If ever youth was served, it was in the making of "All Quiet on the Western Front" as a picture—Laemmle, 22; Ayres, 20; Milestone, 33; Remarque, 30. Producer, star, director, author.

The Picture Tells the Story

There is not a scene in the picture "All Quiet on the Western Front" that is not in the book. Carl Laemmle, President of Universal; Carl Laemmle, Jr., who produced the great film, and Director Lewis Milestone, whose task it was to transfer Remarque's masterpiece of youth to the screen—all have kept faith with the book.

The first step was the engagement of two celebrated authors to make the film adaptation and write the dialogue. Maxwell Anderson, co-author of the stage play "What Price Glory?" and George Abbott, co-author of "Broadway," wrote the dialogue, while Anderson made the adaptation and Abbott wrote the screen story.

Nothing was added; no tricks were performed.

The greatness of Remarque's work was there in the book, intact. "We have simply changed written words to a picture," says young Laemmle. "Our reasoning was that if the book was such a tremendous success the picture must be, if it was truthfully adapted and produced."

In choosing the players for the seven schoolboy soldiers of Remarque's story, youths of almost the same age as the comrades of the book were selected. Every soldier of the 2,000 appearing in the picture was an ex-service man. Most of them were American Legionnaires and there were Germans, French, English, Canadians, Russians and Italians fighting side by side in the battle scenes staged by Milestone, himself a war veteran. All wore the German uniform.

Remarque wrote: "The greatest thing that came out of the war was comradeship." The filming of the picture proved it. The hatreds of war were forgotten. Keeping faith with Remarque meant, among other things, getting the spirit of comradeship on the screen. It was done by the very employment of men who were once in contending armies. They lived together for several months in the great military camp built by Universal on the Irvine Ranch in Southern California.

Universal bought the greatest of best-sellers; the greatest human document ever written. It gave that book the finest production possible—faithfully, truthfully.

The picture tells the story!

A schoolboy vision of war before the enlistment *seven comrades. One of them went because he p* *tured himself an officer, popular with charmi* *women.*

"Then we lie down again to play cards. We know how to do that— to play cards, to swear, and to fight."
(From the Book)

Task Superbly Accomplished

How triumphantly "All Quiet on the Western Front" has been transposed to the screen was told by an editorial in *The Los Angeles Record* on April 12. It was written after a private viewing of the masterpiece. Let it speak for itself:

" 'All Quiet on the Western Front'——

"The dictionary hasn't enough superlatives to describe the massive and sensational quality of this Universal Production.

"When Erich Maria Remarque's daring book was purchased by the film company, countless predictions were made to the effect that it could not be transferred to the screen successfully. It has been transferred to the screen—and most succssfully.

"Lewis Milestone, the director, had a tremendous task before him—a job few would have tackled with the same spirit of truthfulness he has shown.

"Everyone concerned with the making of this strange and remarkable film epic is to be praised and congratulated for their fine work. Maxwell Anderson and George Abbott prepared the dialogue, adhering faithfully to the original lines and theme.

"Lewis Ayres, a newcomer, rises to tremendous heights with the important role of Paul. John Wray is outstanding as Himmelstoss. Louis Wolheim plays Kat, a strange character, to perfection. William Bakewell does his best film work to date as one of the German boys who is spirited into the war, hoping for adventure and finding nothing but tragedy. Slim Summerville portrays a German soldier with a dry sense of humor. He is a relief to the sordid things of war. Slim comes near to stealing the honors of the picture. Russell Gleason gathers many new laurels. Ben Alexander and Owen Davis, Jr., are two others who achieve much with their parts.

" 'All Quiet on the Western Front' will blaze a new trail for Universal. It will startle the public and the industry. Carl Laemmle, Jr., produced this picture against the advice of many so-called wise men of Hollywood. They warned him that it couldn't be done. Junior Laemmle can now take a grand bow and the applause should be quite deafening.

" 'All Quiet on the Western Front' is the most startling, realistic production since 'Birth of A Nation.' "

We were due to leave next morning. In the evening we prepared ourselves to square accounts with Himmelstoss."

(From the Book)

"My sleeve is torn away by a splinter ... No pain. I feel the arm all over, it is grazed but sound."

(From the Book)

Lewis Ayres
The Screen's New Find

Only twenty years old, and he plays a leading role in the greatest picture of the year, "All Quiet on the Western Front"!

Lewis Ayres—the outstanding screen find of the past five years!

When Hollywood heard that Universal would picturize Remarque's masterpiece, the best of filmdom's younger stars bid against each other for the role of "Paul Baumer." But back in the heads of Carl Laemmle and the Universal executives, and Lewis Milestone, who had been assigned as director of "All Quiet," lurked the thought and the hope of a new face, a new character, a new hero.

That hope was gratified in Lewis Ayres, the personification of clean, romantic American youth. Ayres asked for a test. Two days later, he was offered the part of "Paul"—admittedly the greatest role of the year in pictures.

Ayres, always a lover of music, was playing in an orchestra at the Cocoanut Grove, Los Angeles, when a new ambition seized him. Nightly, the greatest stars in filmdom danced before him and stopped to listen as he sang the soft refrains of the orchestra renditions. He dreamed that one day a beautiful star, who had heard him sing, would remember and aid him in getting into pictures.

By chance, an agent who managed a number of well-known players saw him dancing at the Hotel Roosevelt, Hollywood, one afternoon with Lily Damita, and at once divined his picture possibilities. The result was that he got a contract with one of the big companies, but played only a "bit" in one picture.

Then came the opportunity that took his breath away. He was cast to play the youthful lover of Greta Garbo in "The Kiss." He made a great impression in the role.

Lewis Ayres is something "new" in pictures. He isn't a "hoofer," or a "sheik," or a jazz party clown. He is simply a boy—the kind of a boy that Richard Harding Davis wrote about. He lives alone in a modest Hollywood apartment.

One of the first productions of the new season, in which Ayres will be featured, is "Saint Johnson," the novel by W. R. Burnett, which will be published next Fall. It will be filmed by Universal as an outdoor epic. John Wray, who plays "Himmelstoss" in "All Quiet on the Western Front," will be co-featured with Ayres.

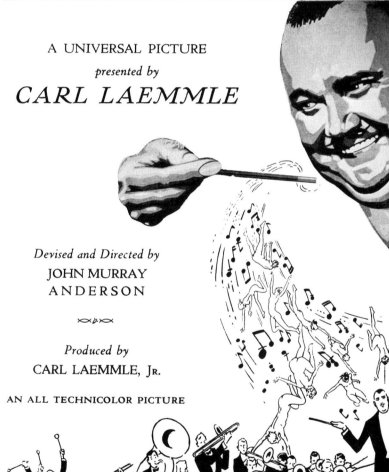

ALL QUIET ON THE WESTERN FRONT
A UNIVERSAL PICTURE

GARBO
John
BARRYMORE
Joan
CRAWFORD
Wallace
BEERY
Lionel
BARRYMORE
in
GRAND
HOTEL

PRICE TWENTY-FIVE CENTS

METRO GOLDWYN MAYER

presents

GRAND HOTEL

Based on William A. Drake's Adaptation of the Play by Vicki Baum

An Edmund Goulding Production

Recording Director: Douglas Shearer
Art Director: Cedric Gibbons
Film Editor: Blanche Sewell
Photographed by William Daniels
Gowns by Adrian

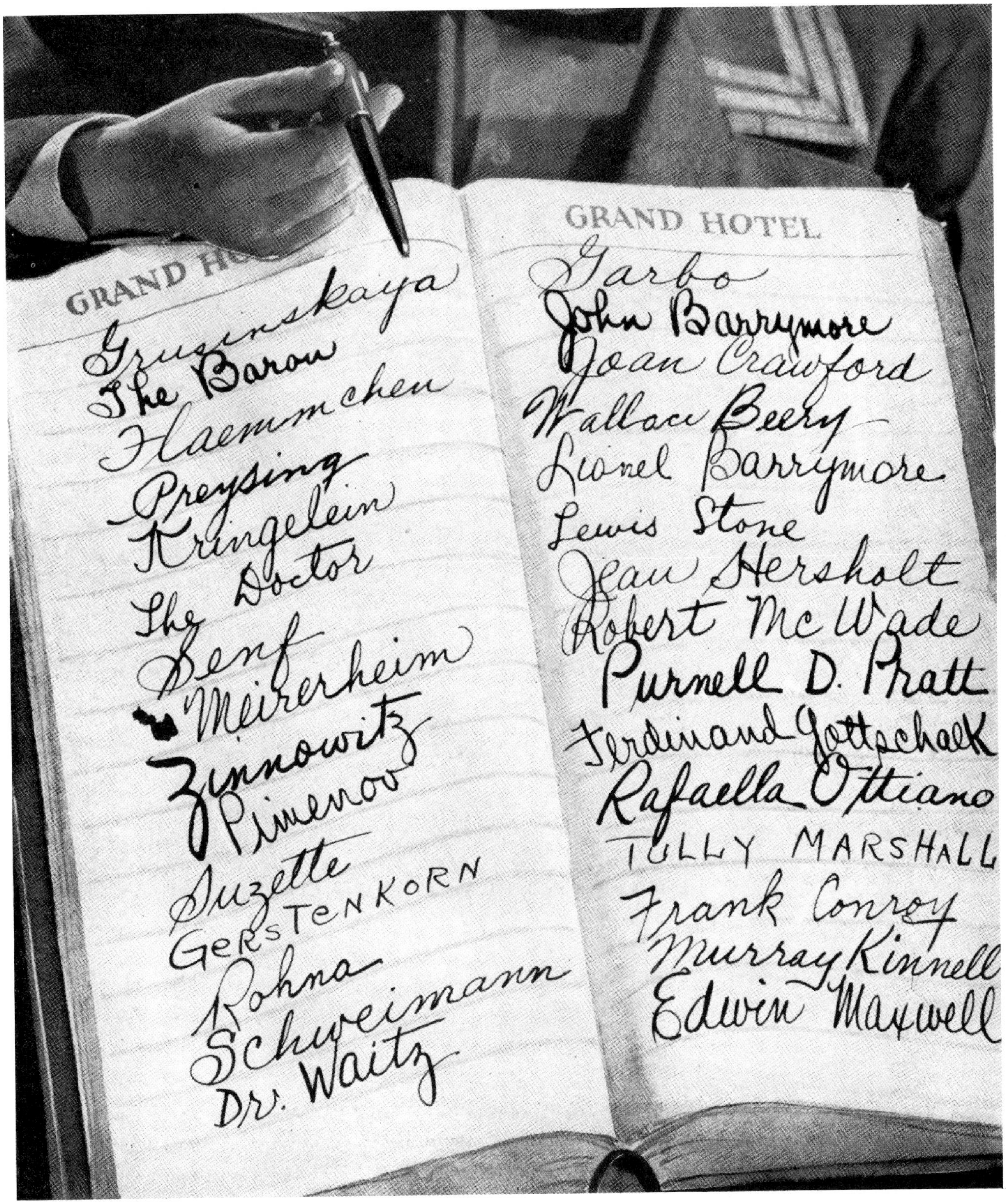

GRAND HOTEL

Gruzinskaya
The Baron
Flaemmchen
Preysing
Kringelein
The Doctor
Senf
Meierheim
Zinnowitz
Pimenov
Suzette
Gerstenkorn
Rohna
Schweimann
Dr. Waitz

Garbo
John Barrymore
Joan Crawford
Wallace Beery
Lionel Barrymore
Lewis Stone
Jean Hersholt
Robert Mc Wade
Purnell D. Pratt
Ferdinand Gottschalk
Rafaella Ottiano
TULLY MARSHALL
Frank Conroy
Murray Kinnell
Edwin Maxwell

GRETA GARBO

Greta Garbo, born in Sweden, first attracted attention through being used as a hat model in a store where she was a clerk. Eric Petschler saw her and gave her a screen test. Then Mauritz Stiller, at that time the greatest director in Sweden, directed her in several pictures. Metro-Goldwyn-Mayer brought her to the United States and she was rapidly recognized to be one of the most magnetic personalities on the screen. She appeared last in "Mata Hari" and "Susan Lenox."

The Story of GRAND HOTEL

AT midday in the Grand Hotel in Berlin there is the usual stir and bustle of people arriving and departing. In this center of metropolitan life men and women tarry for a while with their fears and desires—and deposit them for a night or a week or a month in the rooms they occupy there.

Tragedy, adventure and romance are next door to each other: Grusinskaya, a beautiful dancer who has known success and fame, languishes sorrowfully in her suite because her popularity is waning; Kringelein, who has been told that he has but a short time longer to live, is determined to salvage as much as possible from his remaining hours, and to forget his former under-dog life as a clerk in an orgy of spending; Preysing, the textile magnate who was Kringelein's employer, has turned his apartment into a business conference office in an attempt to settle a merger, knowing that failure will bring complete ruin; Flaemmchen, a lovely young secretary, is forced by circumstances to be the plaything of men; and Baron von Gaigern, black sheep of his family, is in financial straits and determined to steal the dancer's pearls so that he may extricate himself from his difficulties.

Each of these individuals, of such widely different temperaments, is immersed in his or her world of affairs, oblivious to the troubles of others, until the skein of fate draws them together.

Meanwhile the Doctor, a scarred war veteran, inquires fruitlessly of the desk clerk for messages, and, because there are none, thinks that nothing ever happens in the Grand Hotel—nothing but the usual routine.

That evening Grusinskaya is so upset that she refuses to appear at the theatre. It is only when she is told the theatre is crowded and many have been refused admittance that she consents to go. At the same time the Doctor and Kringelein are together in the clerk's gorgeous room, the latter pathetic in his attempts to find a way to forget his bodily ills. In the hall, where he has been waiting to see the dancer pass, the Baron meets Flaemmchen. They start a conversation, and the Baron invites her to a dance the next afternoon. When she leaves him to take dictation from Preysing, the Baron goes to his own room.

From his apartment he hears Grusinskaya leave, and after a talk with his chauffeur, one of the thieves who are forcing him to steal the pearls, the Baron manages to enter the dancer's room by the hazardous route of the outside balcony. He finds the pearls, which Grusinskaya has refused to wear because she imagines they have brought her bad luck, slips them into his pocket, and then clumsily overturns the telephone. Afraid the desk clerk will become suspicious, he hides, and remains hidden while a chambermaid comes in and arranges the room.

JOHN BARRYMORE

John Barrymore, who was one of the dominant figures on the New York stage before he went to Hollywood to carve out for himself an equally brilliant career in motion pictures, is a Philadelphian by birth. He tried newspaper work as a youth, but, being a Barrymore, drifted naturally to the stage. He appeared in dramas and musical comedies before making his motion picture debut. Recently he has appeared in "Moby Dick," "Svengali," "The Mad Genius" and "Arsene Lupin."

THE STORY (Continued)

Just as the chambermaid leaves, Grusinskaya returns.

The Baron cannot escape, and he watches while the dancer prepares to retire, sees her take a veronal bottle, gasps when she writes a frantic suicide note, and then reveals himself in time to keep her from committing suicide. He explains his presence by declaring that he is in love with her and couldn't withstand the temptation of breathing the air of her room. When he suddenly realizes, as he stands talking to her, that he really loves her, he confesses his theft and returns the pearls. Because she has fallen in love with him, too, Grusinskaya blesses the pearls for bringing them together, and they plan to leave in the morning to start life anew. She offers him money, which he refuses, and, vowing his love, he leaves her early in the morning.

Kringelein, whom the Baron has befriended, calls him as the Baron passes his door, and the Baron goes in to find the poor clerk suffering and the Doctor with him, doing what he can to relieve his pain. Kringelein speaks of the money he has in his possession, and the Baron, watching his chance, steals the sick man's wallet. But the clerk discovers his loss, and appears so crushed that the Baron is remorseful and returns the wallet. When the clerk learns that the Baron needs money, he offers him some, and that afternoon they play

A PRIVATE CONFERENCE

cards. But Kringelein wins—and the Baron loses.

That night the Baron ransacks Preysing's room while Preysing is with Flaemmchen. Preysing, returning, catches the Baron and kills him with the telephone. Flaemmchen, who has been planning to go to England with Preysing, runs to Kringelein with the news, and Kringelein, eager to obtain revenge on his former employer, calls the police to the scene of the tragedy.

In the early morning the Baron's body is taken away from the hotel. Preysing is remorseful and bewildered, totally unable to realize the turn affairs have taken. He is placed under arrest and taken away by the police. Kringelein and Flaemmchen, thrown together, discuss their future. Kringelein asks the girl to accompany him to Paris, and Flaemmchen, who really has become interested in the clerk, consents to this arrangement.

When it is time for the dancer to leave to catch her train, she is worried about the Baron. But Suzette, her maid, assures her that he will be on the train, and Grusinskaya sweeps happily out of the hotel, looking forward to a new life.

The doctor makes his usual morning call at the desk for messages, telegrams or letters that never come, and as he turns away empty-handed, he mutters to himself: "Same thing every day. They come and go—the Grand Hotel—nothing ever happens."

JOAN CRAWFORD

Joan Crawford, who has shown her versatility by equally deft characterizations in serious and light roles, was educated in Kansas City and centered her ambitions on the stage. She made her debut as a dancer in a Chicago revue and came to New York to play in "Innocent Eyes." Signed by Metro-Goldwyn-Mayer, her rise in motion pictures was rapid, and she became a star three years ago. Her most recent appearances were in "This Modern Age" and "Possessed."

Screening "Grand Hotel"

PROBABLY no film of the current season attracted as much advance attention as the picturization of "Grand Hotel," which has enough stars in its line-up to populate a half dozen ordinary screen productions.

The screen version of "Grand Hotel" represents a correlation of salient points in Vicki Baum's novel and stage play, which ran for more than a year at the National Theatre, New York. Action from the novel was blended with the general tempo and structure of the stage play in the screen treatment, which therefore embraces a slightly larger sphere of activity than either of its predecessors. At the same time, Director Edmund Goulding pointed out, none of the action in the film goes beyond the four walls of the Berlin hotel from which the story derives its name.

For some time before actual filming of this photoplay commenced, there was speculation as to how the screen treatment would be handled.

DIRECTOR GOULDING TAKES A CLOSE-UP OF WALLACE BEERY AND JOAN CRAWFORD

Finally it was decided by studio executives to give the picture one of the most unusual casts ever brought together, with equal emphasis placed on various roles. Greta Garbo, John Barrymore, Lionel Barrymore, Joan Crawford and Wallace Beery were all given leading parts, with such notable character players as Jean Hersholt and Lewis Stone added for good measure to this galaxy of talent.

" 'Grand Hotel' is one of the few stories ever written," explained Director Goulding in a backstage chat, "where no single character dominates, but where at least five are equally important to the story structure."

"These five leading parts," he continued, "are uniform. None dominates the other. As a mat-

ter of fact, some of the characters do not meet each other all during the action of the picture and every character has a separate and distinct bearing on the general theme."

The aim of studio executives was to attain something completely novel in the screen treatment in "Grand Hotel." By a combination of the photographic and sound mediums the attempt was made to endow his camera as much as possible with the personality of the audience, permitting the audience, through visual and oral suggestion, to take itself into the Berlin hostelry, and witness the drama through its own eyes and ears.

Hotel architecture from various parts of the world was assembled in the preparation of the unusual settings to be used in the new film. Novelties and fittings used in various hostelries were duplicated, and the hotel carried a distinct Continental atmosphere, but was more or less a composite of many renowned establishments in the great cities of the world.

"Many photographic and sound mechanical innovations were utilized in the making of the unusual shots for the production," said Director Goulding, "but there was no departure from book or play in taking the story away from the hotel for even a moment. The screen treatment, however, allowed a wide camera scope.

"There were no extra players, as such. Every person who appeared before the camera was a distinct and important character. If they did not have an individual importance they would be out of place in the Grand Hotel. We exerted the same care in selecting bellboys, clerks and lesser characters that is usually employed in assigning featured roles."

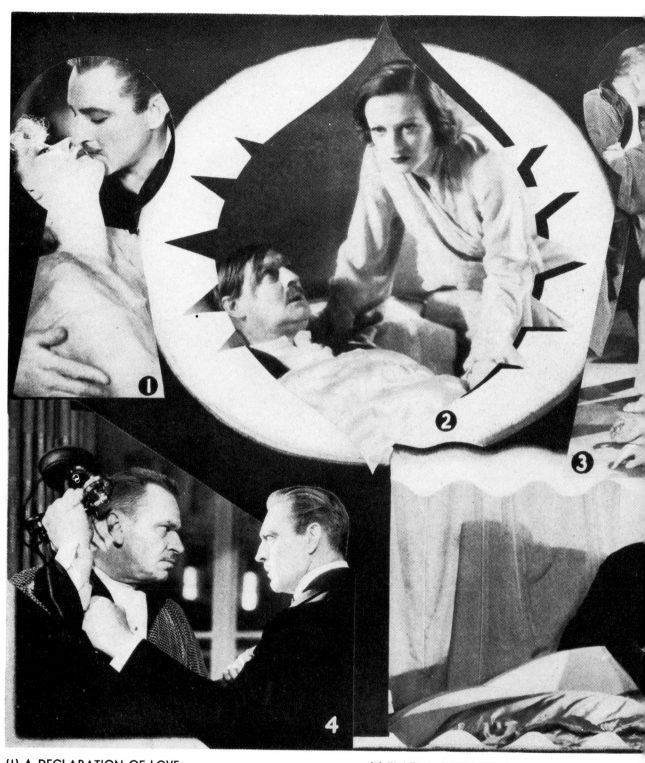

(1) A DECLARATION OF LOVE

(2) FLAEMMCHEN FEELS A SURGE OF SYMPAT

(3) SUDDEN VIOLENCE TWISTS THE PATTERN OF CHANCE

(4) PREYSING THREATENS HIS ANTAGONIST

STIRRING EPISODES FROM THE PICTURE

(5) THE BARON MAKES HIS PRESENCE KNOWN   (6) A TORRID GAMBLING SESSION
(7) THE BARON'S CONSCIENCE GETS THE BETTER OF HIM

WALLACE BEERY

Wallace Beery obtained his start on the New York stage when Raymond Hitchcock, playing in "The Yankee Tourist," couldn't go on. Beery substituted for him and was an immediate success. He went to Chicago to appear in comedies and then was sent to Hollywood as a director. After a variety of screen parts, Beery was signed by Metro-Goldwyn-Mayer, and starred in "Hell Divers" and "The Champ." Other outstandingly successful characterizations, prior to "Grand Hotel," were in "The Big House" and "Min and Bill."

Fraternal Harmony

"GOOD synchronization" is the explanation of the facility of John and Lionel Barrymore in handling characterizations in the same picture, according to Edmund Goulding, who directed the famous brothers in "Grand Hotel."

Director Goulding used this expression in a figurative rather than a technical sense, he explained, when he described the manner in which the Barrymores worked together before the camera.

"Each one seemed to know every slight gesture and expression of the other in advance," said Goulding. "And this wasn't the result of careful preliminary rehearsing, for they studied their scripts separately and hardly exchanged a word about the scenes until after they had actually made the picture. Yet I never saw any two players who could 'time' scenes so accurately. Never in a single instance did one of the Barrymores put in a word too soon or hold it to 'cover' the dialogue of the other."

Although John and Lionel Barrymore played together on the New York stage in "The Jest" and "Peter Ibbetson," they had never been together in the same film until the production of "Arsene Lupin." Both had been working in Hollywood for many years; but perhaps producers felt that one Barrymore per picture was sufficient audience inducement, or perhaps they were afraid that each of the famed brothers would attempt to monopolize scenes and situations.

If the latter suspicion entered their minds, it was so far from the truth as to be almost grotesque, according to Goulding.

"I could name plenty of Hollywood actors who try to 'steal' scenes from each other," he said. "But with the Barrymores the exact opposite is the case. They actually try to 'build up' scenes for each other. Each gets a big kick out of seeing the other get in a particularly effective bit of acting, and they're intensely loyal to each other.

THE BROTHERS BARRYMORE WATCH REHEARSALS ON THE SET

"Each one has a droll but a very keen sense of humor, and John's special delight is to watch Lionel inject comedy touches into his scenes, as he did in several places in 'Arsene Lupin' and in 'Grand Hotel.' John would keep perfect self-control during the photographing of a scene like this, but the moment the cameras stopped grinding he would start shaking with laughter."

John Barrymore likes to tell people about the Barrymore baby—and Lionel always listens with the same quiet, cheerful smile. Lionel is proud of the baby, and John is equally proud of the fact that his brother won the 1931 Academy of Motion Pictures Arts award for the best acting performance of the season in "A Free Soul."

John's favorite anecdote about Lionel concerns the days when the latter was putting on weight to such an extent that it began to be very noticeable.

"You know, he was actually fat," John likes to comment. "That was in New York. I told him that if he didn't do something about it he'd be no good for anything but burlesque parts. Finally, the son-of-a-gun began to agree with me. He took up Vance Thompson's 'Eat and Grow Thin' diet, ran around the Central Park reservoir with four sweaters on, and preserved himself for a future career in the movies."

When John starts springing this anecdote too often, Lionel has one in return. It has to do with the time when John was hustled out of bed at six in the morning when the 1906 earthquake hit San Francisco, and was commandeered into service by army guards shoveling away bricks from the sidewalks. At the conclusion of this story Lionel pauses a moment with a twinkle in his eye, slowly and very carefully crosses his legs while straightening the folds of his trousers and then repeats the late John Drew's comment on the incident:

"It took an earthquake to get him out of bed, and the United States Army to make him go to work!"

LIONEL
BARRYMORE

Lionel Barrymore, winner of the Academy Prize in 1931 for his performance in "A Free Soul," made his stage debut as a child. He later studied dramatic art in Paris, and returned to New York to establish himself as a great character actor in such plays as "The Jest" and "The Copperhead." He came to the screen in 1909 and has directed and acted in motion pictures ever since, proving equally adept at both. "The Man I Killed" and "Arsene Lupin" are among his latest film roles.

Interesting Facts About "Grand Hotel"

Edmund Goulding, director of "Grand Hotel," studied photographs of performers in stage productions of "Grand Hotel" in Berlin, Budapest, Prague, Rome, London, Paris and other cities in deciding on the make-up and wardrobe for his central characters in the picturization of Vicki Baum's play and novel. The director found that although most of the actresses who played Grusinskaya seemed to have accepted similar interpretations of the character, there was a striking individuality of conception of roles as far as Kringelein was concerned.

⚚ ⚚ ⚚ ⚚ ⚚

The fact that Metro-Goldwyn-Mayer's "Grand Hotel" is a most cosmopolitan institution was revealed by the casting office during the filming of the new photoplay. Included in the several hundred persons engaged to provide atmosphere in the expansive hotel lobby built on a sound stage were representatives of many races and nationalities. In one sequence several Japanese, a Russian, a Dane, Swedes, a Lithuanian, an Austrian, a Czecho-Slovakian, Englishmen, Frenchmen, an Armenian, a Spaniard, Italians, a Finlander, two Argentinians, and several Americans took part.

⚚ ⚚ ⚚ ⚚ ⚚

Sixteen thousand square feet of composition flooring was the amount needed to cover a single set built at the Metro-Goldwyn-Mayer studio for the filming of "Grand Hotel." The set represented Cedric Gibbons' conception of the hotel lobby and balconade and included many striking features said to bring new ideas architecturally into the arrangement of hotel facilities.

⚚ ⚚ ⚚ ⚚ ⚚

Lewis Stone wore a felt sole on one shoe and a wooden sole on the other to create a realistic impersonation of a man wearing an artificial limb in his characterization of the shell-shocked doctor in "Grand Hotel." The difference in the soles imparted an unevenness in his tread that sounded convincing when recorded over the microphone.

⚚ ⚚ ⚚ ⚚ ⚚

Lionel Barrymore and Joan Crawford surprised each other with the intensity of their characterizations by bursting into tears in the first scene they played together in "Grand Hotel." In the middle of the touching scene Barrymore's voice broke dramatically and real tears coursed down his cheeks. Joan's tears followed.

"That was the most genuinely touching scene I ever watched," was the comment of Edmund Goulding.

⚚ ⚚ ⚚ ⚚ ⚚

Cecil Holland's file of Continental make-ups was put to a test in the supplying of atmospheric characters as background for scenes in "Grand Hotel." Edmund Goulding required that every person on the set must be a distinct type and no two make-ups must be alike. It was up to Holland, who has for years been recognized as one of the cleverest of make-up experts, to provide distinction of character through the use of special facial contours and tonsorial treatment, based on photographs in his files.

⚚ ⚚ ⚚ ⚚ ⚚

Red flood lights supplied inspirational atmosphere for Garbo during rehearsals of romantic scenes with John Barrymore for "Grand Hotel." With the exception of the diffused lights, the stage was in darkness during rehearsals.

⚚ ⚚ ⚚ ⚚ ⚚

Wallace Beery discovered something new about himself when he clipped his hair and wore glasses for his role of Preysing in "Grand Hotel." When he puts on the spectacles and shows his teeth he bears a striking resemblance to the late Theodore Roosevelt.

LEWIS STONE   JEAN HERSHOLT

Lewis Stone went overseas as an army captain in 1917 and during the war won the commission of major. Before the war he had been prominent on the New York stage, but after his return from abroad he entered the motion picture field and quickly became one of the most popular and versatile character actors on the screen. His excellent speaking voice has made him more in demand than ever before during the past three years.

Jean Hersholt, Danish by birth, wanted to become a painter, and studied art for many years before he decided that he was more interested in becoming an actor. His rise to prominence on the European stage was rapid, and after coming to this country he took a position in the front rank of screen character players. In addition to "Grand Hotel," he has appeared recently in "Susan Lenox," "The Sin of Madelon Claudet" and "Emma."

The Spring Tide of Productions

PRODUCTION executives at the Metro-Goldwyn-Mayer studios approach the peak of the 1932 spring drive with about fifteen pictures under way or in various stages of preparation for the screen. This line-up embraces a wide variety of material.

The new production schedule follows such recent and current M-G-M successes as John and Lionel Barrymore's "Arsene Lupin," Marie Dressler's "Emma," "The Champ," the Garbo-Novarro "Mata Hari," and "Tarzan The Ape Man."

With "Grand Hotel" completed, all the stars who participated in this notable production were again free to resume their normal activities. Joan Crawford has been busy with "Letty Lynton," a new vehicle based on the novel by Marie Belloc Lowndes. Clarence Brown is director of this story and Robert Montgomery co-stars with Miss Crawford. Nils Asther and May Robson are also in the cast.

Garbo's new vehicle is "As You Desire Me," based on Pirandello's character study of an extraordinary woman. George Fitzmaurice, who made "Mata Hari," is director, with Melvyn Douglas and Eric Von Stroheim figuring in prominent supporting roles.

Wallace Beery's next stellar appearance will be in a story of modern Russia, as yet unnamed. George Hill, whose recent films include "Hell Divers" and "Min and Bill," will direct this production.

"Strange Interlude" perhaps challenges "Grand Hotel" for popular interest among new Metro-Goldwyn-Mayer offerings. Eugene O'Neill's vivid characters have been re-created on the screen in the persons of Norma Shearer, Clark Gable, Henry Walthall, May Robson and Ralph Morgan. Robert Z. Leonard, who last directed Garbo in "Susan Lenox," won this directorial assignment.

The name of Norma Shearer's next picture, to follow "Strange Interlude," has not been announced. It will be directed by Sidney Franklin, responsible for "Private Lives." Miss Shearer is also planning to do "Smilin' Through" in the near future.

Current events of the new pages will find their reflection in "China Seas," in which Tod Browning will direct Clark Gable and a strong supporting cast.

Ramon Novarro has just completed "Huddle" under Sam Wood's direction. This is a story of campus life and football romance. This novel, recently featured in a leading national magazine, finds Madge Evans, Una Merkel and Martha Sleeper as an interesting trio of feminine talent.

The adventures of a debonair young man who starts out to marry money, and remains to love, are portrayed in Robert Montgomery's latest starring vehicle, "—But the Flesh Is Weak." This is a comedy based on Ivor Novello's stage play, "The Truth Game." Jack Conway is director, and the star is supported by Nils Asther, Nora Gregor, Heather Thatcher, C. Aubrey Smith and Frederick Kerr.

Jackie Cooper's new starring picture is "Limpy," an adaptation of the William Johnston novel of the same name. Chic Sale, Dorothy Peterson and Ralph Graves are included in the cast which supports the juvenile star.

Marie Dressler's new starring vehicle, in which she again appears with Polly Moran, is "Prosperity," under direction of Leo McCarey. This is an original story especially prepared for the two fun-makers of "Caught Short" and "Politics" and is said to be the most hilarious vehicle they have ever had.

Marcel de Sano will shortly get under way with one of the most discussed stories of the year, Katherine Brush's "The Red-Headed Woman." No cast has as yet been assigned for this important theatrical property, but various leading actresses are being considered for the title role.

Walter Huston heads the cast of "Night Court," a new film dealing with corrupt courts and judges in a great city, with Phillips Holmes and Anita Page in leading roles and directed by W. S. Van Dyke. Lewis Stone, Jean Hersholt, John Miljan and Tully Marshall all have parts in "Night Court."

Charles Riesner, director of those three highly successful comedies, "Caught Short," "Reducing" and "Politics," is preparing to make in talkie form that great comedy favorite, "Turn to the Right."

Other company directors are busy. Edgar Selwyn, responsible for "The Sin of Madelon Claudet," will direct Faith Baldwin's "Skyscraper." Monta Bell has been added to M-G-M's directorial staff to make "Downstairs," John Gilbert's next, from a story suggested by the star himself. Charles Brabin is working on "After All," a picturization of the John Van Druten stage play of the same name, which was seen on Broadway recently. Margaret Perry repeats the role which she had in the stage production.

Buster Keaton and Edward Sedgwick are preparing "Footlights," from Clarence Budington Kelland's Saturday Evening Post story of a college professor who becomes an "angel" for a musical production on Broadway.

Metro-Goldwyn-Mayer has just acquired motion picture rights to "The Claw," Henry Bernstein's melodrama. "The Claw" was produced originally by Arthur Hopkins in October, 1921, at the Broadhurst Theatre. Lionel Barrymore, Irene Fenwick (Mrs. Barrymore) and Charles Kennedy were in the stage cast. This picture will be made in the near future.

CELEBRATION

REGISTRATION

Settings Vitally Important in Filming of "Grand Hotel"

Perhaps in no other film production has the creation of settings been regarded with the importance attached to the designing and construction of the expansive interiors for "Grand Hotel." This, according to Cedric Gibbons, Metro-Goldwyn-Mayer art director, was largely due to the fact that the Berlin hotel in which the entire drama was enacted became a personality rather than a mere background, in the unfoldment of the story.

The Grand Hotel, Gibbons explained, is not an actual place. It is entirely mythical. It just happens to be in Berlin and therefore has a German influence. Otherwise it might be in any other cosmopolitan center anywhere on the globe. It is, in fact, a symbol of life itself. It is the world in which we all are transient guests, with "someone else sleeping in our beds when we leave."

Those who saw the cinema settings, spread over several of M-G-M's biggest sound stages, marvelled at the striking excellence of the architecture and appointments. It is a strictly modern hotel, suggesting the German, yet wholly individual in character. Its personality is its own.

"Motion picture settings usually serve the purpose of a background to the action of the picture," Gibbons relates. "Here, however, the sets take the place of an actor, one of the central figures in the story. The 'Grand Hotel' is bigger than all the people who come and go within its walls. We therefore went about designing the sets with the view of bringing the background forward on the same plane as the players.

"Our settings represent the most modern progress in hotel facilities and appointments. It is modern but not modernistic. The mail chutes all bear an airplane emblem, symbolic of the type of service expected in a 'Grand Hotel.' In the lobby the telegraph counter offers radio service to all ships at sea. As a cosmopolitan institution there is every facility available for translation or stenographic work in any language. There is an international scope about it that makes it at once the stopping place of all kinds of people from all corners of the earth. People are always coming and going. No one stays very long. As Vicki Baum wrote, 'there are a hundred doors on every corridor and no one knows his neighbor.' That is the feeling we tried to express."

DELIBERATION

INFATUATION

EDMUND GOULDING AND VICKI BAUM, AUTHOR OF "GRAND HOTEL," DISCUSS THE PICTURE

Vicki Baum Visits Studio

When "Grand Hotel" was produced at the National Theatre, New York, a year ago last November, Vicki Baum was in Europe and it was not until her creation had been running to capacity houses for many months that she came to New York and witnessed the stage presentation for the first time.

When Metro-Goldwyn-Mayer transferred "Grand Hotel" to the screen, however, the author of the play acted as voluntary technical supervisor. Her first conference with studio production officials and with Director Edmund Goulding took place about a month before any actual camera work on the photoplay.

"My characters didn't come to me by any sudden flash of inspiration," explained the author, "it was a slow process, something like working out ideas and improvements for a country home. I didn't feel like sitting down to write the story for at least three years after the first idea developed.

"My husband, you know, is an operatic conductor. I came to know a certain temperamental ballet dancer when attending his concerts, and I felt that her personality would be a very vivid one for a work of fiction. The characters of Preysing, the financial magnate, and Flaemmchen, the stenographer, were also borrowed from life. The situation involving the two was worked out by me from an actual account in a Berlin newspaper of a similar tragedy. The Baron was the type of lover, in fact, with whom such a person as Grusinskaya might become infatuated. He and Kringelein had no foundation in fact, so far as their origin in my mind was concerned. Kringelein was completely a product of the imagination, and it was really with his character that I started the task of making a detailed outline of my story."

No Jumps in "Grand Hotel"

When final scenes for "Grand Hotel" were photographed, the picture was practically ready for final editing. In the ordinary picture it is customary to begin with any episode which can be made most easily on the day on which the camera starts grinding. Not infrequently the last sequence of a film is photographed first. Director Goulding, however, in two months of advance planning for the job of transferring "Grand Hotel" to the screen, prepared a continuity which was entirely chronological, following the narration of events as presented on the stage with the added scope provided by the eye of the camera.

There was no reason, in the case of "Grand Hotel," with its single focal point of action, to skip from the beginning to the end of the story. The entire photoplay was screened almost exactly as the audience perceives it in final form.

Several times as many as six cameras photographed a single scene of "Grand Hotel," breaking up the action into different "cuts" planned in advance. On the set during the making of key scenes for each sequence was Blanche Sewell, film editor, who was charged with the responsibility of matching the various "cuts" together for a rapid and fluid linking of story and action.

Some of the most difficult shots of the entire picture concerned action that took in seven floors at once. For this scene a spiral staircase seven stories high was constructed, the upper portion representing the seventh floor of the Grand Hotel, the bottom section showing the circular lobby, with special lenses used properly to focus the action.

GRETA GARBO AND JOHN BARRYMORE CHAT WITH EACH OTHER DURING A "REST PERIOD"

A Metro-Goldwyn-Mayer PICTURE

PRINTED BY PACE PRESS, INC., N.Y.C.

Dinner at 8

A Metro-Goldwyn-Mayer
PICTURE

TWENTY-
FIVE
CENTS

101

METRO-GOLDWYN-MAYER

Presents

DINNER AT EIGHT

•

From the SAM H. HARRIS Stage Play by GEORGE S. KAUFMAN and EDNA FERBER

Screen Play by FRANCES MARION and HERMAN J. MANKIEWICZ

Additional Dialogue by DONALD OGDEN STEWART

Produced by DAVID O. SELZNICK

Directed by GEORGE CUKOR

THE CAST

Carlotta Vance . . . . MARIE DRESSLER

Larry Renault . . . . JOHN BARRYMORE

Dan Packard . . . . WALLACE BEERY

Kitty Packard . . . . JEAN HARLOW

Oliver Jordan . . . . LIONEL BARRYMORE

Max Kane . . . . LEE TRACY

Dr. Wayne Talbot . . . . EDMUND LOWE

Mrs. Oliver Jordan . . . . BILLIE BURKE

Paula Jordan . . . . MADGE EVANS

Jo Stengel . . . . JEAN HERSHOLT

Mrs. Wayne Talbot . . . . KAREN MORLEY

Hattie Loomis . . . . LOUISE CLOSSER HALE

Ernest DeGraff . . . . PHILLIPS HOLMES

Mrs. Wendel . . . . MAY ROBSON

Ed Loomis . . . . GRANT MITCHELL

Miss Alden . . . . PHOEBE FOSTER

Miss Copeland . . . . ELIZABETH PATTERSON

Tina . . . . HILDA VAUGHN

Fosdick . . . . HARRY BERESFORD

Mr. Fitch . . . . EDWIN MAXWELL

Mr. Hatfield . . . . JOHN DAVIDSON

Eddie . . . . EDWARD WOODS

Gustave . . . . GEORGE BAXTER

The Waiter . . . . HERMAN BING

Dora . . . . ANNA DUNCAN

ART DIRECTORS . . . . . . HOBE ERWIN and FRED HOPE
PHOTOGRAPHY . . . . WILLIAM DANIELS
FILM EDITOR . . . . BEN LEWIS

NOTE: The Kaufman-Ferber stage play, "Dinner at Eight," was produced by Sam Harris, and opened at the Music Box Theatre, New York, on October 22, 1932. The cast included Constance Collier, Conway Tearle, Marguerite Churchill, Ann Andrews, Judith Wood and Paul Harvey.

LIONEL BARRYMORE, winner of the Academy Prize in 1931 for his performance in "A Free Soul," made his stage debut as a child. He later studied dramatic art in Paris, and returned to New York to establish himself as a great character actor in such plays as "The Jest" and "The Copperhead." He came to the screen in 1909 and has directed and acted in motion pictures ever since, proving equally adept at both. "Stranger's Return" and "The Late Christopher Bean" are among his latest film roles. His chief interest outside of pictures is etching, and several of his works have been exhibited.

MARIE DRESSLER, who is generally voted Hollywood's most popular actress, was born in Coburg, Canada, and made her first public appearance when she was five as the particularly enchanting Cupid of a church celebration. At fourteen she joined a roving theatrical troupe. Miss Dressler has played in almost every imaginable type of theatrical presentation. Her characterization in Greta Garbo's "Anna Christie" established her as one of the leading screen character stars. Among later vehicles are "Let Us Be Gay," "Caught Short," "Prosperity," "Min and Bill" and "Tugboat Annie."

DINNER AT EIGHT

THE STORY

MILLICENT JORDAN, wife of Oliver Jordan, the shipping magnate, plans a formal dinner at her New York home in honor of Lord and Lady Ferncliffe of London. Jordan himself takes no interest in the affair other than to request his wife to invite Dan Packard, a hard-headed business man with important connections in the shipping business. Dan's wife, Kitty, is a voluptuous and flirtatious former hat-check girl who has social ambitions and who utilizes her spare time to seek romance outside her husband's jurisdiction.

Larry Renault, a movie star who has lost his popularity and has reached the point where he is being pressed by his hotel manager for a long-overdue bill, is invited to the dinner, although it is certain that Mrs. Jordan would never have dreamed of inviting him had she known that he was carrying on a secret affair with her daughter, Paula. Paula is nineteen and infatuated with the fading cinema hero, who is more than twice her age; at the same time she is engaged to Ernest DeGraff, a young man of good social connections whom she finds far less interesting than the glamorous Larry.

Carlotta Vance, a theatrical star of the "gay 'nineties," who has lost her beauty but still retains a reputation for wit and candid speech, has just arrived in New York from abroad and is invited by Mrs. Jordan to her dinner party. The same day Carlotta visits Jordan, who used to be an ardent suitor and is still one of her closest friends, in his private office. She tells him that she wants to sell her stock in his company because she is hard-pressed for money. Jordan reluctantly agrees to try to help her dispose of it.

Dan Packard, working through confidential agents, secures Carlotta's stock and also that of the majority of large holders in the Jordan Steamship Line. Rumors of the financial instability of the corporation aid Packard in carrying out his design, which is to amalgamate the line with another and turn over a handsome profit for himself, though it means Jordan's ruin.

When Dan is told by his wife of the Jordan's invitation to dinner, he flatly refuses to have anything to do with it.

"I can't go and eat his dinner!" he exclaims. "If he's a sucker that's his funeral. Business is business, but I can't go walking into his house."

DAN PACKARD SOUNDS OUT OLIVER JORDAN ON THE PRECARIOUS CONDITION OF HIS FIRM

WALLACE BEERY obtained his start on the New York stage when Raymond Hitchcock, playing in "The Yankee Tourist," couldn't go on. Beery substituted for him and was an immediate success. He went to Chicago to appear in comedies and then was sent to Hollywood as a director. After a variety of screen parts, Beery was signed by Metro-Goldwyn-Mayer, and starred in "Hell Divers" and "The Champ." Other outstanding successful characterizations, prior to "Grand Hotel," were in "The Big House" and "Min and Bill." He is an experienced air pilot, with a government transport license.

JEAN HARLOW first gained the attention of motion picture audiences with her performance in "Hell's Angels." Visiting a casting office with a friend who had movie ambitions, Miss Harlow was persuaded to accept extra work. The casting director for the Hal Roach studios happened to see some "rushes" and a contract with Roach followed. Later Miss Harlow played a bit in Clara Bow's "The Saturday Night Kid." Then Ben Lyon and James Hall introduced her to Howard Hughes and the latter tested her for the "Hell's Angels" role. Her most recent pictures were "Red-Headed Woman," "Red Dust" and "Hold Your Man."

THE STORY [Continued]

Kitty, however, is determined that nothing shall thwart her social ambitions, and uses all her resourcefulness to make Dan change his mind. She threatens a disclosure of some of his shady business deals if he turns down the dinner, and ends up by pointing out to him the obvious advantages of a personal introduction to the wealthy and influential Lord Ferncliffe. Her husband capitulates.

Dr. Wayne Talbot, who is summoned daily by Kitty to the Packard home on various pretexts, is more than a professional visitor there. For some time he has been Kitty's lover, but it is now becoming rather evident to her that her company does not interest him as it once did. Lucy, the doctor's wife, is tolerant and understanding in the matter of his affairs with women patients; nevertheless Talbot feels intense remorse when she discovers his relationship to Kitty, and he secretly resolves to have done with it.

When Oliver Jordan, hurrying home from an exhausting day at the office, is seized by a sudden heart attack, he barely manages to stumble into Talbot's office. The doctor quickly discovers that his old friend is suffering from a complicated cardiac condition that may at any time prove fatal, but he conceals the truth from Jordan.

Mrs. Jordan, meanwhile, is notified that her prize guests of honor, the Ferncliffes, have left unexpectedly for Florida and will be unable to attend the dinner. She is frantic with anger and disappointment, but can do nothing except invite her socially unacceptable sister and her husband as substitutes.

Larry Renault's press agent brings to the actor's hotel suite a theatrical producer who has tentatively agreed to give Renault a small part in a stage play. Under the influence of drink, the former movie idol makes himself so obnoxious to the visitor that he withdraws his offer. This is the last straw . . . no further chance of a job, less than a dollar in his pocketbook and an impossible affair with Paula Jordan make Larry realize the futility of going on. He dismisses his press agent, locks his room, stuffs the crevices in the door and turns on the gas.

Before they start for the Jordan dinner, Kitty Packard and her husband engage in a violent quarrel, during which Kitty boasts of the fact that she is having a secret love affair, and dares Dan to do anything. She further adds that unless he releases Oliver Jordan from the web he has wound around him, she will tell everything she knows about his business transactions.

Dan, on arriving at the Jordan home, goes up to the shipowner and in a tone of affected cordiality tells him he has unearthed a plot to corner his stock and undermine the business. Jordan is astonished at the news, particularly when Dan tells him that every share of stock will be restored.

"I've been looking the proposition over," Dan adds. "I was just saying to my wife tonight it looks like a good place for me to sink a little dough, didn't I, honey?"

"You certainly did, lamb," Kitty rejoins.

The news is a wonderful tonic for Jordan. He and Millicent lead the way into the dining-room, where, their strange preliminary cross-dramas ended, the mixed group finally assembles for dinner.

PAULA RELUCTANTLY PARTS FROM LARRY

BILLIE BURKE was born in Washington, D. C., but received much of her early education in England, and made her stage debut in a London musical comedy. It was in "My Wife," opposite the late John Drew, that Miss Burke made her Broadway theatrical debut. She scored a great hit, and was subsequently starred in a long list of successes, including "A Marriage of Convenience," "Caesar's Wife" and "Intimate Strangers." She played in a number of silent films and made her talkie debut in "A Bill of Divorcement," following this with "Christopher Strong."

JOHN BARRYMORE, who was one of the dominant figures on the New York stage before he went to Hollywood to carve out for himself an equally brilliant career in motion pictures, is a Philadelphian by birth. He tried newspaper work as a youth, but, being a Barrymore, drifted naturally to the stage. He appeared in dramas and musical comedies before going to Hollywood. Recently he has appeared in "A Bill of Divorcement," "Topaze" and "Reunion in Vienna." Whenever he can break away from pictures he goes cruising and fishing aboard his yacht, the Infanta.

Selecting a Super-Star Cast

THE largest number of stars ever assembled for a single dramatic picture—an even bigger name cast than "Grand Hotel's"—are to be seen in leading roles of "Dinner at Eight."

When Metro-Goldwyn-Mayer acquired picture rights to this Broadway stage hit by George S. Kaufman and Edna Ferber plans were at once inaugurated at the studio for a cast that would excel the blue-ribbon one of last season's "Grand Hotel" as well as all previous casts in the history of stage and screen. Twelve stars were recruited for the leading roles of the new production. They included Marie Dressler, John and Lionel Barrymore, Wallace Beery, Jean Harlow, Lee Tracy, Billie Burke, Edmund Lowe, Madge Evans, Karen Morley, Jean Hersholt and Phillips Holmes. Cast in prominent supporting roles were such outstanding players as May Robson, noted character actress, Grant Mitchell and Elizabeth Patterson of the New York stage, and the late Louise Closser Hale.

Perhaps the reception given "Grand Hotel" last season had much to do with the decision of Metro-Goldwyn-Mayer executives to display equal generosity in handing out stars for the leading parts of "Dinner at Eight." Even so, it is doubtful if company officials expected to gather together the talent which was eventually assembled. Various factors entered into the selection of individual players: for example, a Lee Tracy picture was postponed while a new script was being prepared and Tracy was unexpectedly at liberty to do the part of John Barrymore's personal agent; then again, the studio was unexpectedly offered an opportunity to borrow Edmund Lowe for the role of Dr. Talbot, a part which had tentatively been assigned to a lesser-known actor; and the fact that Billie Burke was to remain on the coast and had just decided to defer plans for future theatrical activities made it possible to enlist her services for the film.

Marie Dressler was the first player selected for the cast of "Dinner at Eight." She was picked out for the role of the retired actress, Carlotta Vance, within twenty-four hours after a company executive had seen the premiere of the play "Dinner at Eight" at the Music Box Theatre, New York. After securing an immediate option on the film rights, it was agreed that Miss Dressler would be the right party to play Constance Collier's stage role. John Barrymore was the next player to be selected for the cast to play the role of the fallen movie star in which Conway Tearle scored on the stage. The rest of the cast was selected during the ensuing six weeks.

Today, if such pictures as "Dinner at Eight," "Grand Hotel" and "Night Flight" are to be taken as criteria, only one thing counts—has the story sufficient vivid characterizations to support a number of outstanding stars? If so, it will be popular. Such stories are rare, but Metro-Goldwyn-Mayer's current production of "Dinner at Eight" happens to fall in the category.

The remarkable part of the picture is that its episodic narrative offers each of the celebrities in the cast a choice role. Just as there are enough stars in "Dinner at Eight" to equip more than a dozen film vehicles, so its story has enough plots and sub-plots to furnish any number of separate cinema narratives; but the picture is so cleverly contrived that it interweaves the various tales into one gripping climax in which the majority of characters are brought together.

SHOOTING A SEQUENCE WITH LIONEL BARRYMORE AND MARIE DRESSLER

1. CARLOTTA VANCE, FEARING FOR PAULA, TRIES TO ADVISE HER.
2. THE DOCTOR'S ATTENTIONS PROVE A LITTLE MORE THAN PROFESSIONAL.
3. LARRY'S PRESS AGENT TRIES TO PREVENT A *FA*
4. KITTY PACKARD THREATENS DISCLOSURE OF

AND'S SHADY BUSINESS DEALS.

5. PAULA'S INFATUATION FOR LARRY RENAULT LEADS TO COMPLICATIONS.

6. THE DOCTOR DECIDES TO TELL MRS. JORDAN OF HER HUSBAND'S REAL CONDITION.

GEORGE CUKOR'S OBSERVATIONS

THE director of "Dinner at Eight," George Cukor, has transferred to the screen some of the leading Broadway theatrical properties of recent seasons. In addition to "Dinner at Eight," these include "The Royal Family," "A Bill of Divorcement" and Somerset Maugham's comedy, "Our Betters."

"There are only a very few stories, plays or novels," explained Director Cukor, "which legitimately offer a place for a group of stellar roles. You rarely find a story where there are more than three or four dominant parts, but in 'Grand Hotel' and even more in 'Dinner at Eight' there are many more than this. Both of these stories, although utterly different, were of episodic character, combining compact characterization with action. In 'Grand Hotel' the background was a Continental hotel with the action shifting abruptly from one room to another. In 'Transatlantic' the action was set in various cabins aboard an ocean-going steamship. In 'Shanghai Express' the point of action was even more restricted, being confined to the cars of a fast-moving cross-country train. In 'Dinner at Eight' the focal point of action is less important than in any of these other pictures, for the characters never assemble at this central point until the close of the story. The picture is entirely concerned with events preceding a New York dinner party, and the interwoven relationships of the persons invited to this party.

"When I was assigned the direction of 'Dinner at Eight' all my friends began dealing out condolences on the difficulties that were to confront me in handling so many stars. Conflicting temperaments, they pointed out, had caused more trouble for directors than anything else. I actually began to get quite worried, in spite of the fact that 'Grand Hotel' with its dozen star names, had been made with a surprising lack of friction and argument.

"The first few days' shooting on 'Dinner at Eight' eliminated all these advance worries. Marie Dressler and Billie Burke greeted each other like long-lost sisters, and were apparently overjoyed to play in the same picture for the first time. Wallace Beery and the Barrymore brothers, all of whom had been in 'Grand Hotel,' went about arm in arm on the set, like the Three Musketeers. Jean Harlow, Madge Evans and Karen Morley seemed to go out of their way to help each other. One would have thought that I was directing a Rotary convention instead of a motion picture, judging by the amicable relationships prevailing on the set. From now on I shall advise directors who want to protect themselves against temperamental flare-ups to crowd their casts with stars."

WHAT THE STUDIO CAT HEARD

● An inquisitive studio cat is reported to have prowled about the "Dinner at Eight" set while the big array of stars in the picture were lounging about between shooting of scenes. This is what the feline listener overheard:

Wallace Beery and Edmund Lowe were talking about boxing. They "post mortemed" all the bouts held at the Hollywood Stadium for the past ten years.

John Barrymore and Lee Tracy discovered a mutual interest in fishing. They brought their tackle to the set and compared experiences encountered on their coast angling expeditions.

The conversation between Marie Dressler and Jean Harlow concerned themselves. Although the two had worked for years in the same studio they had never met until the filming of "Dinner at Eight." Immensely interested in each other, they conducted a mutual cross-examination.

Billie Burke and Grant Mitchell were stage stars at the same time in New York. They chatted without end about scores of mutual friends in the theatre. Miss Burke also had much pleasure in renewing an acquaintance with Madge Evans. They had both played together on the stage in "The Marquis."

DIRECTOR CUKOR COACHES JEAN HARLOW

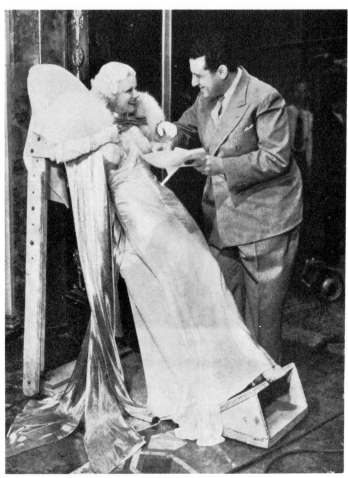

PICTURE TREND IS TOWARD MORE SELECTIVE AUDIENCE, SAYS PRODUCER

"DINNER AT EIGHT," which has become one of the most discussed films of the past several years, is the first picture turned out by David O. Selznick following his recent affiliation with Metro-Goldwyn-Mayer. The signal accomplishment of bringing this all-star transcription of the Kaufman-Ferber play to the screen has served to focus public attention on the young executive producer, whose success has been so extraordinary, and whose earlier photoplays include "Topaze," "Our Betters," "Christopher Strong" and a long list of other outstanding films.

Asked recently to state his views on the artistic standards of the motion picture, and how they had been affected by the coming of talkies, Mr. Selznick drew a sharp contrast between the period of silent films and the present-day era.

"It is my conviction that the screen attained literacy with talking pictures," he said. "We very quickly advanced past the excellent but artistically incomplete pantomime of silent days, and after a year or two of transition I feel, we have made faster progress than at any previous period.

"I believe that the quality of present-day screen writing is comparable to the best writing to be found in the legitimate theatre or among contemporary novelists. A majority of the leading playwrights, novelists and short story writers of the country have been contributing to this development through their presence in Hollywood. The great improvement in pictures attracted a new and more adult audience. I think the day is not so far off when pictures will be made for selective audiences as well as for general release.

"It was with some misgivings that my staff approached the screen production of 'A Bill of Divorcement' when I decided to make it after it had been shunned for ten years because it was thought 'too adult.' Consequently it was most gratifying when the picture turned out to be a great commercial success, as well as one which was praised highly by critics. This, more than any other one thing, strengthened my feeling that an adult picture could be financially successful if it possessed outstanding dramatic merit. I think we have achieved this ideal in 'Dinner at Eight,' which is certainly adult and at the same time has a positive down-to-earth appeal."

After completing "Dinner at Eight," Mr. Selznick did another all-star production. This was the adaptation of the French prize novel, "Night Flight," with John and Lionel Barrymore, Helen Hayes, Clark Gable and Robert Montgomery. The young producer is particularly interested in new and distinctive types of screen entertainment, and is at the moment supervising the production of "Meet the Baron," in which Jack Pearl and Jimmy Durante will both be seen.

BILLIE BURKE, LOUISE CLOSSER HALE AND MAY ROBSON IN THE "DINNER AT EIGHT" KITCHEN

Gaining fame on the New York stage through his roles in "Broadway" and "The Front Page," **LEE TRACY** came to the screen and became known as one of the fastest-talking young men in films. Born in Atlanta, Georgia, Tracy received his education at the Western Military Academy and at Union College, New York. During the war, Tracy served as a lieutenant. Afterwards he entered vaudeville and finally turned to the legitimate stage. His pictures include "Blessed Event," "Washington Merry-Go-Round," "The Nuisance" and "Turn Back the Clock."

JEAN HERSHOLT, Danish by birth, wanted to become a painter, and studied art for many years before he decided that he was more interested in becoming an actor. His rise to prominence on the European stage was rapid, and after coming to this country he took a position in the front rank of screen character players. He was an intimate friend of the late Lon Chaney, sharing the same dressing room for years. In addition to "Grand Hotel," he has appeared recently in "Susan Lenox," "The Sin of Madelon Claudet" and "Emma."

DINNER AT EIGHT

William Daniels Has "Lucky Dollar"

● William Daniels, ace cameraman for Greta Garbo, the Barrymores and other film stars, is not without his superstitions. He has a lucky talisman, though it isn't a rabbit's foot.

Six years ago he was only partially successful, just one of many photographers striving to gain a foothold in Hollywood. Today he is considered an outstanding leader, and he gives the credit to a "lucky dollar bill."

In 1927 Marie Dressler, then comparatively obscure, played in "The Callahans and the Murphys." Inasmuch as her salary at that time was a meagre one, her gift to the technical crew when the picture was completed was a simple one. Each man received a leather wallet containing an old-fashioned, full-sized "blanket" dollar bill, the kind which is now exceedingly rare.

Luck began to shower itself on Daniels from that point on. It was shortly afterwards that he became Greta Garbo's cameraman, climbing upwards in his profession via that star's pictures.

During the filming of "Dinner at Eight" Daniels showed the billfold and the dollar bill to the original donor, Marie Dressler, and expressed his thanks for the good fortune it had brought him.

The cost of repairing the wallet has already exceeded its original price, but Daniels intends to keep it and the bill until both fall to pieces from old age.

Famous Curios in Shipowner's Office

● A set to delight the heart of anyone nautically inclined was built at the Metro-Goldwyn-Mayer studio for "Dinner at Eight."

It represents the office of Lionel Barrymore as head of the old Jordan Steamship Line. There is nothing in it of the modernity or shining mahogany which might characterize the lair of a twentieth century captain of industry. It had to have a mellow quality to typify a firm which had proceeded from grandfather to father to son over a period of more than a century.

Fourteen magnificent ship models were used in the setting. Since the best models can no longer be purchased but are held as private property, David O. Selznick, the picture's producer, arranged for them to be loaned individually. To protect these valuable works of art a special officer was kept on the sets night and day.

A California museum loaned another nautical art piece, the genuine log of a Spanish galleon. Also loaned were three ancient maps. One of these, issued in the seventeenth century, shows South America as being a third wider than we know it today.

Rare Chinese lamps, an old map of Java done in batik, and other similar tokens of world-wide travel complete the atmosphere of this unusual office, designed under the supervision of the noted decorator, Hobe Erwin.

FIFTH TIME TOGETHER

● John and Lionel Barrymore appear together in a picture for the fifth time in "Dinner at Eight." The two famous brothers, members of America's first theatrical family, first played together on the screen in "Arsene Lupin." Then followed joint roles in "Grand Hotel," "Rasputin and the Empress" and "Night Flight." They are expected to appear together again in "The Paradine Case," filmization of Robert Hichens' novel.

MULTI-STAR FILMS POPULAR

THE trend toward multi-star casts, or the grouping of several stellar names in a single production, is perhaps the outstanding characteristic of the new season at several of the coast studios. In particular is this trend in evidence at Metro-Goldwyn-Mayer, where ten photoplays on the new year's schedule may now be definitely assigned to the multi-star classification, with the likelihood of others being added later. Since the total output of this company for the 1933-34 season will be forty-six pictures, it is evident that approximately one-quarter of these productions will "have the benefit," as the publicity writers put it, of several star names.

A star, in Hollywood parlance, is an actor or actress whose contract specifies that his or her name must be placed ahead of the title of the production on the theatre marquee or in the billing of the picture. If you go into a movie just as a picture is starting and read on the screen, "Percival Pendennis in 'The Grand Duchess and the Iceman'," you know that Mr. Pendennis is a star. A featured player, conversely, is one whose name follows the title of the photoplay, so if your title reads: " 'The Grand Duchess and the Iceman,' with Percival Pendennis and Lavinia LeGrand," it is obvious that Mr. Pendennis and Miss LeGrand are merely featured members of the cast. Some featured players are catapulted to stardom overnight by an unpredicted success (as was the case with Greta Garbo following "The Torrent" and Jean Harlow after "Hell's Angels"). Some players flash forward to stardom, only to fall back to the featured ranks the next season. The life of the star is uncertain, and fate is likewise capricious when it comes to age: Jackie Cooper becomes a star at seven, Marie Dressler one at sixty.

Multi-star productions had been tried now and again with fair success, particularly films on the order of "The Hollywood Revue" and "The Paramount Parade," but it was not until "Grand Hotel" that such films came dominantly to the fore. Then there was "Rasputin and the Empress," with the three Barrymores, "Smilin' Through," with Norma Shearer, Fredric March and Leslie Howard, "The Sign of the Cross" and others with a trio of stars apiece. New season Metro productions which will go in the same category include "Dinner at Eight," "Soviet," an original story of contemporary Russia; "Two Thieves," based on Manuel Komroff's novel of ancient Palestine; "The Late Christopher Bean"; "The Paradine Case," with Diana Wynyard, John and Lionel Barrymore; "Meet the Baron," with Jack Pearl and Jimmy Durante; "Broadway to Hollywood," with favorite theatre stars of three generations; "Night Flight," with the two Barrymores, Helen Hayes, Clark Gable and Robert Montgomery, and "The Hollywood Party," with Joan Crawford, Marie Dressler, Jimmy Durante, Lupe Velez, Jean Harlow, Charles Butterworth, and many other stars.

"WHY DON'T YOU GET SOME EXERCISE?" DAN ASKS HIS WIFE

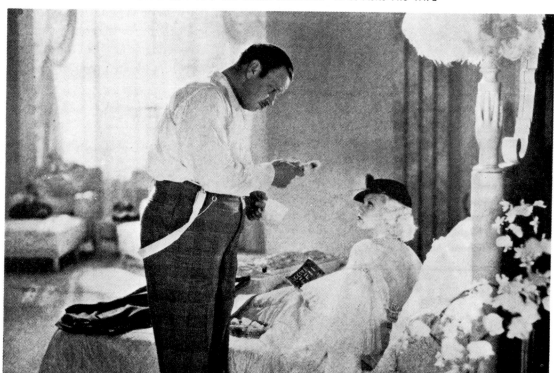

It was while he was attending Princeton University that **PHILLIPS HOLMES,** son of the theatrical star, Taylor Holmes, received his start in motion pictures. Given a part in "Varsity," he went to Hollywood during his summer vacation for interior scenes. He received other featured parts and rapidly climbed to prominence. For Metro-Goldwyn-Mayer he has played in "Night Court," "Men Must Fight," "Storm at Daybreak," and many other pictures. Holmes has travelled all over Europe and the United States, attending classes at Cambridge University in England.

Considered one of the most beautiful women in the motion picture colony, **MADGE EVANS** has been associated with the screen from childhood. In 1917, as a very young child, she appeared in a film starring Robert Warwick. Other early stars with whom she played juvenile parts included Alice Brady, Montagu Love and Holbrook Blinn. In 1925 she played the lead opposite Richard Barthelmess in "Classmates." After that she was given a stage contract. Since she has been in talking pictures she has been seen in "Son of India," "Are You Listening?" "Huddle," "Fast Life," "Hell Below," "The Nuisance" and other films for Metro-Goldwyn-Mayer.

KAREN MORLEY is an Iowa girl who served her theatrical apprenticeship in the Pasadena Community Playhouse. Sent by the Metro-Goldwyn-Mayer office to read lines in place of Greta Garbo in tests for masculine players for roles in "Inspiration," she so impressed Director Clarence Brown that she was given the role of Liane in the picture. Since then she has been selected a Wampas Baby Star and has appeared in such pictures as "The Sin of Madelon Claudet," "Susan Lenox," "Mata Hari," "Arsene Lupin" and "Gabriel Over the White House."

EDMUND LOWE disproves the theory that juvenile prodigies may not afterwards attain successful careers, for he received a B.A. from Santa Clara University at the age of eighteen. He set another record when he joined the university faculty at nineteen. Becoming interested in dramatics, he appeared in a couple of coast productions, then starred on Broadway. His first leading role in pictures was opposite Clara Kimball Young in "Eyes of Youth." Some of his greatest successes were scored in "The Fool," "What Price Glory" and "The Cock Eyed World."

» » » » News Items « « « «

SPINACH PREFERRED

The exigencies of a picture production frequently tax the digestive powers of an actor or actress. In a scene of "Dinner at Eight," for example, Jean Harlow was required to lie comfortably abed while she read movie magazines and took liberal helpings from a box of chocolates at her side. During the taking of "repeat shots" and close-ups, Miss Harlow consumed almost two pounds of confectionery in one morning. When she visited the studio lunch room that noon she confined her meal exclusively to spinach.

•

BILLIE BURKE'S CAREER

Picturegoers may be under the impression that Billie Burke, who has the role of Millicent Jordan in "Dinner at Eight," is a comparative newcomer to films, having begun her screen career with "A Bill of Divorcement." The wife of the late Florenz Ziegfeld, however, has evidence to prove otherwise. She first visited Hollywood in 1916 to play the lead in "Peggy," a picture produced by Thomas H. Ince.

•

USES OF A YACHT

When the earthquake struck Long Beach, California, twenty-five men, women and children of that community sought refuge aboard John Barrymore's yacht, which was anchored at a wharf in the beach city. They seemed to feel that the sea was a safer place than on land. Barrymore, when informed of his unexpected visitors, tersely replied: "They're all welcome. I'd like to join them, but I have two pictures to finish first."

•

HIDES FROM HOLLYWOOD

Greta Garbo isn't the only recluse in Hollywood. Grant Mitchell, noted stage star, who has the part of Ed Loomis in "Dinner at Eight," spends every bit of time when not working in pictures at his secluded desert bungalow. This retreat, in Mitchell's own words, is "seventeen miles from a telephone and can be reached only by a dirt road that will ruin any respectable car."

TRACY'S SORROW

Lee Tracy, the genial comedy star, says that he has had but one major sorrow in his life. He loves tap dancing but he has never been able to master the art. "I took lessons for four months," he explained, "but I only learned two steps, and I decided that I just wasn't born with the right kind of feet."

•

WHISTLING SHOES

Lionel Barrymore, for one, firmly believes that there is something new under the sun, after an experience that occurred during "Dinner at Eight." Following a sick room scene in which Lionel lay on a bed and moved slightly from side to side, everyone relaxed until the voice of the sound technician came from above: "It will have to be done over," he said. "Mr. Barrymore's shoes whistle." The character star changed his shoes, and the scene was taken successfully.

A CANINE QUARTET IN TOW

Printed in the U.S.A.

Pace Press. Inc., N.Y.C

A Metro-Goldwyn-Mayer PICTURE

CAPTAINS COURAGEOUS

Metro-Goldwyn-Mayer

RUDYARD KIPLING

(At left) The monument in Gloucester, Mass., erected in memory of fishermen and mariners lost at sea. (Above) The late Rudyard Kipling.

THE intense interest currently being shown by motion picture producers in the stories of Rudyard Kipling was inevitable. Kipling's canvas was that of the world. His books were as unorthodox, as far removed from the ordinary restrictions of plot and structure, as he alone could make them. His characters were as rare, human and engrossing as the subjects about which he chose to write.

The difficulty confronting screen adaptors of his work lay in the fact that each Kipling work took on qualities of grandeur and epochal achievement. His vigorous Odysseys of the sea, the British soldier and the Far East obviously had to be handled in a manner befitting their heroic conception. There was something about them which forbade any half-hearted or incompetent approach. So it came about that when "Captains Courageous" was finally made, it required two years of preparation and inspired, determined endeavor. "Kim," the fascinating story of India which will be produced on similar scale by Metro-Goldwyn-Mayer, is another one of the late British author's masterpieces. And there is still the whole wide range of the two "Jungle Books," "The Phantom Rickshaw," "The Light That Failed," "Plain Tales from the Hills," "Soldiers Three," and the beloved "Barrack Room Ballads" from which to draw.

Few persons ever think of Rudyard Kipling in association with the United States. Every reference to his life, and most references to his books, place him in far off India, where he was born, or in some secure place in the British Isles.

Yet Kipling lived in New England for a considerable time, making his headquarters in a house called Bliss Cottage, in Brattleboro, Vt., where he did a good deal of writing. His residence in this country came as the result of chance circumstances. Shortly after his marriage in London, he set out with his wife on a world tour, stopping first in Canada, delaying in snow-bound North Vancouver, and then going on to Japan, where the wisteria and peonies were in bloom.

One day Kipling decided to go to the Yokohama branch of his English bank to draw out some money. When he arrived there he discovered, to his consternation, that the bank had failed and swallowed up his funds. All his plans from that moment on had to be changed. The young married couple salvaged the remainder of their world tour trip tickets, rushed back to Canada, then proceeded to New England. Here they lived in Bliss Cottage in what approximated poverty. According to Kipling's descriptions, the cottage was only one and a half stories high, with a water supply dependent on a single half inch lead pipe which froze during the winter. Sometimes, stray skunks would enter the damp cellar and force both the Kiplings to make a hurried exodus.

Kipling's American physician, Dr. Conland, collaborated, in a sense, with the English author on "Captains Courageous." Kipling did the writing and Dr. Conland, who had served on a fleet in his youth, supplied the details.

In order to give an authentic atmosphere to the scenes and situations, they made many trips to the Massachusetts shore front, visited Boston Harbor, dropped in on sailors' eating houses and consulted tug-masters. In order to assure themselves of having all the details of the story accurate, they boarded schooners and studied charts and navigation implements. When it was all over one of the greatest sea stories of all time had emerged.

CAPTAINS COURAGEOUS

Metro-Goldwyn-Mayer
PRESENTS . . .

John Carradine as "Long Jack."

Melvyn Douglas, appearing as Harvey's father.

Mickey Rooney, as the son of Captain Disko.

(Right) Jack La Rue in the role of the priest.

Spencer Tracy as Manuel, Freddie Bartholomew as
Harvey, and Lionel Barrymore as Captain Disko.

The Players:

Charley Grapewin as
Uncle Salters.

HARVEY .... Freddie Bartholomew

MANUEL .... Spencer Tracy

DISKO .... Lionel Barrymore

MR. CHEYNE .... Melvyn Douglas

UNCLE SALTERS .... Charley Grapewin

DAN .... Mickey Rooney

"LONG JACK" .... John Carradine

CUSHMAN .... Oscar O'Shea

PRIEST .... Jack La Rue

DR. FINLEY .... Walter Kingsford

TYLER .... Donald Briggs

"DOC" .... Sam McDaniels

CHARLES .... Billie Burrud

Directed by *Victor Fleming* ● Produced by *Louis D. Lighton* ● Based on the Book by
Rudyard Kipling ● Screen Play by *John Lee Mahin, Marc Connelly* and *Dale Van Every*
Musical Score by *Franz Waxman* ● Songs: Music by *Franz Waxman* ● Lyrics by
Gus Kahn ● Art Director: *Cedric Gibbons* ● Associates: *Arnold Gillespie* and *Edwin
B. Willis* ● Marine Director: *James Havens* ● Photographed by *Harold Rosson, A.S.C.*
Film Editor: *Elmo Veron* ● Recording Director: *Douglas Shearer*

HISTORY: *Based on the book, "Captains Courageous," by Rudyard Kipling. First English
publication by MacMillan, London, 1897. First American publication by Century Company, New York, 1897.*

THE STORY OF
CAPTAINS COURAGEOUS

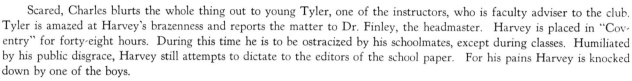

ONLY son of a millionaire industrialist, ten-year-old Harvey Cheyne has been thoughtlessly pampered by his father. The elder Cheyne, a widower, devotes almost his entire attention to business rather than to the proper rearing of the boy, and Harvey has become spoiled and is under the impression that money can buy for him anything he desires. Since Harvey's great ambition is to become a member of a certain exclusive school club, to which he has thus far been denied entrance because of his snobbishness, he makes plans to invite Charles, the club president, to the Cheyne home for the spring holidays. Scheming to put Charles under obligation to him, Harvey presents him with a rare edition of "Treasure Island," which the other boy accepts with misgivings.

En route to Connecticut and school, Harvey bluntly demands that Charles return the Cheyne favors by nominating Harvey for admission to the club. When Charles refuses, Harvey goes so far as to threaten to have Mr. Cheyne see to it that Charles' father loses his job.

Scared, Charles blurts the whole thing out to young Tyler, one of the instructors, who is faculty adviser to the club. Tyler is amazed at Harvey's brazenness and reports the matter to Dr. Finley, the headmaster. Harvey is placed in "Coventry" for forty-eight hours. During this time he is to be ostracized by his schoolmates, except during classes. Humiliated by his public disgrace, Harvey still attempts to dictate to the editors of the school paper. For his pains Harvey is knocked down by one of the boys.

Unable to endure such treatment, Harvey smears ink over his face and clothes and runs away from school. Bursting into his father's office, he blurts out a tale about having been imprisoned and tortured. Mr. Cheyne immediately summons both Dr. Finley and Tyler to his home, and from them learns of Harvey's high-handedness and precocity for lying. Realizing at last he has neglected the boy, Mr. Cheyne decides to take him to Europe for several months of travel to make up for their previous lack of companionship.

* * * *

On board ship, Harvey tries to impress his youthful fellow passengers with his father's importance and with his own capacity for ice cream sodas. Six of these, and Harvey, feeling ill, heads for the rail. But he leans over too far and, unobserved by any one on board, falls into the ocean.

Fortunately, the liner is now in the path of the Gloucester fishing boats. Manuel, a Portuguese fisherman, is out in his dory not far from where the liner has passed, and rescues the boy, taking him to the schooner, the *We're Here,* of which he is a member of the crew.

When Harvey recovers consciousness, the gruff, kindly fishermen welcome him, but the boy chooses to be most obnoxious. He immediately orders Captain Disko Troop to take him to his father. Disko patiently explains that it is impossible to take Harvey anywhere for three months, until the "catch" is in the hold.

Remaining sulky, Harvey is ostracized by the crew; all but Manuel, who attempts to reason with him. The others,

"Persons in Coventry do not speak after a class is dismissed."

Harvey is Defended by Manuel.

for the most part, look upon him as a "Jonah," and to pacify them Captain Disko places Harvey's name on the books as a member of the crew, at three dollars a month. Not until he consents to do actual work is Harvey accepted by the men and by Dan, Captain Disko's young son.

In the days that follow, Harvey learns to worship Manuel, the only real friend he has ever known. His one great desire, now, is to go out fishing with Manuel in the latter's dory. Not since the death of his father has Manuel accepted a dory mate. At last, however, Manuel brings joy to Harvey's heart by taking him along. There is a contest with another dory, that of "Long Jack" and his mate, as to who can bring in more fish. Harvey, anxious to win, secretly snarls "Long Jack's" nets, and when the truth is discovered Harvey is again a "Jonah." But when he admits his crime, Manuel softens. At last the hold of the *We're Here* is filled with fish and they put about for Gloucester. Each schooner desperately strives to be the first into port. One of Captain Disko's rivals, Walt Cushman, has managed to get under way first, but by daring and skillful sailing, the *We're Here* soon overhauls the *Jennie Cushman,* Walt's ship.

Disko knows that in order to stay in the lead he will have to break out more canvas, a dangerous procedure because of the strain it will put on the mast. It is Manuel who offers to go aloft to tend the topsails. The entire crew is horror-stricken when the mast begins to crack under the pressure. Manuel falls into the water, entangled in rope and canvas. Using Portuguese, his native language, so that the tearful Harvey may not understand, he shouts for Disko to cut him loose. He knows he is dying, having been almost sawed in half by the rope.

Realizing it is the only course to take, Disko himself takes an axe and severs the rope. The waves close over Manuel's head. Harvey is inconsolable in his grief.

*   *   *   *

When port is reached, Harvey is given Manuel's vielle, the sailor's beloved musical instrument, to keep. Overjoyed that his boy is alive and well, Mr. Cheyne flies to Gloucester, but Harvey, heartbroken because of his bereavement, wants to stay with the fishermen. Out of the nine dollars he receives for his wages he buys a candlestick for Manuel's father, and one for Manuel, which he takes to the church.

Memorial services are performed for those who gave their life at sea. When Manuel's name is pronounced, Captain Disko, Dan and Harvey all throw wreaths onto the water. Mr. Cheyne, understanding, also has brought a wreath. As the two wreaths float on the water, side by side, Harvey turns to his father for comfort, and Mr. Cheyne knows he has made the first step toward a new understanding of his son.

In "David Copperfield"

David Copperfield Steps Along

TEN THOUSAND came—but only one was chosen. And a happy choice it was, millions of film devotees agreed, when Freddie Bartholomew was selected, from among ten thousand applicants throughout the English-speaking sections of the world, to bring to life the youthful David Copperfield in Metro-Goldwyn-Mayer's highly applauded film version of the Dickensian classic novel.

That was two short years ago. Overnight, ten-year-old Freddie became a film luminary of the first water. With each succeeding picture, the boy continued to amaze critics and the public alike with his poise, charm and sheer ability. He played Greta Garbo's son in "Anna Karenina," followed with performances in "Professional Soldier" and "Little Lord Fauntleroy," and then returned to the M-G-M studio, where he remained under long-term contract.

Young Bartholomew was born in London, on March 28, 1924. Reared from infancy by his aunt, Millicent Bartholomew, Freddie received all his schooling from her. His curriculum was not limited to the studies ordinarily found in school books. Indeed, almost as soon as he learned to talk he was reciting poetry and prose with a prodigality that amazed his hearers. At the age of three he was already appearing in public in amateur theatricals in the Wilts area; and when he was only slightly older he could recite from memory long passages from Shakespeare, and entire chapters from Charles Dickens.

In the spring of 1934, when Metro-Goldwyn-Mayer was conducting extensive screen tests in the search for a boy David, Freddie, discovering through the newspapers the story of the film studio's quest, began to coax his aunt to take him for an interview. She demurred, and not until the M-G-M representatives had returned to the Culver City studios was she won over.

And so Freddie and Aunt Millicent made the 6,000 mile trip to Hollywood. At least, the boy's guardian thought, they would have a pleasurable excursion.

In due time, Freddie stood before the cameras, and was making a screen test. Studio executives needed no more than a glance at the "rushes" to realize they had reached the proverbial "gold at the end of the rainbow." He was immediately placed under contract.

What is perhaps most important of all is the fact that, despite his meteoric success and the adulation that followed, Freddie has not been spoiled. He remains the same unaffected boy who won the hearts of the townsfolk in his Warminster home.

Freddie is tremendously popular with his juvenile playmates in Hollywood, and his interests are approximately the same as the normal, physically active American boy's. He's fond of bicycles, roller skates, swimming and kite-flying. He's a match for anybody his age on the tennis court, and he's just been made a member of a California Boy Scout-troop.

Metro-Goldwyn-Mayer plans many important roles for Freddie, leading off with the title role in "Kim," which, like "Captains Courageous," is another masterpiece from the pen of Rudyard Kipling.

In "Anna Karenina"

In "The Devil Is a Sissy"

Judy Garland, who will be seen in M-G-M's "Broadway Melody of 1938," and Jackie Cooper accompany Mickey Rooney to a "Captains Courageous" preview at Grauman's Chinese Theatre, Los Angeles.

THE SERIOUS BUSINESS OF EDUCATION goes on between scenes—as does a boy's love for sport. Freddie Bartholomew and his stand-in, Ray Sperry, get some football pointers from their tutor, R. Van Scoyk, ex-varsity star at Kentucky.

Hail the "Iron Egg"

THE "iron egg" and the "self-wiping windshield" are the two amazing inventions which make possible filming of storms at sea, hazards of sailors on fishing schooners, and thrilling marine rescues, on a scale never possible before.

They are the newest equipment for operation of cameras on boats, developed by John Arnold, president of the American Society of Cinematographers, for use in "Captains Courageous."

The "iron egg" is a heavy egg-shaped mass of solid iron suspended from a framework, and to which the camera is attached, permitting it to swing like a pendulum. The result will be stability within five degrees, no matter how a boat may toss.

"This at last removes the effect of the ocean careening all over the screen as a boat rocks," explains Arnold. "As a matter of fact, utilizing gravity, the camera automatically steadies itself."

The "self-wiping windshield" is a disk of plate glass, about eight inches in diameter, rotated before the camera lens at high speed, by a motor. Pressure plates about its circumference keep it wiped and polished at all times, so that spray, waves, or drops of sea water can never obstruct the lens.

Both were installed on the Gloucester fishing schooner *We're Here* and used for location work throughout the picture, under supervision of Director Victor Fleming.

Long Distance Direction

A NEW and ingenious wrinkle was added to the technique of modern motion picture production when a director sitting on a Hollywood sound stage supervised an important sea episode, being photographed twenty miles away, by means of short-wave radio-telephone.

Taking advantage of a sudden clouded sky needed for scenes at sea, Director Victor Fleming ordered a second unit of his "Captains Courageous" company to set sail in the schooner *We're Here,* while he continued directing inside shots at the Metro-Goldwyn-Mayer studio.

A telephone line was held open between the set and a short-wave radio transmitter on the Santa Monica pier. His own receiver was tuned to the wave length of a transmitter on the vessel.

Assistants took directions for setting up the scene, then held the microphone so that the director could hear the dialogue in M-G-M's version of the Kipling sea story.

In the meantime Fleming continued with indoor scenes between Lionel Barrymore and Mickey Rooney.

CONFERENCE ON LOCATION. Director Victor Fleming and Spencer Tracy talk over a scene before the cameras "roll."

129

Captain Disko and the crew take desperate measures.

Juvenile mutiny on the "We're Here."

Harvey sets out to establish ice-cream soda supremacy.

(Above) In tribute to those who go down to

(Below) Mr. Cheyne

The Doctor gives Harvey's "injury" the once-over.

Harvey is enthralled by Manuel's musical prowess.

A friendly competition.

Memorable Scenes

from the

Production

(Right) "Long Jack" accuses Manuel of foul play.

...derstand.

...s.

(Lower right corner) Harvey objects to seamen's rations.

Filming "Captains Courageous"—A Director's Own Story

By VICTOR FLEMING

Victor Fleming

THE first step in bringing a story to the screen is to buy the picture rights. The second is to make a screen treatment. But let's start in with the beginning of actual camera work, which with "Captains Courageous" was October 16, 1935. Cameramen Harold Marzorati and Bob Roberts, business managers Frank Barnes and Ewing Scott, and marine technicians Jim Havens and Harry Marble left California that day for Gloucester, Mass., so they might spend the winter with the fishing fleet, filming backgrounds and action shots for the picture in the actual locales of the book.

On October 25, 1935, the two-masted, 110-foot Gloucester schooner, Oretha F. Spinney, which had been the prize vessel of the New England fishing fleet for the past fifteen years, was purchased and rechristened the *We're Here,* to correspond to the famous schooner of the Kipling classic. With Capt. J. M. Hersey at the wheel and our camera crew aboard, it set sail for Newfoundland. It remained up there throughout December before going on to Nova Scotia. Shots of the fishing fleet in every conceivable sort of rough winter weather were filmed. In March the schooner sailed south, through the Panama Canal, and up the Pacific Coast to Los Angeles Harbor.

But though our No. 1 schooner arrived on the west coast in March, it was September before we could gather together all the cast which Producer Louis D. Lighton had in mind for the principal roles. We waited for Freddie Bartholomew to complete work in "The Devil Is a Sissy," for Lionel Barrymore to finish his work with Greta Garbo in "Camille," for Spencer Tracy to complete "Libeled Lady." Melvyn Douglas was still unavailable for the role of the father when we started work with the rest of the cast, but he joined us shortly afterwards.

The *We're Here* had sailed 5,300 miles when it first reached Los Angeles Harbor. The boat that we picked to play its sister ship, the *Jennie Cushman,* was the *Mariner,* also Massachusetts-built, and once John Barrymore's racing yacht. While we were waiting to assemble our cast, the *We're Here* and the *Cushman* left for Monterey, San Francisco Bay, thence for Coos Bay, Oregon, to obtain fog scenes.

On October 1, almost one year from the time our crew first set out for Gloucester, our cast joined the two schooners at Avalon, Catalina Island. We worked throughout the day, then left Long Beach by water taxi late in the afternoon, going to work at sea the next morning. There were seventy-five of us, all told, to crowd onto two schooners which ordinarily have a maximum crew of twenty-seven each, and we had to find space to set up camera and sound equipment, to say nothing of setting aside space in the fo'c'sle for the schoolhouse. Even at sea, youngsters like Freddie Bartholomew and Mickey Rooney must study a legal minimum of three hours a day.

Our schooners, barges, water taxis and speedboats were all in communication with one another by short-wave radio, specially installed. We thought we had taken every advance precaution for obtaining the best results on our cruise. But we could not control the weather. We had purposely set out in October in order to take advantage of the fog. But for days after we began work, either the sun would break through or the wind would cause a break in the mist. The most temperamental cut-up of them all is the weather.

We were getting nowhere. The only thing we could do, we did. We returned to the studio, and filmed scenes of the story having to do with Freddie Bartholomew's school days.

Fortunately, the pictures which are the hardest to make somehow seem to compensate in the final results obtained. Now that shooting is completed, Spencer Tracy has confessed to me that there used to be days when he prayed that production would be called off. It was his first dialect part, also his first role requiring any singing. He was certain that everything, including his own role as Manuel, the Portuguese fisherman, was going wrong.

The day came when we were ready to put back to sea. We had brought down thirteen other schooners, many from Seattle and Alaska, for the close-ups of the fishing fleet. At this point the Pacific Coast maritime strike broke out. Though we were not operating our ships commercially, and theoretically were not affected by the strike, it was impossible to get complete crews. So we sailed short-handed.

But probably our most baffling problem was the fish. We needed thousands of pounds of codfish, dead and alive, to show authentically the Gloucester fishermen's work. Two members of the original crew of the Spinney, Olaf Olsson and Joe O'Neill, were our technical experts on that. From Boston was shipped case after case of frozen cod, but we still needed live cod and halibut for the fishermen to haul into their dories. In specially constructed sea-water tanks we tried to ship fish from Alaska, but by the time they reached Seattle they were dead. We tried again, with fewer fish in larger tanks. At last, after weeks of waiting, we received a sufficient number for our purpose.

We needed racing shots between the two schooners, with a storm background. The *We're Here* and the *Cushman* sailed thousands of miles, seeking just the right atmospheric conditions. Off the Oregon coast, the sky was too dark. Off the California coast, we had no storms at all. Off the southern Mexican coast, the sky, the clouds and the lighting were perfect, but the seas were not heavy enough. With instructions not to return until he had what was needed, Jim Havens set sail from Mazatlan, Mexico, with two months' provisions, ready to sail to Honolulu if necessary. Meanwhile, taking no chances, we sent another camera crew on to Galveston.

More weeks of waiting. We were getting desperate. Then the worst storm in more than twenty years hit the Pacific Coast. Havens made the most of it, photographically. But off Cape San Lucas, Lower California, we came near losing the *We're Here*. In a terrific hurricane she heeled over on her side and looked in danger of capsizing. Cameraman Marzorati, with his apparatus set up on the *Cushman,* obtained a perfect film record of the whole occurrence.

We were just congratulating ourselves on this, when the winter siege of flu hit our cast broadside. One by one they were forced to take to their beds. Even John Lee Mahin, who helped adapt the script, was a victim. Lionel Barrymore hung on nobly, but at last he and Charley Grapewin both caught the bug. And I, who had escaped the flu, had to go to the hospital for an operation which was supposed to keep me from work for just two days. It was better than three weeks before I ducked away from that hospital bed. Then Jack Conway, who was pinch-hitting for me, came down with the flu himself.

When we got back to work, it was in the midst of the coldest weather ever recorded in California. And that was the time when we had to film the close-ups of the wreck. Special rubber suits, lined with cotton, and water-tight at neck, wrists and ankles, were made to keep out the icy sea-water. In the spray and the wind, the cast took severe punishment. Spencer Tracy went to the hospital for three days before we made the scenes showing him facing death in the water. This was to give him a complete rest before the ordeal of spending hours at a time with waves pounding over his head. John Carradine, who had suffered the longest grippe siege of any of us, still looked as pale as a ghost.

Somehow, taking the fewest possible chances, we cleared up everything. It was late in the afternoon when we got finished, and I had another hospital trip ahead of me. A different hospital this time. At four o'clock the next morning, my second daughter put in her appearance. Maybe that's what you'd call anti-climax. Anyway, having survived the picture, I managed to get through the second ordeal.

Finally, our film, representing seventeen months of work and a tremendous financial investment, was pieced together. When we screened it, in rough form, everything we had gone through seemed worth-while. Of all concerned in its making, I think Producer Louis D. Lighton was the only one who never doubted that we would do credit to the Kipling story and bring an equally thrilling and inspiring film to the screen. If audiences agree with him, then the seventeen months and the production budget were well invested.

Sentenced to Stardom

In "They Gave Him
a Gun"

SPENCER TRACY was kept so busy with film assignments the past three years that until recently he found it impossible to come East even for the briefest sort of vacation. But finally there was a chance for a flying visit. After all scenes in "Captains Courageous" had been photographed, it happened that further background shots were necessary. While a technical crew was on the high seas filming these, Tracy and his wife spent a few days in Manhattan.

Practically all of their time was taken up by visits to the legitimate theatre, where the actor got his own histrionic start. It was a little over six years ago that he scored a tremendous success as "Killer" Mears in John Wexley's play, "The Last Mile," and emigrated to Hollywood.

One of those modest, down-to-earth young men not associated with Hollywood "glamour," Tracy was very much surprised to find himself stalked by autograph hounds in New York. In fact, this was the most startling and disturbing thing about the whole trip to him. He says he can now understand the tribulations chaps like Clark Gable and Robert Taylor are forced to endure while on vacation trips.

Incidentally, Tracy is a great believer in giving young players a chance to show their mettle. Having attended a performance of "Dead End," he was especially anxious to put in a good word for two of the young understudies in the Kingsley production, who were filling in that day. He thought both of them gave excellent performances, and wired the studio to that effect.

Like most expatriates, Tracy would like to come back to the stage, if only for a while. But Hollywood producers do not see eye to eye with him on this subject. Four new assignments were awaiting him upon his return to the Culver City studios. The first was in "They Gave Him a Gun," with Gladys George and Franchot Tone, which has just been released. Other possibilities for forthcoming films include "The Foundry," with Jean Harlow and Wallace Beery as his co-stars, "Tell It to the Marines," with Robert Taylor and Miss Harlow, "Three Comrades," Erich Remarque's great post-novel, with James Stewart and Robert Taylor, and "Test Pilot," with Clark Gable.

Born in Milwaukee, Wisc., Tracy attended public schools there until his family moved to Kansas City, Mo., when he was not yet sixteen. The following year, the Tracys returned to the city of Spencer's birth and the youth was installed in the West Side High School. Came the war, and young Tracy decided it would be more romantic than Latin verbs. He tried to join the Marines, but was rejected because of his youth. He finally managed, however, to be accepted in the Navy, and fought the war from Norfolk, Va., hoping for an overseas call that never came.

The armistice found him back in school, this time at Marquette Academy. From there he went to Northwestern Military Academy and Ripon College, where he spent two years. It was here, under the influence of one Professor Boody, that he first became interested in dramatics, taking part in school plays.

He came to New York and attended the American Academy of Dramatic Art, meanwhile getting a bit role in the Theatre Guild's production of "R.U.R." There followed a season of stock, with Leonard Wood, Jr., in White Plains, and a jump to another repertory organization in Cincinnati.

He appeared on Broadway in "Yellow" and then, in turn, in "Baby Cyclone," "Dread," "Conflict" and, finally, "The Last Mile." His films, prior to his great role in "Captains Courageous," include "Up the River," "Young America," "The Power and the Glory," "Whipsaw," "Murder Man," "Fury," "Libeled Lady" and the unusual role of the young priest in "San Francisco." Response to his recent characterizations has been so enthusiastic that the ex-"Killer" Mears was sentenced permanently to Hollywood stardom.

Tracy has two main off-set interests, racing horses and motorboats. It was the late Will Rogers who suggested the former: Tracy had been fretting about his parts, worrying about not doing the best possible job, and Will recommended getting out in the open air more. He said horses were the perfect antidote for any kind of mental friction.

As for boating, Tracy has always been an ardent water sports enthusiast. He has one of the speediest motorboats on the coast, which he runs, stocks, repairs and stokes for himself. And no matter how fast and furious the picture pace, he finds time to slip away for a spin a couple of times a week.

In "San Francisco"   In "Fury"

A Few Flashes from Hollywood

ONE ON LIONEL—The "Captains Courageous" unit had worked all morning without recess on storm scenes for the picture. Director Fleming finally called a halt and Lionel Barrymore, water dripping from face and neck, squatted on the deck of the ship for a much-needed rest.

"Boy, how I hate directors!" he grunted at Charley Grapewin, John Carradine and Spencer Tracy, eyeing Fleming with a sly smile.

"Listen to that!" Spencer exclaimed, turning to Fleming. "You know the famous story about Lionel, don't you, Victor? Hunt Stromberg told it to me.

"When Lionel first turned to directing, several years ago, his first assignment was 'Madame X,' with Ruth Chatterton. It was tough going and, after the first day's work, Lionel sank into a chair on the set and shook his head.

" 'Gosh,' he groaned, 'how I hate actors!' "

EIGHTY-SIX "HEAVIES"—Jack La Rue, who plays the part of the priest in M-G-M's "Captains Courageous," enacted eighty-six "heavy" roles in the two years previous.

WATER-TIGHT SUITS—For Spencer Tracy's final scenes in "Captains Courageous," the M-G-M wardrobe department was called upon to supply two specially constructed water-tight suits, lined with cotton, to protect him against the icy waters into which he is flung from the *We're Here*.

WANT TO BUY A VIELLE?—Everyone whose curiosity has been aroused by the strange-looking instrument which Spencer Tracy plays in "Captains Courageous" will be interested to learn that it is a vielle, an ancient Portuguese instrument. Stringed, and resembling both a mandolin and a piano-accordion, the vielle was popular as far back as the sixteenth century.

It operates on the same principle as the present-day hurdy-gurdy, played by turning a crank at the base, musical tones resulting when revolving picks strike the strings while the fingers choose the correct notes. The crank—or wheel—is rosined, like a fiddler's bow.

Several may be seen at museums, especially in European countries. Few are to be found in the United States. The vielle used in the picture was obtained from a Los Angeles collector. A search by the studio's music department discovered a man who was able to teach Tracy to play one.

A MODEL SON—John Lee Mahin, writer, used his eleven-year-old son, Graham, as his "model" while working on an adaptation of Kipling's "Captains Courageous" in which Freddie Bartholomew was to play the leading role. Mahin tested the dialogue and the action on his son to determine whether it was acceptable for a boy of his age.

VERSATILE MICKEY—Mickey Rooney's twelve-piece orchestra played its first engagement of the season recently at the Girard Country Club, California, with Mickey alternating between piano, trombone and baton.

A Golden Harvest

In "The Gorgeous Hussy"

BORN and brought up in the atmosphere of the American theatre, Lionel Barrymore has contributed even more to the films than he did to the stage. He was one of the first great names in the Broadway theatrical galaxy to see the potenialities of the rudimentary moving picture. It was 'way back in 1910 that Barrymore was induced by his friend, D. W. Griffith, to play a role in an early feature production called "Friends." Although he did not devote himself wholly to pictures, he played in a great many from that time on, alternating with such memorable stage portrayals as those in "The Copperhead" and "The Jest."

It was with the development of talking pictures that Barrymore came to be recognized as one of the really great names in Hollywood, and since his first speaking role in "The Lion and the Mouse" he has had more demands on his time and talent than he could possibly attend to. For a short time he abandoned acting in favor of directorial work, but the public refused to let their favorite isolate himself behind the cameras—and he returned to acting.

The current season is his twenty-eighth in the motion picture field, and the list of great cinematic characterizations during that time is legion. Among those that would have to be included are his Rasputin in "Rasputin and the Empress," the film in which his brother John and sister Ethel both appeared, his Kringelein in "Grand Hotel," his role as the father-lawyer, with Norma Shearer, in "A Free Soul," his re-creation of Andrew Jackson in "The Gorgeous Hussy," his father in "Ah, Wilderness!" and—most certainly—his great role as Capt. Disko in "Captains Courageous."

Barrymore was born in Philadelphia, made his stage debut at the age of five with his parents (who were famous actors) and then received his education in New York. He was given a chance to go abroad to study art, and took it. He studied for a while in Paris with the intention of becoming a painter, and on his return to New York, followed the calling of an illustrator for nearly a year before concentrating on the stage. Today his etchings are on display in famous galleries and he always finds time to do more. He is also a composer and musician of some note.

Barrymore's philosophy of acting may be expressed in two typewritten lines. He said recently:

"An actor's brain must be a sort of a warehouse, and the more goods stored in it, the better the business of acting. The goods are recollections."

Barrymore's own recollections are many and varied, ranging from life as a child backstage in the theatre to world-wide travels, adventures, associations with famous people, and a host of unusual acting roles.

"Recollections of personal experiences, of people, and of impressions made by plots and stories," he said, "are the most important equipment of the actor. With a mind filled with these, he can draw, as from a card index, the reactions and emotions necessary for the situations created by the playwright, just as the musician takes a sheet of music, and from it plays what he reads. The aptest description of the function of an actor was voiced by Wilde, when he called Sir Henry Irving 'a trumpet set for Shakespeare's lips to blow.'"

Besides being a fine character actor, Lionel Barrymore must rated a prophet of the first water. Back in the early 'twenties, when sound pictures were admittedly on their way, the veteran stopped off in a middle western town for an interview. Speaking to reporters there, he remarked:

"Well, when sound comes there will have to be a new name for pictures. Maybe they'll call them 'talkies.'" And "talkies" they became. On the basis of his past record, Barrymore was asked for some comment on the future of motion pictures. He stated:

"Now, let's get away from this 'prophet' angle. As one who has been in pictures for so long a time, I can only say that they must go ahead, they must constantly improve. There's no question of it. We'll have opera, and we'll have nothing but color, eventually. They'll come slowly, but they'll come."

What are the best subjects for pictures? Barrymore flashes one of his wry, half-concealed smiles when you ask him that, and says there are only two kinds of stories available for Hollywood: good ones and bad ones. "I'll take the good ones, whenever I can find them," he said. "I don't care whether they're about sailors, or bankers, or jailbirds or Indian maharajahs, just as long as they're good."

In "Treasure Island" In "Ah, Wilderness!"

M-G-M's Greatest Year

Clark Gable

Norma Shearer

Robert Taylor

Joan Crawford

Spencer Tracy

Eleanor Powell

James Stewart

Wallace Beery

Greta Garbo

William Powell

Myrna Loy

Lionel Barrymore

Helen Hayes

Nelson Eddy

Gladys George

Charles Laughton

THE new season of 1937-8, which will start in September, promises to be the greatest in the history of Metro-Goldwyn-Mayer. Twenty-four stars, the largest group ever assembled under contract at any of the West Coast studios, will figure prominently in the schedule.

Emphasis is placed on the fact that stories rivalling in magnitude and importance such outstanding successes of the current year as "The Great Ziegfeld," "The Good Earth," "Romeo and Juliet," "Camille" and "Captains Courageous," will occupy an important place on the new season schedule.

One of the biggest productions, from the standpoint of advance preparation and technical detail, will be the adaptation of Rudyard Kipling's "Kim." This will co-star Freddie Bartholomew, juvenile star of "Captains Courageous," and Robert Taylor. Jean Harlow, Robert Taylor and Spencer Tracy are to be starred in "Tell It to the Marines."

"Rosalie" will be a musical play by William Anthony McGuire, author of "The Great Ziegfeld," and Guy Bolton, in which Eleanor Powell and Nelson Eddy will be starred; "Three Comrades," Erich Maria Remarque's companion piece to "All Quiet on the Western Front," will star Robert Taylor, Spencer Tracy and James Stewart; "The Girl of the Golden West," based on David Belasco's stage play, will co-star Jeanette MacDonald and Nelson Eddy, who were teamed in "Maytime," "Naughty Marietta" and "Rose Marie."

The film version of "Idiot's Delight," Pulitzer prize play by Robert E. Sherwood, will star Clark Gable in one of the most coveted film roles of the new season. Three stars, Jean Harlow, Robert Taylor and Wallace Beery, will appear in "Spring Tide," play by J. B. Priestley and George Billam. Jeanette MacDonald and Allan Jones, the tenor of "Show Boat," will be seen in "The Firefly," musical opera by Otto Harbach and Rudolf Friml. William Powell and Myrna Loy, co-stars of "The Thin Man" and "After the Thin Man," will be paired in a third story of the same genre, titled "The Return of the Thin Man," written for them by Dashiell Hammett. They will also be co-starred in an adaptation of the Ferenc Molnar comedy, "Great Love."

Comedy melodrama centered about the Spanish civil war is the motif of "Spanish Omelet," in which Robert Montgomery will be starred. The western plains of 1845 provide the locale for "Stand Up and Fight," a Wallace Beery starring vehicle.

Clark Gable will appear in "The Great Canadian," story of a famous hockey player. Gable and Spencer Tracy will head the cast of "Test Pilot," aviation tale by Lt. Comm. Frank Wead. Jean Harlow will be starred in "The Best Dressed Woman in Paris." Joan Crawford, who played the title role in "The Gorgeous Hussy," will have another historical characterization in "Lola Montez," in which she will be seen as the famous nineteenth century dancer, in a picture adapted from T. Everett Harre's "The Heavenly Sinner."

Robert Montgomery will star in "Wedding Dress," a comedy-drama of modern marital complications. Eleanor Powell will be the star of "Hats in the Air," a musical film, by Dwight Taylor. "Merry Christmas," by Norman Krasna, author of "Fury," will star Luise Rainer in a story written especially for her.

Other outstanding story properties from which new season Metro-Goldwyn-Mayer productions will be selected include: "The American Flaggs," by Kathleen Norris; "The Foundry," by Albert Halper; "Pride and Prejudice," by Jane Austen; "Anchor Man" and "The Four Marys," both by Fanny Heaslip Lea; "As Thousands Cheer," musical by Moss Hart and Irving Berlin; "Bright Girl," by Vina Delmar; "Declassee," by Zoë Akins; "The Distaff Side," by John Van Druten; "The Far Off Hills," by Lennox Robinson; "Goodbye, Mr. Chips," by James Hilton; "The Harbourmaster," by William McFee; "Her Excellency's Tobacco Shop," by Laszlo Bus-Fekete; "I've Married an Angel,"

Luise Rainer

Robert Montgomery

Jeanette MacDonald

The Marx Brothers

Freddie Bartholomew

Jean Harlow

by Joseph Vaszary; "Johann Strauss," an original story; "La Tendresse," by Henri Bataille; "A Lady Comes to Town," by Clements Ripley; "Ma Pettingill," by Harry Leon Wilson; "Merrily We Roll Along," based on the Broadway stage hit by George Kaufman and Moss Hart, "Nancy Stair," novel by Elinor Macartney Lane; "No Hero," by J. P. Marquand; "Not Too Narrow, Not Too Deep," novel by Richard Sale; "One Came Home," by Grace Norton; "The Paradine Case," novel by Robert Hichens; "Party," by Ivor Novello "Presenting Lily Mars," novel by Booth Tarkington; "Rennie Peddigoe," novel by Booth Tarkington; "Sari," the Viennese operetta; "Sehoy, Ahoy!" Cosmopolitan Magazine serial by Clements Ripley; "Silas Marner," by George Eliot; "Timberline," by Gene Fowler; "Tish," by Mary Roberts Rinehart; "The Wind and the Rain," play by Merton Hodge; "A Couple of Quick Ones," by Eric Hatch; "Pitcairn's Island," by Charles Nordhoff and James Norman Hall, a sequel to "Mutiny on the Bounty"; "The Red Mill" and "Rose of Algeria," Victor Herbert musicals; "I Love You Again," by Octavus Roy Cohen; "Pierre of the Plains," play by Edgar Selwyn; "All the Brothers Were Valiant," novel by Ben Ames Williams; "Caprice," by Dalton Trumbo; "Courthouse Square," by Hamilton Basso; "Green Grow the Lilacs," play by Lynn Riggs; "The French Quarter," by Herbert Asbury; "Katinka," operetta by Otto Harbach and Rudolf Friml; "Race the Sun," novel by Dale Collins; and "Sea of Grass," by Conrad Richter.

The list of directors under contract for the coming M-G-M season comprises Dorothy Arzner, Frank Borzage, Clarence Brown, George Cukor, Jack Conway, George Fitzmaurice, Victor Fleming, Sidney Franklin, Robert Z. Leonard, Gustav Machaty, Edwin L. Marin, J. Walter Ruben, George Seitz, Edward Sloman, John M. Stahl, Errol Taggart, Richard Thorpe, W. S. Van Dyke and Sam Wood.

The group of featured contract players stands out as the most impressive in company history. The roster of one hundred and twenty scenarists and musical composers is also the largest ever assembled at the beginning of a new season.

Included in the list of featured players are: Elizabeth Allan, Robert Benchley, Ray Bolger, Virginia Bruce, Billie Burke, Bruce Cabot, Lynne Carver, Jean Chatburn, June Clayworth, Henry Daniell, Melvyn Douglas, Buddy Ebsen, Cliff Edwards, Madge Evans, Betty Furness, Reginald Gardiner, Judy Garland, Charles Gorin, Charley Grapewin, Julie Haydon, Ted Healy, William Henry, Betty Jaynes, Allan Jones, Guy Kibbee, Miliza Korjus, Elissa Landi, Tilly Losch, Una Merkel, Frank Morgan, Della Lind, Stanley Morner, George Murphy, Edna May Oliver, Maureen O'Sullivan, Reginald Owen, Barnett Parker, Cecilia Parker, Nat Pendleton, Juanita Quigley, Jessie Ralph, Florence Rice, May Robson, Mickey Rooney, Rosalind Russell, Lewis Stone, Franchot Tone, Sophie Tucker, Johnny Weissmuller, Cora Witherspoon, Dame May Whitty, Robert Young, Warren William.

Metro-Goldwyn-Mayer short product for 1937-38 will include eighty-one one-reel pictures, sixteen two-reelers, and 104 issues of the news reel, "News of the Day." Both features and shorts will be inclusive of product from the Hal Roach studios.

THIS BOOK SOLD ONLY IN THEATRES SHOWING

"CAPTAINS COURAGEOUS"

THE GOOD EARTH

Metro-Goldwyn-Mayer

• It is deeply regretted that IRVING THALBERG could not witness the many brilliant openings of his outstanding producing effort. "The Good Earth" had been under his supervision nearly three years, and the faithful artistry of its translation to the screen was the dearest concern of his last days. This production is a monument to his memory and to him it is dedicated.

Pearl S. Buck

a prologue by the author

*T*HE GOOD EARTH began not as a single book, but as the story of the entire span of a Chinese family rising, as nearly all great families do, out of the earth. The story told is not the story of a farmer, but a man far more than the average farmer, a man whose home was upon the land and would always be, but who used the land as a foundation upon which to build a family. Nothing in Chinese life, and indeed in human life, is more significant than this rise and fall of families. The founder is often a strong, naive, clever, simple man, whose children swiftly grow beyond his environment and carry his vigor far and wide into other lines. The original vigor of Wang Lung is carried later through his children into war and into trade and money-getting and money-spending, and that vigor, first bound in his one figure, is dissipated, as time goes on, into many sons and many places, and at last is quite scattered. Accustomed riches, remoteness from the land, the complicated forces of modern existence, tempered and even destroyed the strong, ruthless, unconscious selfishness of the founder, and the family is not only physically but mentally and spiritually scattered. Some day it will again be revived and again brought together by the rebirth of a simple and ambitious man somewhere upon the earth, but not yet. Such has been the history of the great Chinese families.

IN China today, this history runs horizontally and perpendicularly. That is, although the story begun in THE GOOD EARTH covers half a century of time-years, every part of it is being lived now also, and will be lived for a long time to come. For China is living both in the past and in the present, in ages medieval and modern. She is great enough to be able to do so. Other nations and peoples may struggle for uniformity, but she does not. Upon the land men still live and work exactly as their ancestors did, in the same sort of houses and with the same tools. Only today they may pause in the ploughing and look up for a moment to see an aeroplane across the sky. But if they look up it is but for a moment. For them the real things are still the earth, the plough, the potential famine always looming, and so the struggle for more land and more food. Yet in the aeroplane rides that third generation, grandsons of Wang Lung, looking down curiously and often carelessly upon that minute blue-coated figure which crawls along the dark brown surface beneath them. Each has his meaning and each is fulfilling his place in the enormous pattern of Chinese life.

PAUL MUNI &

" THE

• PAUL MUNI *as the land-hungry farmer Wang Lung*

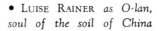

• TILLY LOSCH *as Lotus, second wife of Wang Lung*

• LUISE RAINER *as O-lan, soul of the soil of China*

LUISE RAINER in PEARL S.BUCK'S
GOOD EARTH "

...The Players...

Wang Lung	Paul Muni
O-lan	Luise Rainer
Uncle	Walter Connolly
Lotus	Tilly Losch
Old Father	Charley Grapewin
Cuckoo	Jessie Ralph
Aunt	Soo Yong
Elder Son	Keye Luke
Younger Son	Roland Lui
Little Fool	Suzanna Kim
Ching	Chingwah Lee
Cousin	Harold Huber
Liu, Grain Merchant	Olaf Hytten
Gateman	William Law
Little Bride	Mary Wong

● *Director:* Sidney Franklin ● *Author: Based Upon the Novel by* Pearl S. Buck ● *Adapted for the Stage by* Owen Davis *and* Donald Davis ● *Produced by the* Theatre Guild, Inc. ● *Screen Play by* Talbot Jennings, Tess Slesinger *and* Claudine West ● *Associate Producer:* Albert Lewin ● *Musical Score by* Herbert Stothart ● *Art Director:* Cedric Gibbons ● *Associates:* Harry Oliver, Arnold Gillespie *and* Edwin B. Willis ● *Wardrobe by* Dolly Tree ● *Photographed by* Karl Freund, A.S.C. ● *Montage by* Slavko Vorkapich ● *Film Editor:* Basil Wrangell.

● Charley Grapewin *as the Old Father of Wang Lung*

● Walter Connolly *as the lazy and improvident Uncle*

● Jessie Ralph *as scheming Cuckoo of the Great House*

dwell ye upon the land . . .

DAWN reveals to us a little farmhouse where amidst the turning of water-wheels, the cackling geese, and the crowded footpath on which farmers tread their way laden for market, we find the House of Wang. Wang Lung on his pallet is blissfully expectant: it is the day. Today even Lo, the buffalo, may have an extra handful of straw. And though the querulous Old Father protests that drinking tea is like eating silver, he too feasts on a few leaves: for Wang Lung is to be married. The groom bathes while all the neighbors exchange greetings and jest over his care; his friend Ching wishes him well. Ah, the music of his exultation as he strides toward the Great House. He knocks and knocks until the gateman deigns to answer. Then he is led amidst laughter to the hall where the Ancient One presents him with the slave-girl O-lan. Plain she is and ill-used but Wang can see that she knows correct deportment, for she trots whithersoever he leads and when he bids her lift the heavy box she obeys. But Wang is a farmer and though he is embarrassed to be seen, he takes the chest himself and his bride follows in the pathetic, cowering shuffle of the beaten slave. When they cross the market-place, he presents her with peaches. As he looks at her, she ceases eating; when he throws the stone of his fruit into the rice-field, she retrieves it—"for it will grow."

• *Sometimes Wang searches the passive face of O-lan to learn the meaning of her eternal silence.*

• *(below) They fire a field of ripe grain to drive off the locusts and save the rest for harvest.*

This then is the mute and humble bride that Wang Lung brings home to be his wife, to bear him sons, to tend his father and to do his bidding; this woman who smiles to herself so gently when she is spoken to kindly, her secret joy overcoming slowly her shyness. She is in the kitchen happy that her husband must politely reject his wedding-guests' approval of her cooking. The guests gone after teasing the groom appropriately, Wang finds O-lan in the garden planting the peach-stone of the morning. What are the sorrows of those eyes, why the fear of blows? The night breeze makes the lantern flicker but the glow, dim as it is, is shed upon them both. The sound that Wang makes is not a word nor yet a laugh—it is an exultant call; this woman is his indeed.

Silent and submissive O-lan takes on more than her share of the farmland tasks—they seem to be part of her as we glimpse the water-carrying, the grinding of grain, the hoeing, the fetching of sticks. This air is hers, this land meets her step with new spring. Yes, and she too is fertile and she is to bear when the earth has its harvest. And though such a creature has not spoken, though it would not appear that she has ever dreamed—for this son of hers that is yet to come she speaks a plan. On the first New Year's day after his birth, she will array him in silk and she will take him to see her Ancient Mistress in the house where she, O-lan, was a slave. Wang is puzzled by all this unwonted talk—but he is indulgent.

The year is fat and the harvest is full. O-lan can not go to the field on the last day of her child-bearing. But thunder heralds a storm which menaces the ripened wheat. O-lan exhausts herself to help save the crop. Wang carries her home and in her room, alone and silent as an animal, she bears her man-child. There is silver that year to buy the silk coat and visit the Mistress of the Great House. And though it is daring of him to aspire, Wang is able to add a rice-field to his little grain-corner when the Great House begins to crumble and needs cash. The years pass rapidly and the household grows. Another son comes and then unfortunately a daughter. Wang's fields number six. No more does he dread the destruction of one grain for he has planted several and rice is safe in the lowlands. Prosperity has its burdens: for Wang, a sly lazy Uncle to whom he must pay the respect owing to age.

Somehow there comes a season when industry is not enough. Lo, the buffalo, with whom one toils and lives, the pet of the children, cannot, for all his pawing and stamping, press a drop of water from the caked earth. Nowhere is life stirring. The plants are withered and the wind bears away the soil in clouds of dust. Rootlets become too scarce even for gruel for the child O-lan is yet again bearing. Wang Lung cannot kill his ox, in so many ways his brother, but motherhood gives O-lan a sort of tigerish strength. "We are not hungry!" the children say—but the carcass of Lo staves off starvation a few days longer.

Wang's Uncle wants him to sell his land and Wang refuses. The villagers are incited to raid the hovel when the Uncle argues that a man with so much land would sell it to feed his starving children unless he had a hoard of hidden food. They break in on Wang —even his friend Ching—and find that he has nothing. How gruesome at this moment is the poverty of the spirit, so dry and brittle as the lifeless earth itself! O-lan bears a child—there is one wail—and it is dead. Almost is Wang tempted to sell the fields. But they have become something more than a few pieces of

(Continued on last page)

● *The hunger-crazed villagers raid the house of Wang only to find that he too is without grain.*

● *The soldiers seize O-lan after the looting of the palace in which she found a bag of jewels.*

● *The ox of Wang is called Friend, a trusted ally in the everlasting labors that they must share.*

● Here is a partial list of the titles of foreign editions of the book, presented in their actual type styles. Above, jacket of the first American edition (right) Photograph of the studio collection of foreign first editions, each of them a collector's prize

● This is a page from the actual shooting script used by Sidney Franklin in directing the picture. It deals with the scene on the morning of Wang Lung's wedding day. Note how many directions must be followed at once, the camera instructions, the acting motifs, the synchronization, the rhythm, the emphasis

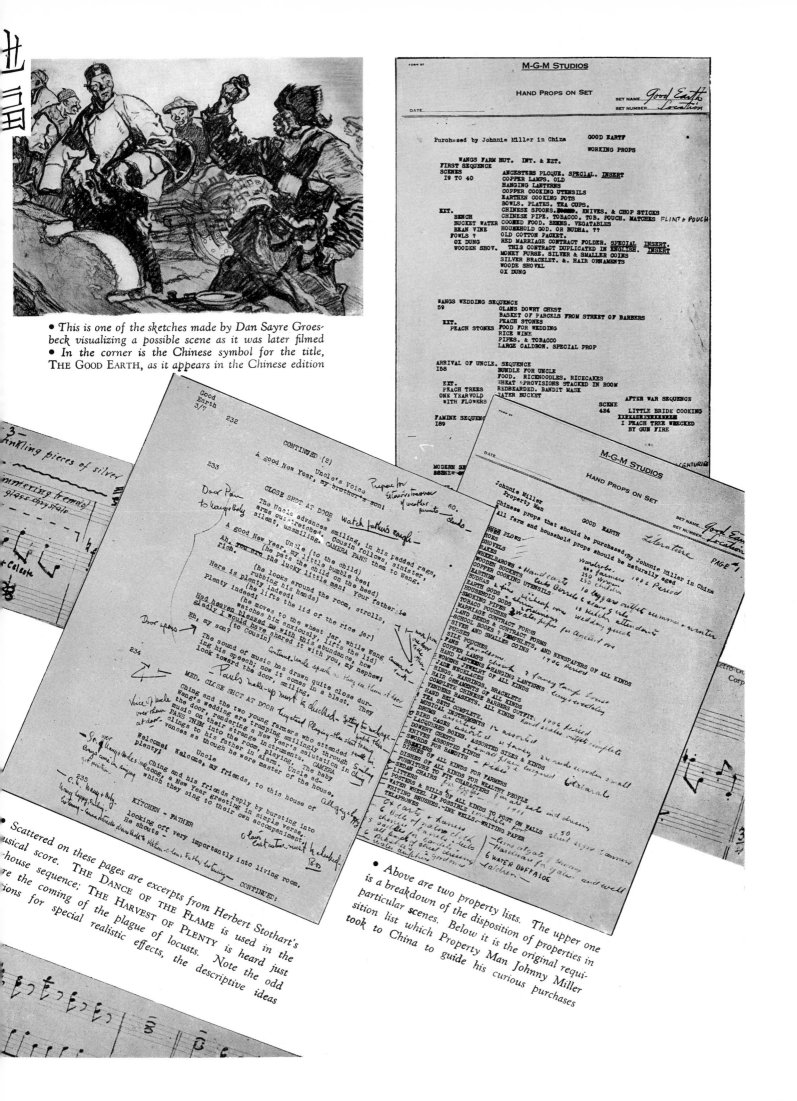

- This is one of the sketches made by Dan Sayre Groesbeck visualizing a possible scene as it was later filmed
- In the corner is the Chinese symbol for the title, THE GOOD EARTH, as it appears in the Chinese edition

Scattered on these pages are excerpts from Herbert Stothart's musical score. THE DANCE OF THE FLAME is used in the farmhouse sequence; THE HARVEST OF PLENTY is heard just before the coming of the plague of locusts. Note the odd directions for special realistic effects, the descriptive ideas

- Above are two property lists. The upper one is a breakdown of the disposition of properties in particular scenes. Below it is the original requisition list which Property Man Johnny Miller took to China to guide his curious purchases

Scenes from
"THE GOOD EARTH

● "With the silver pieces from this harvest and the next perhaps we may go to the Palace and buy even that field!"

● "There be fat years and lean, seasons when the rice is high, and barren times. All of them must we endure"

● "Ever have I hungered for the tinkling sounds of the tea-house, my hands are iron-hard but they know silk-softness"

● (below) "On, Friend, and on! Together we turn up a far furrow of rich loam—no dance is sweeter to the feet!"

● "It is grain we sow, these golden seedlings. Yet when it ripens in the sun, it will be a harvest of happiness"

● "Son of thy father and even thou, Poor Fool, we will be patient yet a little while to see again our distant fields"

● (left) "Whence come so many people? I am borne along with them where they go—oh, for the peace of our land!"

● "Is it needful to speak my pride in thee, O Second Son? Thou hast conquered the plague of locusts—a miracle!"

● "For a few coppers, we bear these endless bitter burdens. I know a land where food is come by more naturally"

how the film was made

JUST as the House of Wang grew to greatness from its roots in the rich earth, so has the book in which is told the tale of the House of Wang grown to be a mighty force—and that because its roots too were sunk in the same living loam. Now that it has been rendered in motion picture form, we look back and find in the history of this production a saga that rivals the epic itself in splendor.

The course of the novel, THE GOOD EARTH, is too familiar to need much reference here. Completed in 1930, it was published in 1931 by the John Day Company. It was hailed in chorus by the critics and for twenty-one months it headed the American list of "best sellers," a record made by no other contemporary book. It was awarded the Pulitzer Prize as the best novel of its year. It was translated and received with similar acclaim in more than twenty languages, including the Chinese, in which there are three different versions. It was adapted for the stage by Owen and Donald Davis and produced in the fall of 1933 by the Theatre Guild in New York with Nazimova and Claude Rains in the cast.

Metro-Goldwyn-Mayer acquired the screen rights and instituted production plans of unprecedented magnificence. Late in 1933 an entire production unit penetrated the sections of China with which the novel deals. Between Shanghai and Peiping this expedition shot nearly two million feet of atmosphere shots. Eighteen tons of properties were purchased outright and shipped back to the studio in more than three thousand bales, baskets, trunks and crates. Entire farmhouses were dismantled and sent back to be reassembled, complete even to the rude tools and threshing implements, worn bedding, cracked kitchen utensils, coffins of authentic ancestors, doors, windows, shrines, and even the stall of Lo, the water buffalo who was brought back with six of his fellows.

In the San Fernando Valley, fifty miles out of Hollywood, on suitable terrain a farm of five hundred acres was purchased and placed in operation by Chinese farmers in simulation of just such farms in China. Seedlings were set to sprout, leek, cabbage, melon and bamboo, and the typical irrigation system duplicated, with its picturesque terraces and water-wheels. City streets were created, lined with more than two hundred individual shops whose wares included preserved duck, reed baskets, musical instruments, teakwood furniture, bone needles, opium pipes, toy dragons and specially inscribed prayers for the birth of sons. While the vegetation matured, engineers carved out a replica of the Great Wall and sailors launched sampans on a moat in the valley. A modern city of more than fifty buildings for the use of the cast and technicians had to be established in the next valley out of camera range.

Sidney Franklin required the services of a loudspeaker to direct scenes in which as many as fourteen hundred players

• Junks brought 18 tons of native props down-river

• Herbert Stothart wrote a score of oriental music

• Director Sidney Franklin and a tool of his trade

• (right) Celestial lunch fifty miles out of Hollywood. • (below) William Law, James Lee and Keye Luke

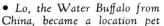

• Lo, the Water Buffalo from China, became a location pet

• (below) Luise Rainer and a member of the company

• (below) Jack Dawn prepares a "facial inlay" for Paul Muni

took part, some as far as three-quarters of a mile from the lens of the camera. General Ting-Hsiu Tu was assigned by the Nanking government to assure the accuracy of settings and historical incidents. It was his military knowledge which drilled the army that appears in the revolution scenes. Casting the sixty-eight speaking parts required a recruiting drive that covered the entire West Coast. English-speaking Chinese, many of them natives of the United States, were drawn from their ordinary pursuits. The cast as it finally appears includes bankers, editors, housewives, students, farmers, miners, writers, sailors, tong officials, laundrymen and actors from the Chinese stage. Coach Oliver Hinsdell organized classes to bring uniformity out of the Babel of accents. Make-up technique was revolutionized by Jack Dawn who developed a system of facial inlays to allow free expression to actors whose racial characteristics had to be fundamentally transformed.

Karl Freund at the camera invented for this production a device nick-named *Rube Goldberg* to accommodate the

• *(left) Extras caught napping.* • *(below, left to right) Cameraman Karl Freund studies the range;* • *Coach Oliver Hinsdell coordinates into English the 80 varied accents of the cast;* • *Paul Muni explains to General Tu the workings of a sightfinder.*

needs of light-mixture, and light-filters were developed that reflect the peculiar dust-laden air of Anhwei province. Cedric Gibbons undertook the task of building and furnishing a lavish palace with material brought from China —a problem complicated by the requirements of the roving camera so that mere duplication of an original was not enough. Dolly Tree took charge of a wardrobe of eight thousand costumes, stocked with shrouds, beggars' tatters, silk raiment and satin, army uniforms and the garments of the idols.

THE screen adaptation, notable for its fidelity to the original text, was completed by Talbot Jennings, Tess Slesinger and Claudine West. Basil Wrangell edited more actual footage than has ever before gone into a motion picture production. An animal department was established on a scale consistent with the scope of the production. It included corrals, coops, barns and a stable near the location. The animal cast included six Asiatic water buffaloes, twenty donkeys, sixteen assorted Chinese mongrel dogs, a flock of two hundred oriental ducks, another flock of pigeons, another of chickens, ten Cochin hogs, an ox and two dozen horses. The depredations of coyotes made it necessary to add two professional hunters to a payroll that already represented virtually every known craft among its seventy-eight hundred names.

A collection of four hundred Chinese musical selections, supplemented by recordings made by the expedition which traversed China, comprised the basis of Herbert Stothart's musical score. Stothart foreswore the superficial tricks of Chinese effects and prepared what is regarded as a major contribution to knowledge of the nature of oriental melody. Many of the scenic ideas were derived from a series of a thousand sketches in which the illustrator, Dan Sayre Groesbeck, visualized possible slants and angles for the film. The curtain of background sound which accompanies some of the speeches is a composite of Chinese tones rehearsed to the exact meter and pitch of street sounds recorded in Anhwei.

The reconstructions of original oriental buildings were complicated by the need to allow for a roving camera. Many of the sequences were dramatized by flying the crew on booms. Dozens of composition shots were completed in the laboratory; none of them are what is known as "stock" material. Perhaps the greatest natural phenomenon ever recorded on the screen is the locust sequence in which a cloud of whirring insects was actually caught in action by the expedition that went to China. The scenes which follow the arrival of the scourge required a technique never before used. Closeups of the insects were shot on what is probably the smallest movie stage ever constructed. The advance of the pest over the grain fields and through the canals were directed by an entomologist in Hollywood.

Here, then is the fruit of a collective effort to which every art was tributary. THE GOOD EARTH as it flashes on the screen is the supreme expression of a vigorous culture as it turns its sensitive and kindly eye upon an aged world. The lustiness of that world as it sheds its dying dream are the drama of this picture as they were the theme of Pearl Buck's book. And because the story is the story of man's eternal hopes and struggles, O-lan in the guise of Luise Rainer becomes our kin; and the strong earthbound Wang Lung, whom we meet in Paul Muni, we recognize for his lowly ways and simple grandeur, one of our own.

the wisdom of the sages . . .

CHINESE thought embodies the accumulated lore of countless centuries. The great faiths have left their print upon the oriental mind in the form of maxims and proverbs attributed to such sages as Mencius, LaoTse and Confucius. These proverbs are used to express thought whenever possible. Even in the most trivial affair of the day, the Chinese sums up his opinion with quotations, acquiring thereby the sanction of prophets he reveres. These are among the most common slogans that govern Chinese conduct:

- By many words is wit exhausted.
- A man thinks he knows, but a woman knows better.
- Moneyed men are always heard.
- Honeyed words and flattery need not be love.
- Talent develops itself.
- He who cheats his appetite saves debts.
- One horse, one saddle.
- The trees in whose shade you sit were planted by your father.
- Mistakes are always embellished.
- There is more virtue in a small kindness than in a thousand-mile journey to burn incense.
- The four seasons follow in their course: need God speak?
- The less you have seen, the more seems queer. (This is spoken so: *Shao chien to kuai;* pronounced *shou* to rhyme with *thou, jane, doe, gwy* to rhyme with *why.*)

a glossary of terms . . .

HERE are a few of the Chinese idioms which became the common property of everybody on the location before the production was completed:

wah see	director (head man)
fong wah see	assistant director
wah gay see	cameraman (man with eye)
yue bay la!	get ready!
a sow la!	go to work! action!
gon jae s'iun	property man (all over the place)
wah min see	make-up man (oil on face)
m'hi gum joe!	you can't do that!
fi dee!	hurry up!
mon jon lan	lunch is ready
sum yun	lonesomeness, heartache
yung kum	native piano
shi - t'ls	actors
yeng pien	film
ding how	very good
ju far'm	breakfast
j'io ch'ong gee	camera
i kwi'r lai	come with me
fuh ti	the good earth

some footnotes . . .

the historical basis . . .

THE events described in the film are historically accurate and they may be dated from the revolutionary sequence which is similar to actual happenings in the course of the republican uprising of 1911. It was in that revolt that a tremendous democratic upsurge, fostered by increasing influence of European traditions and aggravated by drought and famine, unseated the Manchu dynasty which had controlled China for more than three centuries. The present ruler of Manchukuo was then heir-apparent to the throne. The republican leaders under Sun Yat Sen had the support of millions of peasants like Wang Lung, who knew little more than that their plight was intolerable. There followed a period of "expropriation" which got out of hand in some places and resulted in such riots and looting as are shown in the film.

It is interesting to observe that the authenticity of the revolution sequence endows the further portions of the picture with many subtle touches which bring the story down to the present in its social and cultural content. For example, it is only after this period that Wang Lung and his neighbors enjoy a sense of equality and democracy; that the idea of romantic love becomes a serious force in their lives; that woman begins to be treated with humane consideration; that the old caste distinctions between the classes wither; that the complex and hide-bound conventionalities are eliminated. Thus, without introducing a single non-Chinese character—nor any foreign symbol other than an alarm-clock—the film is able to indicate how deeply the social transformations of the time affected the individual lives of the characters. As the House of Wang rises and grows rich, it is not only its development which is described, but also the growth of a new culture more like our own. In the last scenes, Wang Lung and O-lan resemble an aged American farm couple more nearly than they reflect the peasant and slave-girl of their own youth. And that is the true story of their whole generation.

themes . . .

• Stories do not follow blueprints, not even such stories as this, in which the history of a period is part. The theme of this story may be love, the love of O-lan and Wang Lung; or the love of both for the earth; or the love of the earth for its creatures. The theme of this picture might be man's dealings with the earth; his puny grubbing and his helplessness; or the mysterious earth-mother. The theme might be China. Or Man, Man of all time and many places. Let this be said: if you could state a single theme of such a film as this, it would not be the great work it is, but merely the intention of an idea; because all these themes together are entwined and woven into a vast and beautiful fabric, they give this picture its form. When you see it, you do not merely follow the line of an obvious theme to a logical conclusion—but for a space you are planted bodily in the hearts and brains of Wang Lung and O-lan and you look out on their world. What more than this can be the theme of any art?

nature . . .

IT IS a sad fact that the art of our civilization deals so little with nature. Man's conduct from day to day is an accustomed thing and provides the basis of drama. But nature in its season unleashes forces far more theatrical; in repose, the gently riding earth is all that we know of peace or poetry.

So that this film is unique for the account it offers of the way the earth behaved in the valley where Wang dwelt. Two problems are a test of the cinema: those that are too violent and catastrophic and those that are too gentle to be enacted. The scourge of the locusts is as dramatic as any battle scene ever filmed; it is an incident that arrays man against an almost invincible opponent—and awards him a hard-earned victory through what is literally the will of the wind. It is a scene as strong as an earthquake—and its presentation makes screen history.

But let not that spectacle obscure the story of the ordinary cycles, which is even more challenging to tell. When you have seen this picture, try to recall how it was that you gained a sense of the goodness of the soil in one part, the fat fields of waving grain, the bursting pods and the little rills in the rice-fields, the sweet blossoms of cherry and the sleekness of the animals. Then look again to discover whence came the sense of wintriness and desperation, the parching of the sod, the caked soil and the encroaching ice, the shrill wind, withered stalks and crumbling rootlets, the thin light and the whirling dust. When the verdant valley becomes a dustbowl for ghouls, you say with O-lan: "Truly the earth has forgotten us!"

The flight of the refugees from famine sums up the temper of the earth and mutely states the role of man. This, too, is part of nature, this frantic escape from sapped lands. As they reel past the dead under the obscene eyes of buzzards, they are puppets performing on strings pulled by more than mortal fingers. Nature is a leading player in this picture—even after it has assigned its best lines to O-lan.

---

some customs of the Chinese . . .

FEW, indeed, are the differences between the Chinese people and ourselves if we study the ideas expressed by their customs rather than the customs alone. Perhaps they are bound too rigidly to the past and it may be true that the cemeteries of China govern the land more powerfully than its parliament. But even though the manner of expression differs, it is well to note that we express precisely the same things in different ways.

• They can be more romantic than any western race. It is recorded that the poet Li Po drowned while trying to kiss the moon's reflection in a river.

• Because of their religious reverence of ancestors, they regard memory as more important than judgment.

• The most violent sports native to China are kite-flying and shuttlecock.

• Seasons are named after the number of garments which their temperature requires.

• In Chinese grammar all good things are male (yang); all things evil are female (yin).

• Chinese plays, contrary to common notion, are very short. A whole repertory is staged at once without intermissions.

• The Chinese are a people who invented gunpowder—and used it only for firecrackers; invented the magnetic needle—and used it as a plaything; invented paper and printing—and used them only for pictures.

they say . . .

SIDNEY FRANKLIN: Telling the story of a people strange to the rest of the world, telling it in the fashion of these people, and still making it vitally understandable to audiences whose mode of thought is the utter reverse, was the task that filled us all with consternation when we started THE GOOD EARTH. Here, we reasoned, was a case where all precedent and all rules of drama and picture technique must be forgotten and a new structure created. ● Then, as we began to know our Chinese players better, and from them absorbed some of the oriental attitude, we learned that the Chinese people, in their hearts, under the centuries-bred cloak of mannerisms, are exactly the same in their emotions and reactions, as ourselves. This is graphically shown in the splendid performances of Paul Muni, Luise Rainer and the rest of the players who literally breathed life into the complex characters. ● There were many problems, some of them technical, such as make-up, handling of authentic properties and strange mannerisms, to work out. Of tremendous aid was General Ting-Hsiu Tu, who came from China to be our technical adviser. There were many rules that had to be followed for authenticity. ● But the human quality of the characters was no mystery. Drama, we found, was the same in any language, amid any people. So, remembering first and foremost to be human, we found that our problems of deportment and authenticity soon adjusted themselves to our dramatic needs. Pearl Buck's novel was a great human document. I hope we have caught that quality in our picture.

LUISE RAINER: It is always a great happiness to an actress to play a character she loves, and I loved O-lan from the first moment I read THE GOOD EARTH. ● She was strange to me, for I knew little of Chinese women, but she was so intensely human that one could not help absorbing a sort of inspiration from her. ● Many people have asked me if I liked being made up and costumed to avoid being beautiful. To them I always answer that the character could not be beautiful to look at. If O-lan had been beautiful, the whole human quality of her story would have been lost. ● She was a peasant, with knowledge of only a few words. She was stoical, the heritage of centuries. She was almost a clod. Still in her heart was every emotion a woman could have: love, fear, joy, suffering, pride, and a devotion that passes understanding. ● True, to project these to an audience and still retain the lack of apparent emotion of a stoical race, frightened me a little at the outset. The actress essaying such a part has nothing but her eyes and toneless syllables to work with. The secret, I believe, in such a case is to think the meaning —and think it hard. ● Playing with an actor of Paul Muni's artistry is a great aid. Often I mentally absorbed new courage from working with him and noting the certainty of his portrayal. And to our director, Sidney Franklin, we all owe gratitude for the dynamic mind that did so much to keep us constantly imbued with the story and which gave us such a grasp on our characters.

PAUL MUNI: When I approached the task of enacting Wang Lung, it was with frank trepidation. While it is one of the greatest characters in contemporary literature, this character is so foreign to anything an occidental actor has ever played, that my misgivings were great. ● Later I came to love Wang Lung. The more I studied the many facets of his character, and the more I learned of the Chinese psychology which, basically, is like that of any other being, the more insight I gained into the wonders of a people perhaps less known than any in the world. ● The Chinese are fundamentally little different from the occidental but they mask their emotions under a veneer of countless centuries of tradition. Under their stoicism lies the same heart of all men in all parts of the world. Their vein of idealism and poetry is deeply rooted in their thought. Even their speech is largely in metaphor. ● To Sidney Franklin, our director, we owe a debt of gratitude. His insight, patience, and painstaking work made the picture what it is. And to the oriental players, most of them with little or no experience in acting, I pay a sincere tribute. Their fine, natural performance did much to make it a vital, living drama.

CLAUDINE WEST: *(speaking for herself and her collaborators on the screen adaptation, Tess Slesinger, and Talbot Jennings whose picture is on the left).* ● A novel, a play, and a picture are three separate and distinct media, making necessary certain changes when adapting any one form to another. Hence, when we took up the problem of adapting THE GOOD EARTH to the screen, our first concern was to decide just what the straight line of drama would be. We soon found that it must center around the character of O-lan, therefore we end the picture with the natural climax of her death, though the book itself goes beyond that. ● We worried considerably about the character. Here was a being who must always be drab, a clod-like peasant, and still must be interesting. I think, however, that Miss Rainer answered that problem for us by her performance, and answered it beyond our wildest dreams. ● She has that rare quality of making the story her servant, and drawing from it every iota of drama, much of which is not and cannot be expressed in cold type in a script. She clothed the framework of our script with the vivid imagination and intense sensitivity to drama that makes her the artist she is. ● We tried to cling as closely to the book as possible, deviating only to put the picture script into such form as would provide a smooth, straight line story, maintaining necessary tempo and leading to a logical climax. To have gone beyond the story of O-lan, the woman, would have led us into a new story, for there are many stories in Pearl Buck's brilliant novel. And the screen can tell but one at a time.

KARL FREUND: Photography can sometimes be a matter of geography. And the lens of the camera can portray geography, mood of drama, and many other things in addition to the picture it engraves in light upon a moving strip of film. ● Sidney Franklin has a remarkable sensitivity for this phase of photography. Looking at the picture, one will find scenes, such as the exodus of the starving farmers, filmed with the blunt realism of the newsreel. On the other hand, the romantic sequence in the garden, where Paul Muni holds the lantern to Luise Rainer's face and realizes the dawn of love, is filmed with every ounce of artistic quality we could inject into the scene. ● The newsreel technique gave the effect of truth; the impression that a news cameraman was actually there and filmed the scene. The public will subconsciously associate it with accurate film reporting. ● In the love scene, where Luise Rainer, throughout the picture portraying a stolid, clod-like character, becomes for a few seconds radiantly beautiful, as she suddenly appears in her husband's eyes, is another deft bit of Franklin insight. ● Filming THE GOOD EARTH was one of the most interesting experiences I have ever had, technically and because of the remarkable mind of a director who can tell as much in his handling of camera effects as in millions of words. Seldom has a cameraman such opportunity. To me, working with this man was one of the most enlightening episodes in a long life of handling a motion picture camera.

● **TILLY LOSCH:** Oriental dancing, contrary to our impression of the dance, is a mental matter rather than merely enacting drama to music. The oriental dancer seeks to inspire imagination within her spectators which causes them to dramatize the dance, rather than to give a visual exposition of a meaning. ● Studying in the Vienna Opera Ballet, I had of course read much on oriental dancing. But when called upon to perform the traditional Dance of the Flame, I saw for the first time the psychology behind the dance as orientals know it. ● The Flame dance is a series of tableaux, its movements being mainly the manipulation of flame-colored silk sleeves to suggest the movement of fire, starting feebly, rising high, dying out again. But to the Chinese it is more than merely the imitation of a flame. Flame to them represents life. It therefore suggests to the oriental mind a life, starting feebly, rising high, then dying to darkness again as life leaves and the soul ascends to the Dragon. It carries the teaching that, no matter how great the human being, in the end nothing matters. ● Herbert Stothart's admirable arrangement of the Chinese traditional music was in itself most suggestive of the dance's meaning. I am indebted for valuable suggestions by Michio Ito, the talented and widely learned oriental dancer, whose views on the psychology of the dance were most enlightening. I believe that dancers at large would do well to study some of these dances for an understanding that will aid greatly in all forms of the art.

● **WALTER CONNOLLY:** Comedians all have their pet methods of generating laughter. These must be addressed to the type of audience toward which they direct these scenes. When I first essayed the role of the Uncle, I tried to find out what the Chinese consider funny, but soon found that their humor, keen as it is, is usually the reverse of the humor that occidentals appreciate. ● The trick, then, was to envision the character, find what in him would be funny to the occidental mind, and play on that. This uncle was a hypocritical old rascal, protected in his rascality by the age-old tenets of reverence for one's elders, the quality they call filial piety in China. The Chinese would never laugh at him. It would be impolite and disrespectful to age. But the predicament in which he keeps Wang Lung, helpless to resist his sponging, is funny to us. It is funny because it is so far from what we would submit to. ● It was an interesting study in the vagaries of comedy, which nobody will ever clearly understand. I tried to play the old fellow seriously as I envisioned him, aided by the helpful guidance of Sidney Franklin. I never laughed at the character myself. After all, the uncle took himself seriously. I hope audiences will not.

● **HERBERT STOTHART:** Interpreting the color, personality and spirit of China in terms of occidental music, for the score of THE GOOD EARTH, was essentially the same task that a translator has in bringing to the English language a work written in another, and still preserving its psychology, flavor, and meanings. ● Pearl S. Buck preserved China in a book written in the English language by use of a phraseology, and the Chinese system of expressing thought, that indelibly stamped its every paragraph with the spirit of the orient. ● Straight Chinese music, which depends on effect rather than melody, although there are many melodic strains in it, would not have been understood as music by occidental ears. So our problem was to take this music, translate it to European notation, then rearrange and paraphrase it to keep Chinese flavor in a musical form intelligible to the world public. ● This has been done before. Tschaikowsky based his *Danse Chinois* on an oriental strain. Rimsky-Korsakoff and many other composers have done so. ● The work of interpolating Chinese instrumentation in a standard orchestra took much planning. We found many interesting facts, as, for instance, that the shrill falsetto and cymbal music commonly believed to be China's representative music, was the "jazz" of that country, and that the falsetto dated back to centuries when men enacted women on the stage, sang in falsetto, and thus started that phase of oriental music. Their plaintive flute strains and passages for stringed instruments have in many cases a form similar to our music. These facts made a rather gripping entertainment out of the work of embellishing THE GOOD EARTH with its musical cloak.

● **CEDRIC GIBBONS:** Even though authentic scenes, actual portions of buildings, furniture and many integral parts of its settings were imported directly from China, handling of the set and location problem was a task of no small magnitude. ● At the inception of the work, the services of Dan Sayre Groesbeck, illustrator who lived many years in China, were obtained, and he set to work illustrating scenes in the script. These, visualizing actuality, gave us many valuable hints. ● Choice of locations to match the Chinese topography was a matter of several months of search, and the engineering problems, including building an artificial river, installing an irrigation system, laying out fields and gardens and actually "growing" the farmlands, was a matter of eight months' time. ● Artistic placing of buildings, Chinese water wheels, laying out of streets in the village and the great city, combined architectural, engineering and pictorial skill, and our art department responded with what I believe are exceptional results to the problem before it. To Harry Oliver, Arnold Gillespie, and the staff that carried out and completed one of the largest set and location operations in years, I voice my sincere thanks and congratulations. ● Authenticity, of course, was observed to the finest detail under expert technical supervision, in addition to so designing the sets as to accentuate the drama of whatever was to be enacted within them. Aside from their dramatic quality, I feel that these sets have a distinct educational value. We have, I think, shown much of China as it is.

● **JESSIE RALPH:** The role of Cuckoo almost made me a pajama addict. There is nothing quite so comfortable as the garb of a Chinese woman. ● But there is probably nothing so exacting as the task of portraying one. I have in my life played many roles, but never one more difficult, or more interesting. ● She was an odd character, sly, scheming, sometimes sinister, but under it all she had deep human quality. For instance, there is the scene where O-lan brings her first-born to be seen by the Ancient Mistress. Cuckoo is stern, preserving the manner she should toward a former slave in the palace. Then the thought crosses her mind that she herself never bore a child. She looks at the cooing baby, and for a moment the mask falls, as she gazes on the child, playfully remarks, "A sickly thing, your child!" The next moment she is again the mistress of the slaves, hard, aggressive, again the clever schemer. ● Pearl Buck's character is made human and believable by just such a touch. The most artificial character on the screen is one shown as either totally bad or totally good. Every person has some human instinct, concealed somewhere, that crops out. It is this that makes life interesting, and that makes a character interesting. ● A play, as Lionel Barrymore once remarked, can consist of nothing else than interesting people saying interesting things.

● **CHARLEY GRAPEWIN:** A Chinese father may be ruler of the home, but it is amazing to note how many things he cannot do. Playing the Old Father gave me many a laugh at the oddness of the Chinese point of view as compared with ours. ● For instance, in the original script, when O-lan is about to become a mother, I had a line, "She is with child. Soon I shall be a grandfather." General Tu, our technical adviser, protested. The father-in-law, he explained, can never discuss his daughter-in-law, especially in so delicate a matter. But it was permissible for me simply to say, "Soon I shall be a grandfather," for then I would be speaking only about myself, and not about her. ● Playing the Old Father was an interesting study in customs as well as a problem in portrayal. The old father was sharp of wit, despite his absent-mindedness. He is really, in the story, the only person who remained always faithful to O-lan. And he had a certain native humor. ● I have known many Americans who resemble this old fellow almost to duplication. And that, I think, was the most satisfactory thing about playing him. He was a mighty human old man. When the actor knows the character he is playing exists somewhere, he is a long way ahead toward making others believe in him. ● I cannot fully express the inspiration we drew from our director, whose patience, especially with inexperienced Chinese players of whom he made fine actors, I shall never forget.

for it is good . . . (Continued)

silver to O-lan. She had rather go south with the stream of refugees and save the land to come back to when drought and famine have passed.

So it is that they join the endless rout that leaves a trail of corpses for the buzzards. The old man on his back, Wang brings his family to the railroad track, where passes that mythical steam-belching monster which "climbs along the iron poles" and will take them to the city. Wang builds a shelter against the wall of a huge Palace. O-lan teaches her children to beg—even the little daughter, whom hunger has reft of reason, thenceforth the Little Fool. There is marching in the street and proclamations everywhere. But nothing to eat. When a coolie drops dead from overwork, Wang eagerly takes his job. The Eldest Son is able to steal, but that Wang does not allow.

Revolution comes. The republican army in seizing power lets slip a few hours when no authority is immediately in control. Looting and pillage are rife. Wang is swept away with one crowd, O-lan with another. She is drawn with the mob into the Palace. The house is stripped bare. As the crowd runs when police shots are heard, O-lan is felled and kicked. She is alone there hours later in the darkness, faint. She has received the wound that will never leave her through her remaining days. But as she rises, she sees a bag of jewels, priceless gems, either lost in the scuffle or rejected as worthless baubles by some ignorant fellow. This fortune she places in her bosom. The army is executing looters and O-lan steps directly into the group of prisoners. They are being shot mercilessly without trial or pause. But just as O-lan comes to the head of the line, the soldiers race off, needed elsewhere.

SO THEY are back again on the land with the money from the jewels of O-lan and they will never know hunger nor cold again. O-lan asks to keep two little pearls. Wang Lung gives them to her—though he doesn't understand why such a plain face needs pearls. She promises humbly only to look at them sometimes. Wang is able to buy the Great House and all its lands. Ching is taken to be steward and the sons of Wang are put to work. Wang himself is immersed in business in the city and his crafty Uncle, finding him very tractable through idleness and distance from the soil, initiates him into the seductive delights of the tea-house. Wang is easily fascinated by the Flame Dancer, Lotus. He goes to O-lan and speaks to her of the gnawing hunger for this girl he cannot deny himself. O-lan, O-lan, as you surrender the pearls which are to be given your rival, do you see in this Wang a helpless child? What is the wisdom of your eyes that is deeper than your sorrow?

The House of Wang becomes an embittered gloom with the arrival of Lotus as Wang's second wife. She demands and gets fabulous gifts. Wang mortgages his crops to get cash. But Lotus is enamored of the Eldest Son. The Younger Son has gone to an Agricultural College and Eldest Son is supposed to be in charge of the land until Wang discovers from Ching that he rarely comes to the land. Wang is incensed by the gossip and orders Ching to leave after a lifetime of friendship and years of stewardship. Wang races back to the House in time to discover his Eldest Son in the inner court with Lotus. Wang falls upon his son and beats him mercilessly, then orders him from the House. It is just at this moment that the first of the plague of locusts appears. The farmers assemble to hear the Younger Son plan an attempt to beat off the locusts by means of a fire-lane and ditches. His strategy is to limit the area the locusts can devastate until the wind veers and carries them off. Oh, the ugly milling myriads of whirring pincers and blade-wings as they come over the hill and are sucked down into the beautiful ranks of grain! Black grows the furrow and there are no blades left, just skeletons of stalks in the light of the blaze the farmers light to break the advance. But there too many of the ugly little beasts; they smother the fire with their bodies. Wang gives up that field and retreats to the rice-lands. Here, too, the bodies of the locusts soon fill the ditches. Just as they break through again, Wang Lung encourages the farmers to use their hands and feet, their shovels, anything to hold them back. It is in the midst of this scene that Wang Lung recognizes the Son he has beaten and ordered from the House, fighting valiantly by his side. Does Wang's face say that such things don't matter on the soil, that that was indeed another world? Even Ching is faithful, rushing in to get a light on his torch from the flame of Wang's. The lines hold firm until the barely perceptible waving of the grain becomes a deep whisper—and with that signal the horde of locusts departs.

This is reunion. They celebrate their victory with work—and Wang has come back to the soil. That night is the wedding of their Son to the daughter of Liu, the Grain Merchant. O-lan lies dying as she receives her new daughter-in-law. She bids her in kindly tones follow the precepts of wifeliness. Ah, what have they brought thee, O-lan, that you urge them on another now? Wang comes to her and restores her pearls. That is the symbol of her hopes, womanliness knows no other. She dies—but only after begging forgiveness of Wang for dying. As Wang steps out and touches the peach-tree planted so many years before, he knows at last what it is that he has always wished to hear in O-lan's silences: "Thou art the Earth!"

地
福

THIS BOOK SOLD ONLY IN THEATRES SHOWING

"THE GOOD EARTH"

It May Be Purchased in Quantities From

AL GREENSTONE ● 145 West 45th Street, New York

COPYRIGHT 1937 BY METRO-GOLDWYN-MAYER

Printed in U.S.A. by Pace Press, Inc., N.Y.C.

RONALD COLMAN
IN
FRANK CAPRA'S
PRODUCTION OF
LOST HORIZON
BY ROBERT RISKIN FROM JAMES HILTON'S NOVEL
A COLUMBIA PICTURE

Foreword

I read "LOST HORIZON" when it was first published and immediately I wanted to do it. I saw in the book one of the most important pieces of literature in the last decade. The story had bigness. It held a mirror up to the thoughts of every human being on earth. It held something of greatness. Any story that reaches into the hearts and minds of all humanity is a story that can be put on the screen successfully as good entertainment.

Frank Capra

COLUMBIA PICTURES CORPORATION

PRESENTS

RONALD COLMAN

IN

FRANK CAPRA'S

PRODUCTION OF

LOST HORIZON

WITH

EDWARD EVERETT HORTON   MARGO
H. B. WARNER   JANE WYATT
SAM JAFFE   JOHN HOWARD
THOMAS MITCHELL   ISABEL JEWELL

SCREEN PLAY BY
ROBERT RISKIN

FROM JAMES HILTON'S NOVEL

PHOTOGRAPHY BY
JOSEPH WALKER, A. S. C.

MUSICAL SCORE BY		MUSICAL DIRECTOR
DIMITRI TIOMKIN	* * *	**MAX STEINER**

THE CAST

Ronald Colman..*Robert Conway*

Jane Wyatt ....*Sondra*

Edward Everett Horton..*Lovett*

John Howard..*George Conway*

Thomas Mitchell..*Barnard*

Margo ....*Maria*

Isabel Jewell..*Gloria*

H. B. Warner..*Chang*

Sam Jaffe..*High Lama*

Lovely Jane Wyatt
Posed in the Huge
Shangri-La Set

The Story of "LOST HORIZON"

Robert Conway (*Ronald Colman*) had been found! Aboard the S.S. Manchuria, steaming toward England, men and women were tensely excited over the reappearance of their famous fellow passenger. More than a year before Conway had disappeared from his diplomatic post in Baskul. Little had been said in the press of a certain uprising of native bandits, but after it Conway had utterly vanished. He had returned as mysteriously. Where had he been? What had happened? Lord Gainsford, his friend, tried his best to shield him from the mob. Conway, as if in a daze — apparently suffering from amnesia — looked upon the whole proceedings with a detached air.

Then, that night, Sieveking, the pianist, gave a concert in the ship's salon. Conway attended. As the program developed he appeared to be a man groping for something, trying to remember. At the close of the concert he sat at the piano and played while Gainsford, Sieveking and a few others lingered.

What Conway played was so unusual that Sieveking asked what it was. Conway replied that it was something of Chopin's, to which explanation the pianist took exception. Conway insisted he was right; that it had never been published and said he had learned it from a pupil of Chopin's.

"Why, that is impossible," retorted Sieveking. "If a pupil of Chopin's were alive today he would be more than 120 years old!"

"What of it?" shot back Conway. Sieveking withdrew rather than continue what appeared to be a ridiculous discussion.

But to Conway, who continued to play the haunting melody, it was far from ridiculous. Suddenly he stopped.

"Now I remember," he cried. "Shangri-La! That melody brings it all back to me. I've got to get off the ship. I've got to go back."

Before Lord Gainsford could stop him, Conway was out on deck, shouting for the steward to pack his things. The ship was approaching Chaing Chow. There was no time to lose. Gainsford finally caught up with Bob and tried to reason with him. It was then that Conway told a tale of experiences so strange as to leave his lordship bewildered and not a little doubtful as to the narrator's mental condition.

* * * *

It all began at an airport in Baskul during a bandit uprising when Conway and his brother, George, (*John Howard*) were evacuating the population in planes before an approaching horde of bandits. Everything was pandemonium. The powerhouse had been blown up and the field was in darkness, preventing the landing of additional rescue ships. Bob, with George and several others, piled into the last plane, an immense thing sent by General Wong. Fenner, a crack pilot, had been sent along to fly it. As the plane took the air and noses were counted, there was discovered in the party: Barnard, an American of whom little was known; Alexander P. Lovett, a rather fussy archæologist and Gloria Stone, an embittered, wan looking young woman, whose occupation and mode of life had made her the enemy of all men. It was an odd collection of humans, but circumstance had thrown them together in a common danger and they made the most of it.

Exhausted from their experiences, they fall off into a slumber, to awaken to the startling realization that the plane was off its course. Instead of flying toward Shanghai it is going north. Investigation disclosed that at the controls, instead of the British pilot Fenner, there is a strange looking Oriental. An attempt to remonstrate is met with the threatening display of a revolver, so they withdrew to discuss means of meeting the situation. Plainly, they were being kidnaped. For what reason or to what destination they were headed remained a mystery. Higher and higher the plane ascended until the occupants suffered from the altitude. After hours in the air Conway found a map and sought to learn their whereabouts. The information was a terrible shock. They were a thousand miles beyond the line of civilization, headed in the direction of the Tibetan plateaus!

Then, suddenly, the trip came to a terrifying end. It was a swift descent and a precarious landing in a wild and apparently limitless country. The

plane nosed up but, by some miracle, no one was hurt. That is, no one except the pilot, the man they were to know later as Talu — and he was dead!

Just when their situation seemed hopeless, there appeared in the distance a caravan, headed by an elderly Chinese. His name was Chang and he appeared to be expecting them. Mysterious as it was, Conway and his friends followed willingly when Chang led them over miles of tortuous cliffs. Bruised and suffering they trudged on wearily until they had ascended the highest cliff on the landscape. Then, in the valley, they beheld the most beautiful sight they had seen. Chang said it was Shangri-La, a garden of contentment, a spot free from the greed and fears of a world gone mad with avarice.

But why were they there? Why had they been kidnaped? Bob's young brother, with the impulsiveness of youth, threatened dire things to Chang unless he found out. Barnard, the American, was content to find a place to rest. Lovett, (*Edward Everett Horton*) sputtered something about protests to the English government. Gloria Stone (*Isabel Jewell*) who had been dragged through the dregs of life, just didn't care.

Conway soon was to learn the reason for their presence. He also was to learn that they never could leave Shangri-La. The High Lama told him that he had been kidnaped at the suggestion of Sondra Bizet, (*Jane Wyatt*) a girl who had read his books and had gleaned from them that he was a man searching for peace — that he needed Shangri-La. He learned other things, too. For instance, the High Lama was none other than Father Perrault, who had founded Shangri-La in 1713, more than two hundred years before — and he was still alive!

"The purpose of Shangri-La," said the High Lama, "is to preserve the treasures of beauty. The time will come when brutality and lust for power must perish by its own sword. Against that time is why you were brought here. You cannot leave."

But young George was adamant. He was intent upon returning to civilization. The others began to like the place. Its peace and contentment grew upon them. Barnard, who it was learned, was wanted by the police for a gigantic stock swindle, forgot his craving for gold. He set to work putting in a modern plumbing system in Shangri-La, while the natives smiled. Gloria took an interest in music and Lovett started a class in geology among the native children.

Conway had met Sondra Bizet and had fallen in love with her. There was a romance budding between Gloria and Barnard. And Maria, a little Russian girl, had fallen madly in love with George. The story that Maria had come to Shangri-La in 1888 and was in reality nearly sixty years old could not be believed and did not matter.

But, in spite of it all, George was not content. He insisted upon leaving.

Then an amazing thing happened. The High Lama called Robert Conway before him and announced that he, the Lama, was about to die. He had finished his work and saw no need for lingering upon this earth.

"I place in your hands, my son, the destiny of Shangri-La," he said, and then peacefully lapsed into eternal slumber.

He! Bob Conway! The High Lama of Shangri-La! It all seemed too fantastic, unbelievable. But then, why not? Chang confirmed the sincerity of the High Lama.

But young George still thought differently. He insisted that it was all a fake, that the High Lama was not Father Perrault and that there was some ulterior motive in keeping them there. He said he would prove it. He brought in Maria, the little Russian girl, to back him up. She did. She said Father Perrault, the founder of the colony, died years ago, and she showed a locket with the inscription "To my dear one on her sixteenth birthday . . . 1932" to prove that she herself was not an old woman, preserved by the charm of Shangri-La. She would leave with them, because she loved George.

Convinced that he had been duped, Conway started out on the return to civilization, with a band of native porters. Gloria, Barnard and Lovett were content to remain. It was a disillusioned man who turned his back on that garden where he had found such contentment. It was difficult to leave his beloved Sondra, but he did.

After a few days of travel over almost impossible land in their fight to return to the mad whirl of civilization, a strange change came over Maria. Her face began to wither and her hands became wrinkled. She was actually becoming old! Her lie caught up with her. She *was* an old woman, preserved by the charm of Shangri-La! She confessed as much. Then, in remorse, George realized what he had done to his brother. He took a natural course. His body was found at the bottom of a ravine.

* * * *

"That is the story," Conway told Gainsford aboard the ship. "So you see, I must go back. I must get off the boat. I must go back to Shangri-La."

Conway rushed to his stateroom and began packing his things. Desperate to stop him, Gainsford locked the door and although Conway protested, refused to unlock it. But when his lordship did open the door, Conway was gone. He had climbed through the porthole and lowered himself over the side of the ship.

For a year Gainsford searched for Conway, but never caught up with him. He followed the trail through the East and heard the most amazing stories of a desperate man who fought and even robbed to reach his destination. The trail was lost at the border of civilization. Whether he reached it or not, Gainsford never knew.

At a club, later, Lord Gainsford lifted his glass.

"I give you a toast, gentlemen," he said. "Here is my hope that Conway finds his Shangri-La . . .; Here is my hope that we *all* find our Shangri-La."

An informal shot

Mr. Capra   Margo   Mr. Colman   Miss Wyatt   Mr. Howard

FRANK CAPRA

CAPRA . . . *PICTURE MAKER*

The ability to make an audience laugh is an accomplishment of no mean proportions . . . to make an audience cry . . . is again something else . . . to make an audience laugh and cry without a hangover of the lighter scene . . . without a continuance of that risibility which prevents the heart from pounding up into the throat at exactly the right split second . . . is Capra.

Much has been written of this Sicilian-born immigrant boy who pounded his way from obscure poverty to preeminence in the production of motion pictures; but no more sincere tribute has been paid him than a recent one by an admirer, who said that Capra was the "first novelist of the screen" inasmuch as he produced living novels, with each sequence a turning page and that when one has finished seeing a Capra picture, it is as if the wee hours of morning had come after complete submersion in a fascinating book and that the time had arrived to turn off the light and call it a day.

And just as immersed as the average spectator is in his pictures, so is Capra completely submerged in their making.

In a recent production: "MR. DEEDS GOES TO TOWN," there is a scene, now familiar to hundreds of millions of picture lovers the world over. Mr. Deeds, after his acquittal, escapes from the mob. He rushes back to the courtroom to find the girl of his heart, who has silently remained weeping in her seat, rising and rushing toward him. He lifts her in his arms and covers her face with kisses. Capra, standing very quietly beneath the camera, almost impercetibly directing the film, as Gary Cooper carefully put Jean Arthur on her feet, said quietly:

"Try it again."

Once more Mr. Cooper dashed into the courtroom scene, torn and disheveled from the mob, and again Miss Arthur rushed into his arms, in happy submission to the demands of the scene. At its end both stood and looked at Capra who soberly and without expression, ejaculated:

"Again!"

Somewhat reluctantly Miss Arthur returned to her chair, and without quite as much sprightliness, Mr. Cooper disappeared to prepare for his return.

Seven times the scene was played before it suddenly occurred to Capra that something was amiss somewhere and he turned and looked questioningly at a bystander he had permitted on the set.

"Does it occur to you," the bystander mildly interrogated, "that Miss Arthur is sincerely and devotedly attached to her husband and that Mr. Cooper is very much in love with Mrs. Cooper?"

"Oh, hell!" was Capra's response, "this is serious, we're making a picture!"

It was important to Capra to shoot that scene just that many times so that he would have his selection from the "takes" of the precise one of the seven which would have the greatest semblance of naturalness, freshness, enthusiasm and sweetness in its contribution to the whimsy of that particular part of "MR. DEEDS GOES TO TOWN."

Capra, of course, claims that he doesn't direct actors. From his appearance on a set one would think that he hardly directed anything. He never raises his voice, and aside from a funny little whistle which is characteristic of him, he hardly makes himself heard.

He selects his casts with infinite care; his players are given lines to read and he asks them to read them with the utmost naturalness. He has the gift, emotionally, of putting them into a friendly state; by his own completely friendly attitude, he robs them of awkwardness, hesitancy, falsity or anything that might sound an unnatural note.

He pats a "bit" player on the back encouragingly and quietly says "Good work," when all the bit player has done has been to grimace in complete correctness at the proper moment.

His relationship with the important players is invariably friendly. He respects them for their abilities and they respect him for exactly what he is — the industry's top producer-director.

He is a modest yet withal a rebellious fellow — this Capra. Before the flower of the motion picture industry assembled to witness the awards of the Academy of Motion Picture Arts and Sciences he embarrassedly tucks the prize award of the year under his arm and literally flies back to his seat without comment and yet will defy the tradition of the industry by taking as his subject matter for a picture that which his confreres label "anti-boxoffice."

He declares he made pictures according to formula up to a few years ago, when he decided that certain fetishes regarding particular types of pictures were basically unsound. He saw no reason, for instance, why a story that had charm and fine characterization but with the dominant character an elderly woman, he had to listen to the insistent cry: "The public does not want that sort of a picture." It was about then that he became interested in Damon Runyon's story, "MADAME LA GUIMP," which Capra transposed to the screen under the title of "LADY FOR A DAY."

An acceptance had been pretty well established that motion picture patrons of the world did not want racehorse pictures, but when Capra analyzed "BROADWAY BILL," he saw in it everything that he later put on celluloid, and kicked over another precept which really wasn't a precept at all.

*Interesting Scenes
from Frank Capra's
Production of "Lost
Horizon" starring
Ronald Colman*

The Making of a Great Picture

To bring Tibet to Hollywood: to present in living reality the ancient civilization of a land which has remained, throughout world history, inviolate in its mountain fastnesses — was Frank Capra's task in bringing to the screen James Hilton's novel, "LOST HORIZON."

Hollywood — and Capra — are used to challenges. The problem of crystallizing dream into tangibility is an every-day affair in the cinema capital of the world. But the challenge of Hilton's "LOST HORIZON" presented problems which might have given pause even to Capra. For here was a land of mystery, shrouded by drifting mist and driving snow: a challenge of an author's idealism which required, in its meeting, not only the most patient and far-reaching of research, the utmost in technical skill and resourcefulness, but a high order of creative imagination.

More than a year of intensive study went into the making of "LOST HORIZON." Long before Columbia decided to produce the picture, Frank Capra had commissioned his London agent to buy him the original manuscript. He drew it out of a desk drawer on Hilton's first visit to the Columbia lot, and the only regret of the young novelist was that he had been so pressed for funds when he wrote "LOST HORIZON" that he had written it on the cheapest available copy paper. "It would," mourned the British novelist, "have cost me only the price of another meal or two to have written it on better paper."

With the author himself on the ground to bring his own knowledge and enthusiasm to the making of the film; with Columbia resolved that the production must be as perfect as skill could make it; with Robert Riskin as scenarist, and Harrison Forman, American explorer and authority on Tibet, engaged as technical adviser, it was inevitable that "LOST HORIZON" would become an important picture.

Capra and Riskin worked together on the script as they have worked together on "LADY FOR A DAY," "IT HAPPENED ONE NIGHT," "BROADWAY BILL," and "MR. DEEDS GOES TO TOWN." Strangely enough, consid-ering the fantastic, dream-quality of the novel, they retained more of the original book than in any other story which they have adapted. A few minor changes in characterization were made to fulfill the demands of motion picture technique. Hilton was fully in accord with these changes. He said, in fact, that if they had occurred to him, he would have made them himself in writing the novel.

With the story completed, research in the technical problems of the film could go forward. Forman had brought with him from Tibet a bewildering assortment of articles, varying as widely as wigs with 108 separate braids of long hair, drums made from the halves of two human skulls, and primitive swords, spears and firearms — muzzle-loaders exploded in a flashpan ignited by a wick.

Lama costumes, the everyday, holiday and ceremonial costumes of Tibetan peasants, the implements of primitive farming and handicraft and day-to-day living of this far-away and archaic civilization of the roof-top of the world, had all come in the crates and boxes and trunks stamped with the exotic lettering of Tibet.

Bucket-hoops of native silver, studded with coral and turquoise, gold and silver charm-boxes, bracelets and necklaces heavy with clumped masses of gems, a sorcerer's trumpet made from a human thigh-bone — these were only a few of the items of Tibetan booty brought by Forman from Tibet. There were, too, in Forman's possession, innumerable photographs of life as it is lived in Tibet, innu-

merable notebooks filled with scrawled data of needed details.

Search through the properties of Hollywood's costume companies failed to reveal anything that even remotely approximated duplications of these costumes and properties. Capra called in the property men and assigned to them the task of creating what was needed. A special department of ten expert property makers was installed in the studio, to fashion the more than 700 unique props.

In the meantime, Stephen Goosson, art director of Columbia studios, with his assistants, Lionel Banks and Paul Murphy, was at work creating the magical backgrounds for "LOST HORIZON." The lamasery of Shangri-La, that stronghold of the best that man's mind and spirit have brought forth of beauty and art; the Valley of the Blue Moon, in which, under the beneficent dominance of the lamas, lived the Tibetan peasants of this harmonious world — these were two of the major assignments of Goosson and his staff of artists.

Scale models, complete to the minutest detail, were made of the lamasery of Shangri-La — this lamasery which, upon its completion on the Columbia lot, measured one thousand feet long and almost five hundred feet wide, was one of the largest and most elaborate sets ever built in Hollywood.

There were, too, the Chinese city of Baskul, to be seen in the picture during a military uprising and the evacuation of its citizens and American residents; the snow-piled field on the mountainous borders of Tibet; the plane, in which the principals of the cast were being kidnaped, landed; the lounge, smoking-room and library of a great ocean liner;

these and innumerable other necessary scenes offered to Goosson and his assistants problems which piled one upon another, like the thunderous mountain landscape of Tibet itself.

While these sets were being created, costume impressions of lamas and peasants were being painted by the facile brush of Dan Grossbeck, the distinguished illustrator. Cary Odell, one of Hollywood's youngest and most promising artists, worked on eighteen colored set sketches of "LOST HORIZON," while, when the sets were actually completed, Schuyler Crail, a young photographic artist of Hollywood, made Contax studies of every set.

Actual work on the Shangri-La set began March first, and took one hundred and fifty workmen two months to complete. With its background of piled, dark peaks, overwhelming in their snow-covered majesty, the lamasery is presented, in Hilton's own words, as hanging upon the mountain side "with the chance delicacy of flower petals impaled upon a crag."

"It was superb and exquisite," Hilton wrote. "An austere emotion carried the eye upward from milk-blue roofs to a gray rock bastion above, tremendous as a Wetterhorn above Grindelwald. Beyond that, in a dazzling pyramid, soared the snow slopes of Karakal. It might well be, Conway thought, the most terrifying mountainscape in the world."

And so here stands Shangri-La! The delicate pavilions are reached by soaring flights of shallow marble stairways, and stand surrounded by rambling gardens of luxuriant foliage, with sparkling lily-covered pools, fountains, and flower-filled terraces. Two hundred doves were oriented to the

garden, that their peaceful comings and goings might add to the harmony of the scene.

The interior sets of Shangri-La match the exterior in the size and splendor of their scale. The quarters of the High Lama are strikingly beautiful. The library, music rooms, bedrooms and gigantic hallways and staircases all combine to match the picture of a palace inconceivably lovely and luxurious. The dining-room, for instance, is almost weirdly beautiful, with walls of creamy parchment, sewed together with strips of rawhide, intricately interwoven. Furniture, hangings, table appointments, each makes its own contribution to the ensemble of dignity and richness.

Even the lamasery was not, of course, sufficient to give the whole picture of Hilton's dream world. It was necessary to bring forth for camera reproduction the Valley of the Blue Moon, the downward prospect to be seen from the serene plateau heights of Shangri-La. Sherwood Forest, about forty miles from Hollywood, was chosen as the perfect realization on earth of the happy valley.

It was a real stroke of luck for Capra that Sherwood Forest was so near Hollywood. Secluded as it is, it carried the atmosphere of isolation implicit in Hilton's description. Important features were a natural basin which could be transformed into an artificial lake, and certain flattened heights which have the aspect of Tibetan plateau-land. A rigid policing system to keep airplanes from zooming into the picture, was required. Here, surrounding the artificial lake, there arose a complete Tibetan village. Primitive houses, crude picturesque bridges, chortens or mausoleums that hold the sacred ashes

of departed lamas, thousands of orchids in bloom — these and innumerable other characteristic details of the forbidden country nestling in the Asiatic eaves of the world, helped to make up this rare setting.

It is in this idyllic country that hundreds of Tibetan types will be seen in the picture, following their happy existence, farming, spinning, weaving, practicing their primitive handicrafts. The difficulty of the casting problem encountered may be inferred from the fact that not a single Tibetan has ever been known to take out a passport for America. Capra and Forman interviewed literally hundreds of hopeful extras of every possible ethnic type, before finding any which approximated the Tibetan racial characteristics.

Even the selection of an airport for "LOST HORIZON" offered difficulties. The book places the field somewhere in Manchuria. Obviously, the up-to-date airports of Los Angeles, located as they are in the heart of building development, could not be used. This field required a mountain background, plenty of room to build Chinese hangars, and a crude headquarters building. The luck that hovers over Hollywood supplied the answer in Metropolitan airport, twenty miles from Los Angeles. It is a field that has been unused commercially for several years. Secluded, overgrown with weeds, and with a natural background of towering San Bernardino mountains, it answered every requirement of novelist, script writer, and director.

It was here that a thousand Chinese extras, from every strata of Chinese life, from high Manchu to lowliest denim-clad coolie, were used in one of the most thrilling sequences of the picture, the

evacuation of Baskul. One of the spectacular shots was the burning of an immense Chinese hangar. Twenty-five thousand dollars depended on that shot, for if anything went wrong with the scene, it meant that the hangar would have to be rebuilt; more than a thousand extras would have to be called back for retakes, and an entire night's work with an expensive cast of stars and featured players would have to be done over again.

There was to be great confusion in this scene. The planes would take off; trucks, filled with shouting, shooting rebels, would follow in a mad rush, while excited Chinese hordes, some leading cows, driving horses, herding squealing pigs, battled to get out of the way of the take-off. All this was to follow the tossing of the firebrand into the flimsy Chinese hangar, built to ignite like tinder. But it was a Capra scene, in a Capra production, perfectly conceived, perfectly rehearsed. Nothing went wrong. For this scene, the ubiquitous modern touch was present, although it will be unseen in the picture: an entire company from the Los Angeles Fire Department was on hand to see that no dread fire calamity started during the making of the sequence.

For the landing of the plane carrying the kidnaped principals when it is surrounded by strange tribesmen who refuel the plane in the snow-covered wastes on the Tibetan borderland, dangerous terrain was required, with a dried water-bed large enough for the landing and taking off. Lucerne Dry Lake, about a hundred and fifty miles from Hollywood, supplied the site, after weeks of search-

ing through California, Nevada and Arizona. It fulfilled every possible technical and artistic demand — all but one. That was how to take care of a company of three-hundred-and-fifty men, women and children, with scores of camels, horses, pigs, cows, and other living things that comprise the populace of a primitive nomadic settlement. And so a complete young city, with living shacks, messhall, hospital, recreation rooms, dark rooms for cameramen, property rooms, dressing rooms, and other necessary shelters was erected, just outside of camera lines.

While the cameras filmed Hilton's description, the Granite Mountain, Pickaniny Buttes, San Gorgonion and San Anononia "standing in" for Tibetan peaks, a reverse shot would have revealed one of the most complete mushroom cities that ever sprang into being.

And so it went, with every background in Hilton's book coming alive under the brilliant direction of Capra, and the work of his staff. The British foreign office, airplane cabins, ships' radio cabins, and innumerable other sets were evolved, and became the stages, large and small, on which Hilton's characters lived their lives.

In casting "LOST HORIZON," Capra had many problems. The Tibetan and Chinese types were eventually found. There had been the problem of finding a star who would incarnate, in physical appearance, and in certain indefinable qualities of mind and spirit, the Conway of Hilton's book. Ronald Colman, inevitably, became the star of the production. In assigning his other important roles, Capra reversed his usual formula in casting: with the exception of Colman, Edward Everett Horton, and H. B. Warner, who play the important parts of Lovett and Chang, a lama, Capra drew, not upon the ranks of players whose previous achievements had proved their ability, but upon those of

the young, untried players — actors and actresses whose careers are still before them, and who show brilliant promise of taking their places among the great names of the screen. Jane Wyatt, who plays opposite Ronald Colman, has appeared in only two pictures. John Howard has been in Hollywood less than two years. Isabel Jewell, who gave her most important performance in "A TALE OF TWO CITIES," is given her biggest opportunity. Margo, from the stage, who has shown brilliant possibilities in her few pictures, plays Maria, and Thomas Mitchell, although a veteran of the theatre as actor, author and stage director, makes his first screen appearance in "LOST HORIZON."

Capra found his greatest difficulty in casting the role of the High Lama. Since Kipling wrote "KIM," the lama has not figured prominently in occidental literature. Here, moreover, was a lama, who, although he had taken on some of the characteristics of the people with whom he had cast his life, was himself an exotic, an outlander. He, like Conway, must be of a certain type, distinctive, unique: he must be a man with a rich background of worldly culture, and yet one who was dedicated to priestlike sincerity, to the life of harmony, peace and infinite understanding. The role was the last one cast, and was assigned to Sam Jaffe, who first made himself known to Broadway by his outstand-work in "GRAND HOTEL."

Thus, the desire for perfection in every phase of the making of this great picture resolves itself into a series of perfections, great and small — perfection in casting, perfection in backgrounds, settings, props. It is a big job that Capra has done — but after all, that's Capra.

Sam Jaffe, who plays the High Lama, in a scene from "Lost Horizon"

A tense moment as the refugees flee from the Chinese bandits

This book may be purchased from the publisher, AL GREENSTONE, 145 West 45th Street, New York, N. Y.

Gone With The Wind

Clark Gable *as* Rhett Butler.

Clark Gable, the popular choice for Rhett Butler, was born in Cadiz, Ohio. He attended Hopedale High School (Ohio) and night school at the University of Akron. He joined a traveling road company, barnstorming the West Coast and Middle West. His first legitimate show was Jane Cowl's "Romeo and Juliet," followed by "What Price Glory," "The Copperhead" with Lionel Barrymore, "Madame X" and "Lady Frederick." In between stage work, he got a few extra movie jobs. One of them was in "The Merry Widow" with John Gilbert and Mae Murray. After playing the comedy lead opposite Nancy Carroll in "Chicago," he left Los Angeles for a year's stock engagement in Houston, Texas. Arthur Hopkins cast him in the leading role of "Machinal," followed by "Conflict," "Gambling," "Hawk Island," "Blind Windows" and "The Last Mile." His first picture, "The Painted Desert," followed this engagement. He made his M-G-M debut in "The Easiest Way," followed by "Dance, Fools, Dance," "The Secret Six," "Laughing Sinners" and "Sporting Blood." Then came "A Free Soul," "Hell Divers," "Susan Lennox, Her Fall and Rise," "Possessed," "Polly Of The Circus," "Strange Interlude," "No Man Of Her Own," "The White Sister," "Dancing Lady," "It Happened One Night," "Men In White," "Manhattan Melodrama," "Forsaking All Others," "After Office Hours," "Mutiny On The Bounty," "Wife vs. Secretary," "San Francisco," "Cain and Mabel," "Love On The Run," "Parnell," "Saratoga," "Test Pilot," "Too Hot To Handle," and "Idiot's Delight."

Vivien Leigh *as* Scarlett O'Hara.

Vivien Leigh, who plays the part of Scarlett O'Hara, was born in Darjeeling, India. Her father was French, her mother, Irish. She attended London's public schools, a French convent in Italy, and finishing schools in Paris and Bavaria. She joined the Academy of Dramatic Art in London when 19. Her first legitimate stage role was in "The Green Sash," followed by "The Mask of Virtue," "The Happy Hypocrite," and "Henry VIII." "Fire Over England" was her first major picture, followed by "Dark Journey," "Storm In A Teacup," "St. Martin's Lane" and "A Yank At Oxford." Meanwhile on the London stage she played "Bats In The Belfry," "Hamlet" and "A Midsummer Night's Dream." Her casting as Scarlett O'Hara happened fortuitously. After all efforts and tests had been made with the issue still in doubt David O. Selznick actually started filming his picture without his heroine. Miss Leigh was a guest witness at the opening scene when the producer was struck by her resemblance to the Scarlett as described by Miss Mitchell.

DAVID O. SELZNICK'S
production of
MARGARET MITCHELL'S
Story of the Old South

GONE WITH THE WIND

IN TECHNICOLOR, *starring*

CLARK GABLE

as Rhett Butler

LESLIE   OLIVIA
HOWARD · de HAVILLAND

and presenting

VIVIEN LEIGH

as Scarlett O'Hara

A SELZNICK INTERNATIONAL PICTURE

Directed by VICTOR FLEMING

Screen Play by Sidney Howard

Music by Max Steiner

A Metro-Goldwyn-Mayer Release

THE PLAYERS

in the order of their appearance

AT TARA,
The O'Hara Plantation in Georgia:

BRENT TARLETON . . . . FRED CRANE
STUART TARLETON . . . . GEORGE REEVES
SCARLETT O'HARA . . . . VIVIEN LEIGH
MAMMY . . . . HATTIE McDANIEL
BIG SAM . . . . EVERETT BROWN
ELIJAH . . . . ZACK WILLIAMS
GERALD O'HARA . . . . . THOMAS MITCHELL
PORK . . . . OSCAR POLK
ELLEN O'HARA . . . . BARBARA O'NEIL
JONAS WILKERSON . . . . VICTOR JORY
SUELLEN O'HARA . . . . . . EVELYN KEYES
CARREEN O'HARA . . . . . . ANN RUTHERFORD
PRISSY . . . . BUTTERFLY McQUEEN

AT TWELVE OAKS,
The nearby Wilkes Plantation:

JOHN WILKES . . . . HOWARD HICKMAN
INDIA WILKES . . . . ALICIA RHETT
ASHLEY WILKES . . . . LESLIE HOWARD
MELANIE HAMILTON . . . OLIVIA DE HAVILLAND
CHARLES HAMILTON . . . . . . RAND BROOKS
FRANK KENNEDY . . . . CARROLL NYE
CATHLEEN CALVERT . . . . MARCELLA MARTIN
RHETT BUTLER . . . . CLARK GABLE

AT THE BAZAAR IN ATLANTA:

AUNT "PITTYPAT" HAMILTON LAURA HOPE CREWS
DOCTOR MEADE . . . . . . HARRY DAVENPORT
MRS. MEADE . . . . LEONA ROBERTS
MRS. MERRIWETHER . . . . . JANE DARWELL
RENE PICARD . . . . ALBERT MORIN
MAYBELLE MERRIWETHER . . MARY ANDERSON
FANNY ELSING . . . . TERRY SHERO
OLD LEVI . . . . WILLIAM McCLAIN

OUTSIDE THE EXAMINER OFFICE:

UNCLE PETER . . . . EDDIE ANDERSON
PHIL MEADE . . . . JACKIE MORAN

AT THE HOSPITAL:

REMINISCENT SOLDIER . . . . . CLIFF EDWARDS
BELLE WATLING . . . . ONA MUNSON
THE SERGEANT . . . . ED CHANDLER
A WOUNDED SOLDIER IN PAIN
                    GEORGE HACKATHORNE
A CONVALESCENT SOLDIER . . . . ROSCOE ATES
A DYING SOLDIER . . . . . . JOHN ARLEDGE
AN AMPUTATION CASE . . . . . ERIC LINDEN

DURING THE EVACUATION:

A COMMANDING OFFICER . . . . . . TOM TYLER

DURING THE SIEGE:

A MOUNTED OFFICER . . . . WILLIAM BAKEWELL
THE BARTENDER . . . . LEE PHELPS

GEORGIA AFTER SHERMAN:

A YANKEE DESERTER . . . . PAUL HURST
THE CARPETBAGGER'S FRIEND . ERNEST WHITMAN
A RETURNING VETERAN . . . WILLIAM STELLING
A HUNGRY SOLDIER . . . . LOUIS JEAN HEYDT
EMMY SLATTERY . . . . ISABEL JEWELL

DURING RECONSTRUCTION:

THE YANKEE MAJOR . . . . . ROBERT ELLIOTT
HIS POKER-PLAYING CAPTAINS . GEORGE MEEKER
WALLIS CLARK
THE CORPORAL . . . . IRVING BACON
A CARPETBAGGER ORATOR . . . ADRIAN MORRIS
JOHNNY GALLEGHER . . . . . J. M. KERRIGAN
A YANKEE BUSINESSMAN . . . OLIN HOWLAND
A RENEGADE . . . . YAKIMA CANUTT
HIS COMPANION . . . . . BLUE WASHINGTON
TOM, A YANKEE CAPTAIN . . . . . WARD BOND
BONNIE BLUE BUTLER . . . . . CAMMIE KING
BEAU WILKES . . . . MICKEY KUHN
BONNIE'S NURSE . . . LILLIAN KEMBLE COOPER

PRODUCED BY DAVID O. SELZNICK • DIRECTED BY VICTOR FLEMING
BASED ON MARGARET MITCHELL'S NOVEL "GONE WITH THE WIND"

SCREEN PLAY BY SIDNEY HOWARD

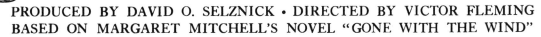

The Production Designed By . . . *William Cameron Menzies*	Assistant Director . . . . *Eric G. Stacey*
Art Direction By . . . . *Lyle Wheeler*	Second Assistant Director . . . . *Ridgeway Callow*
Photographed By . . . . *Ernest Haller, A.S.C.*	Production Continuity . . . . *Lydia Schiller*
Technicolor Associates . . . . . *Ray Rennahan, A.S.C.*	*Connie Earle*
Wilfrid M. Cline, A.S.C.	Mechanical Engineer . . . . *R. D. Musgrave*
Musical Score By . . . . *Max Steiner*	Construction Superintendent . . . . . . *Harold Fenton*
Associate . . . . *Lou Forbes*	Chief Grip . . . . *Fred Williams*
Special Photographic Effects By . . . . . *Jack Cosgrove*	In Charge of Wardrobe . . . . . . *Edward P. Lambert*
Associate: (Fire Effects) . . . . *Lee Zavitz*	Associates . . . . *Marian Dabney*
Costumes Designed By . . . . *Walter Plunkett*	*Elmer Ellsworth*
Scarlett's Hats By . . . . *John Frederics*	Casting Managers . . . . *Charles Richards*
Interiors By . . . . *Joseph B. Platt*	*Fred Schuessler*
Interior Decoration By . . . . *Edward G. Boyle*	Location Manager . . . . *Mason Litson*
Supervising Film Editor . . . . *Hal C. Kern*	Scenic Department Superintendent . . . . *Henry J. Stahl*
Associate Film Editor . . . . *James E. Newcom*	Electrical Superintendent . . . . *Wally Oettel*
Scenario Assistant . . . . *Barbara Keon*	Chief Electrician . . . . *James Potevin*
Recorder . . . . *Frank Maher*	Properties:
Makeup and Hair Styling . . . . . *Monty Westmore*	
Associates . . . . *Hazel Rogers*	Manager . . . . *Harold Coles*
Ben Nye	On the Set . . . . *Arden Cripe*
Dance Directors . . . . *Frank Floyd*	Greens . . . . *Roy A. McLaughlin*
Eddie Prinz	Drapes . . . . *James Forney*
Historian . . . . *Wilbur G. Kurtz*	Special Properties Made By . . . . . . *Ross B. Jackman*
Technical Advisers . . . . *Susan Myrick*	Tara Landscaped By . . . . *Florence Yoch*
Will Price	Still Photographer . . . . *Fred Parrish*
Research . . . . *Lillian K. Deighton*	Camera Operators . . . . *Arthur Arling*
Production Manager . . . . *Raymond A. Klune*	*Vincent Farrar*
Technicolor Co. Supervisor . . . . . . *Natalie Kalmus*	Assistant Film Editors . . . . . . *Richard Van Enger*
Associate . . . . *Henri Jaffa*	*Ernest Leadley*

FACTS *about the* PRODUCTION

DAVID O. SELZNICK, *Producer of*
GONE WITH THE WIND

DAVID O. SELZNICK bought the motion picture rights of "Gone With the Wind" on July 30, 1936, for $50,000, the highest price ever paid for a first novel . . . The title is a quotation from Ernest Dowson's poem about Cynara . . . The book, which consists of 1037 pages, had surpassed fifty thousand copies on the first day of sale, shattering all existing fiction records . . . It was begun by Margaret Mitchell in 1926 . . . Most of the book had been completed by 1929. In the succeeding years until its publication in 1936 much additional work was done in filling in missing chapters, rewriting certain others and checking the thousands of historical and other factual statements for accuracy . . . It has now been translated into 16 foreign languages and has sold around two million copies of which one-and-three quarter millions were sold in the United States . . .

Of established stars mentioned for the part of Scarlett O'Hara, Bette Davis, Katharine Hepburn, Margaret Sullavan, Miriam Hopkins, Norma Shearer, Carole Lombard and Paulette Goddard were most prominent . . . Oscar Serlin, Maxwell Arnow and Charles Morrison, talent scouts, and Director George Cukor conducted a national search for a girl to play the part . . . Their records show that 1,400 candidates were interviewed; 90 screen-tested; 149,000 feet of black and white film and 13,000 feet of Technicolor shot in these tests . . . The cost of the search has been computed by studio accountants at $92,000, of which about two-thirds represents cost of the screen tests . . . Magnitude of this figure is apparent by comparison with the cost of casting the other 59 principal characters, which totaled "only" $10,000 . . .

The burning of the military supplies of Atlanta, one of the major spectacular scenes in the picture, was filmed on the night of December 15, 1938, at which time David O. Selznick met Vivien Leigh, a spectator, who had accompanied his brother Myron, the well-known talent representative, to the studio . . . Struck by her physical resemblance to the Scarlett described by Miss Mitchell, in that she has the green eyes, narrow waist and pert features, he suggested a test . . . It was made and on January 16, 1939, he signed her for the role . . .

To insure her mastery of the Southern accent, Selznick engaged Will A. Price of McComb, Mississippi, an expert in Southern dialects, and Susan Myrick of Macon, Georgia, known as the "Emily Post of the South," to assist her in her cultivation of it . . . Miss Myrick was also entrusted with the job of technical adviser in the matter of Southern customs and manners . . . To authenticate all details of the production historically, Wilbur G. Kurtz of Atlanta, distinguished historian and artist of the South, was added to the staff . . .

Other noted individuals to whom credit must go for exacting chores in the production are William Cameron Menzies, who was given the unparalleled assignment of "Production Designer" . . . Lyle Wheeler, head of the Selznick International art department . . . Joseph B. Platt, one of the nation's foremost industrial designers and head of one of the nation's largest designing firms, who created interiors for the picture . . . Walter Plunkett, one of Hollywood's foremost stylists, who designed the costumes . . .

Sidney Howard worked with Selznick for almost a

"THE production of 'Gone With the Wind' represents the complete devotion to their respective jobs, and the coordinated efforts, of a hundred artists, technicians and department heads. I should like to take this opportunity to express publicly my deep appreciation to those credited on the screen and in the program, including especially Victor Fleming, who, in my personal opinion has forever established himself as one of the great motion picture directors of all time; and, for their brilliant technical achievements, William Cameron Menzies, Jack Cosgrove, and Hal Kern; and also to others too numerous to mention, in particular Katharine Brown, the very first to recognize the film possibilities of the novel...Having had the pleasure and privilege of being associated in close daily collaboration for over a year with that great craftsman, the late Sidney Howard, on the screen play, it is my deepest regret, as it is that of my associates who worked with Mr. Howard, that he did not live to see the realization of his work." —*David O. Selznick*

MARGARET MITCHELL, *Author*

VICTOR FLEMING, *Director*

SIDNEY HOWARD, *Screen Playwright*

year on the script, but died in a tragic accident on his Connecticut farm before he had ever seen a shot of it on the screen . . . Even such well-established artists as Leslie Howard, who plays "Ashley Wilkes," and Olivia de Havilland, who is seen as "Melanie," were tested before being definitely assigned the parts . . . Clark Gable, borrowed by Selznick from Metro-Goldwyn-Mayer, also made costume and make-up tests, though rarely in the history of pictures has an actor been such a unanimous choice of public and press as Gable was for the role of "Rhett Butler" . . .

While no exact percentage has been measured, the dialogue in the picture is predominantly from the book . . . William Cameron Menzies, Lyle Wheeler and the art department prepared more than 3000 sketches, visualizing in full color all the principal scenes in the picture . . . More than 5500 separate items of wardrobe were required to be designed by Walter Plunkett, for which he had to draw more than 400 sketches . . . His task was complicated by the historic fact that during the eleven years covered by the events described in the book, men's and women's fashions underwent three complete changes . . . He thus had to re-create not only the fashions of the hoopskirt era before the war, but the makeshift models of the poverty-stricken war years and the bustle modes of the "reconstruction" period . . .

Production of the long-awaited film was officially begun on January 26, 1939.

Victor Fleming, the director, made the final shot on November 11, 1939, the anniversary of Armistice Day.

It is fair to say that this has been the most important directorial assignment of all time. Fleming's outstanding skill in piloting large casts through fast-moving plots has been gained during the motion picture career that began in 1910. While his directorial talent was well recognized in such productions as "The Wizard of Oz," "Test Pilot," "Captains Courageous," "Treasure Island" and many others, nevertheless he will be remembered for "Gone With the Wind" as far and away the most distinguished directorial job in screen annals.

(*Continued on Page 12*)

On the set—a script rehearsal

Approximately 449,512 feet of film were shot, of which 160,000 feet were printed ... From this length, most of it repetitive, the finally edited film has been cut to 20,300 feet ... Fifteen hundred set sketches were drawn; 200 designed and 90 constructed ... The recreated "City of Atlanta" is the largest set ever built, consisting of 53 full-size buildings and 7,000 feet of streets ... The reconstructed "Peachtree Street" alone is 3,000 feet long ... The amount of lumber that went into the 90 sets is roughly estimated at a million feet.

Eleven hundred horses, 375 assorted other animals (dogs, mules, oxen, cows, pigs, etc.), 450 vehicles (wagons, gun-caissons, ambulances, etc.), were used ... In addition to the 59 members of the cast, there were over 12,000 days of employment given to over 2,400 extra and bit people ... The fact that Technicolor requires exposure of three separate strips of film simultaneously means that 1,350,000 feet of film ran through the cameras to provide a color footage of 450,000 feet ...

Vivien Leigh worked in the picture for 22 weeks with only four days off in that entire time, making her role the longest in history ... She had more than forty costume changes, the largest wardrobe any player has had in one production ... At the "Charity Bazaar" articles of home manufacture, most of them antique, were offered for sale ... Twenty- cameos were bought in the United States and used on Scarlett's dresses ...

color cameras were used to film the duplicate of the actual scene of 75 es 500 feet high leaped from

a set that covered 40 acres ... Ten pieces of fire equipment from the Los Angeles fire department, 25 policemen from the Los Angeles police department, 50 studio firemen and 200 studio helpers stood ready throughout the filming of this sequence in case the fire should get out of hand ... Three 5,000-gallon water tanks were used to quench the flames after the shooting ...

To have filmed every page of the book with the actual conversation and action would have required nearly a million feet of film, which would take a solid week to show with the projector running 24 hours a day ... Nevertheless, the producers believe and hope that every well-remembered scene of the book has been included, either in faithful transcription of the original, or in keeping within the exact spirit of Miss Mitchell's work. Cost accountants estimate that in the preparation of the film, before a single foot was shot, there were 250,000 man hours devoted to preparation ... In actual production there were 750,000 man hours ... Seven bales of cotton went into the 2500 costumes worn by the feminine characters ... The cleaning bill for wardrobe during production—since the State Industrial Board requires studios to clean all wardrobe after each usage — slightly exceeds $10,000 ... Thirty-four different carpet designs were used; 36 wallpaper designs were hand-painted for the picture ... The American Institute of Public Opinion, known as the "Gallup Poll," estimates that 56,500,000 people in this country alone are waiting to see the picture—the largest potential audience any motion picture has ever had ... A total world audience of 100,000,000 is calculated on the basis of world returns of previous Selznick and Metro-Goldwyn-Mayer pictures.

On the set—a consultation

RHETT *by* CLARK GABLE

MY REACTION to playing Rhett Butler is both frank and simple. "The condemned man ate a hearty meal." Now don't get me wrong. As an actor, I loved it. As a character, he was terrific. As material for the screen, he was that "once in a lifetime" opportunity. But as Clark Gable, who likes to pick his spots and found himself trapped by a series of circumstances over which he had no control, I was scared stiff.

This is no alibi. I cannot but honestly admit that the actual making of the picture was one of the most thoroughly pleasant and satisfying experiences I have ever known. During the filming, I was on familiar ground. Once in the atmosphere of the settings, facing a camera in costume, playing scenes that were dramatically realistic, I felt for the first time that I had an understanding of Rhett. The long months I had studied him and tried to know him as I know myself made me believe I was Rhett. These were things I could get my hands on. They were part of my job as an actor. It was those things I couldn't get my hands on that had me worried.

In way of explanation, let me go back to the beginning. I never asked to play Rhett. I was one of the last to read the book. I know, because out of curiosity I have inquired, that I definitely was not Miss Margaret Mitchell's inspiration for creating Rhett. When she was writing her book, Hollywood never had heard of me, and I am certain Miss Mitchell was not interested

in an obscure Oklahoma oil field worker, which I was at the time. The first few times I heard the name, Rhett Butler, it was with growing irritation. Nobody likes to appear stupid. It was annoying to have people say breathlessly, "But, of course, you've read 'Gone With The Wind'," and then look painfully surprised when I said I hadn't. It got to the point where anyone who hadn't read the book was considered illiterate, if not actually a social outcast. Besides, everything in Hollywood out of the ordinary is "colossal." You get used to it. The greatest book ever written that will make the greatest picture of all time appears regularly every week. It is usually forgotten just as quickly. That's what got me about "The Wind." It kept right on blowing.

As I have said before, every minute of the five months the picture was in production was enjoyable. It was the preceding twenty-four months of conversation that had me on my ear. When it got to the point where Spencer Tracy was greeting me with "Hello, Rhett," I read the book. Before that, I had held out even when my best friends told me, "It's made to order for you." I had heard that one before.

In the interest of truth, I became a fan of Miss Mitchell's with the rest of America after going halfway through the book. It was good, too good in fact. Rhett was everything a character should be, and rarely is, clear, concise and very real. He breathed in the pages of the book. He was flawless as a character study. He stood up under the most careful analysis without exhibiting a weakness. That was the trouble.

I realized that whoever played Rhett would be up against a stumbling block in this respect. Miss Mitchell had etched Rhett into the minds of millions of people, each of whom knew exactly how Rhett would look and act. It would be impossible to satisfy them all. An actor would be lucky to please even the majority. It wasn't that I didn't want to play Rhett. I did. No actor could entirely resist such a challenge. But the more popular Rhett became, the more I agreed with the gentleman who wrote, "Discretion is the better part of valour."

My reading of the book enabled me to see clearly what I was in for if I played the part. I decided to say nothing. It became more apparent, anyhow, that it was out of my hands. The public interest in my doing Rhett puzzled me. Long before anyone had been cast for the picture, I was asked for interviews. When I refused comment, the columnists did it for me. My mail doubled and then trebled. I saw myself pictured as Rhett, with sideburns. I don't like sideburns. They itch. I was the only one, apparently, who didn't take it for granted that I was going to play Rhett. It was a funny feeling. I think I know now how a fly must react after being caught in a spider web. It wasn't that I didn't appreciate the compliment the public was paying me. It was simply that Rhett was too big an order. I didn't want any part of him.

To make sure that I hadn't erred in my first impression, I read "Gone" again. It convinced me more than ever that Rhett was too much for any actor to tackle in his right mind. But I couldn't escape him. I looked for every out. I even considered writing Miss Mitchell at one time. I thought it would be great if she would simply issue a statement saying, "I think Clark Gable would be the worst possible selection for Rhett Butler." Perhaps after Miss Mitchell sees my Rhett, or rather what I've done to her Rhett, she'll wish she had. It may be of interest as a sidelight that my own sincere choice for Rhett was Ronald Colman. I still think he would have done a fine job of it.

I found upon investigation that Miss Mitchell, and it was most intelligent of her, didn't care a hang what Hollywood was going to do with her book. All she wanted was peace and quiet. She wrote a book because it was the thing she liked to do, and having innocently caused more excitement than any author in memory, asked only to be left alone. On learning this bit of information, I immediately felt a sympathetic fellowship with Miss Mitchell, whom I never have had the pleasure of meeting. I am sure we would understand one another, for after all, Rhett has caused more than a little confusion in both our lives.

During the months when the casting of "Gone" reached the proportion of a national election, and acrimonious debate was being conducted on every street corner, Rhett became more of a mental hazard than ever. I was still the only one who didn't have anything to say about him. I never did have. For when the time came to get down to business, I was still out on a limb.

I knew what was coming the day David O. Selznick telephoned me. His purchase of the book for a mere $50,000 had started the riot. Our talk was amicable. I did the sparring and he landed the hard punches. David's idea was to make a separate deal, providing my studio would release me to make the picture. I thought my contract was an ace in the hole. It specified that my services belonged exclusively to Metro-Goldwyn-Mayer. I told David that, adding on my own that I was not interested in playing Rhett.

That didn't stop David. Being a friend of long standing and knowing him, I knew that it wouldn't. He pointed out that no actor ever had been offered such a chance. There had never been a more talked-of role than Rhett. That was exactly my reason for turning him down. He put his cards on the table. He was going to try to get me from M-G-M if he could. We shook hands on it.

I could have put up a fight. I didn't. I am glad now that I didn't. Hollywood always has treated me fairly. I have had no reason to complain about my roles and if the studio thought I should play Rhett, it was not up to me to duck out. I had nothing to do with the negotiations. I learned that I was to play Rhett in the newspapers. As a part of the deal, Metro-Goldwyn-Mayer was to release the picture.

I was pleased with the choice of Miss Vivien Leigh as Scarlett. She made Scarlett so vividly lifelike that it made my playing of Rhett much simpler than I had expected. I was equally pleased that Victor Fleming was to direct. He had directed me in "Test Pilot." I had complete confidence in him. One thing stands out in those months of preparation for the picture. There was never any divergence of opinion. No single individual, with the exception of Miss Mitchell, deserves credit more than another. It was teamwork that counted.

There was only one way to make "Gone." That was as Miss Mitchell wrote it. There was only one problem, but it was not an easy one to solve. Miss Leigh and I discussed it a hundred times. We reached the conclusion that Scarlett and Rhett, while definite and powerful characters and individualists, depended on one another for characterization. In this respect, I would like to pay tribute to Miss Leigh. She was Scarlett every minute and I am greatly indebted to her for her contributions to my performance.

"Gone" was different from any picture I have ever made. I often have smiled in the past at actors who "live" their roles. My attitude to making pictures is realistic. But I must admit that all of us, and I am speaking for everyone who had any connection with the picture, had a definite feeling of living it. Miss Mitchell wrote of a period that is typically American, that is inspirational, that is real. When electricians, grips, make-up men and carpenters, who are blase to making movies, stood around and watched scenes being rehearsed, and even broke into spontaneous applause after Miss Leigh had played some of her highlight dramatic scenes, you know you have something. They are the world's severest film critics.

SCARLETT *by* VIVIEN LEIGH

A YEAR has gone by since the night we stood watching the first scenes being made for "Gone With the Wind." It was an awesome spectacle—whole blocks of sets being consumed by flames as Atlanta buildings burned, and I was a little confused by the grandeur of it and what seemed to be a frightening confusion.

That was the night I met Mr. David O. Selznick, the man who was producing "Gone With the Wind," and who had yet to select a Scarlett O'Hara for the film.

In retrospect, it seems to me that the fantastic quality of that tremendous fire, the confusion I felt and the feeling of loneliness in the midst of hundreds of people was indicative of what was to come. I could not know then, of course, what lay ahead—and if someone had ventured to predict it, I probably would have passed it off as nonsense.

The unexpected happened: it made me, for these months at least, and whether I wished it so or not, into the character known as Scarlett O'Hara. Now the difficulty is to view that character objectively. That it was a great role for any actress was obvious, yet I can truthfully say that I looked on Mr. Selznick's request that I take a test for Scarlett as something of a joke. There were dozens of girls testing, and I did not seriously consider that I might actually play the part. Yet once it was decided upon I discovered that there was no joking about playing Scarlett. From then on, I was swept along as though by a powerful wave—it was Scarlett, Scarlett, Scarlett, night and day, month after month.

At once, I was asked two questions, and they persisted. First, everyone wanted to know if I was afraid of the part. And second, what did I think of Scarlett, anyway?

Perhaps if I had struggled, wished and worried about getting the role, I might have been fearful. As it was I had no time to let worry get the upper hand. That, and the sympathetic understanding of Mr. Selznick, eliminated fear before it got started.

As for Scarlett herself—my own views on that headstrong young lady are so bound up with my own experience in playing her that I find it difficult, now, to analyze just how I do feel about her. I lived Scarlett for close to six months, from early morning to late at night. I tried to make every move, every gesture true to Scarlett, and I had to feel that even the despicable things Scarlett did were of my doing.

From the moment I first began to read "Gone With the Wind" three years ago, Scarlett fascinated me, as she has fascinated so many others. She needed a good, healthy old-fashioned spanking on a number of occasions—and I should have been delighted to give it to her. Conceited, spoiled, arrogant—all those things, of course, are true of the character.

But she had courage and determination, and that, I think, is why women must secretly admire her—even though we can't feel too happy about her many shortcomings.

Try as I might to bring these characteristics from Margaret Mitchell's work into reality, there were bound to be times when I felt depressed. With so much painstaking effort going into the filming, every detail worked out to the finest point, days spent in recreating an exact situation, it was inevitable that I should feel sometimes that my work might not measure up to the standards which Mr. Selznick demanded, and which Victor Fleming, the director, strove so hard to reach. Yet Mr. Selznick seemed to sense these moments and was there to lend his encouragement, a help I am deeply grateful for. Mr. Fleming, faced with the task of keeping these thousand and one details coordinated, seemed to have an inexhaustible supply of patience and good humor. I think we all felt that here, above all times, it was imperative that we be good troupers, submerging ourselves to the task at hand.

There were months when I went to the studio directly from my home at 6:30 o'clock in the morning; breakfasted while making-up and having my hair done, then reported to the stage for the first "shot" at 8:45 a.m. And it was the rule, rather than the exception, to leave the studio at 9 or 10 o'clock that night. Needless to say, I saw none of Hollywood's night life!

I do not mean that all the gruelling work was without its compensations and amusements. After so many weeks together, the company had its own jokes, its own forms of fun to lessen the tension. Mr. Fleming could always prepare me for some difficult work with an elaborate bow and a "Now, Fiddle-dee-dee—" which was the name bequeathed me, and Clark Gable's natural humor was always there to comfort us at the moments when tempers were shortest. Leslie Howard, as you can well imagine, is the soul of good humour; rarely upset and apt to come out with a bit of dry wit at the most unexpected moments.

You will recall that Rhett Butler, on a certain night, carries Scarlett up a long flight of stairs. We were ready to shoot this scene late in the afternoon, after a particularly difficult day. As so often happens, a number of things went wrong — and poor Clark had to carry me up the stairs about a dozen times before the shot was satisfactory. Even the stalwart Mr. Gable was beginning to feel it, I'm afraid—the set designer certainly made that stairway long enough.

"Let's try it once more, Clark," said the director. Clark winced, but picked me up and made the long climb.

"Thanks, Clark," said Fleming. " I really didn't need that shot — I just had a little bet on that you couldn't make it."

Even Clark saw the joke, although I'm not so sure I should have if I'd been in his place.

Perhaps the hardest days I spent, hard that is from the point of actual physical exertion, were during the time we made the scene where Scarlett struggles through the populace as it evacuates Atlanta.

Naturally this could not be done all in one continuous "take," and so for what seemed an eternity I dodged through the maze of traffic on Peachtree Street, timing myself to avoid galloping horses and thundering wagons.

And between each shot, the make-up man — he seemed to be everywhere at once—came running to wash my face, then dirty it up again to just the right shade of Georgia clay dust. I think he washed my face about 20 times in one day—and dusted me over with red dust after each washing.

Here, of course, was where the tremendous task of organizing was at its most spectacular. Horses and riders had to cross certain places at just the right time —and so did I. I can assure you that it is not a pleasant experience to see a gun caisson charging down on you —even when you know the riders are experts and the whole thing planned. In fact, I was so intent on being in the right place at the right time all day that I did not realize until I got to bed that night that Scarlett O'Hara Leigh was a badly bruised person.

Oddly enough, the scenes of physical strain were not so wearing as the emotional ones. One night we worked at the Selznick Studios until about 11 o'clock, then went out to the country for a shot against the sunrise, when Scarlett falls to her knees in the run-down fields of Tara and vows she'll never be hungry again. The sun rose shortly after 2 a.m. and I could not sleep, although I had a dressing room in a trailer. We made the shot and I arrived at home about 4:30 a.m., yet I do not recall that I was so terribly tired.

Instead, I think of the day that Scarlett shoots the deserter, and I recall that after that nerve-wracking episode, both Olivia de Havilland, the wonderful Melanie of the film, and myself were on the verge of hysterics—not alone from the tenseness of the scene, but from the too realistic fall as the "dead" man went down the stairs before us.

Yet when the day came that meant the film was completed, I could not help feeling some little regret that our parts were done and that the cast and the crew—who were all so thoughtful and kind throughout—were breaking up. Clark Gable, Leslie Howard, Olivia de Havilland, Tom Mitchell, Barbara O'Neil —fine players all. We should see each other again, of course—but never again would we have the experience of playing in "Gone With the Wind"!

Leslie Howard *as* Ashley Wilkes.

Leslie Howard, who plays the part of Ashley Wilkes, was born in London, England. Schooled privately, he was graduated from Dulwich College. His first professional engagement was in "Peg o' My Heart," followed by "Charley's Aunt," "Under Cover," "The Freaks," "The Title," "Our Mr. Hepplewhite" and "Mr. Pim Passes By." After two more London engagements, "The Young Person in Pink" and "East Is West," Howard sailed for New York to appear in "Just Suppose," "The Wren," "Outward Bound," "The Werewolf" and "The Green Hat." Traveling back and forth across the Atlantic between New York and London, Howard was seen in "The Way You Look At It," "Murray Hill," "Her Cardboard Lover," "Candle Light," "Berkeley Square" and "The Animal Kingdom." His last two legitimate plays before entering pictures were "Free Soul" and "Reserved For Ladies." After appearing in the film versions of "Berkeley Square," "British Agent," "The Lady Is Willing" and "Of Human Bondage" he returned to the stage in "The Petrified Forest." Later Howard appeared in "The Scarlet Pimpernel," "Romeo and Juliet," the screen version of "The Petrified Forest," George Bernard Shaw's "Pygmalion," and "Intermezzo" for Selznick International Pictures.

Olivia de Havilland *as* **Melanie Hamilton.** Olivia de Havilland, who plays the part of Melanie, happened to be born in Tokyo, Japan, moving to Saratoga, California when she was two years old. She attended the Saratoga public schools and the Notre Dame Convent at Belmont, California. Her first legitimate stage experience was in the role of Hermia in Max Reinhardt's "A Midsummer Night's Dream" presented at the Hollywood Bowl. She first gained motion picture fame when Reinhardt directed "Midsummer Night's Dream" for Warner Bros. with Olivia de Havilland playing the same role she had in the legitimate production, followed by "Anthony Adverse," "Captain Blood," "Robin Hood" and "Wings of the Navy." She is five feet, three and one-quarter inches tall and weighs 110 pounds.

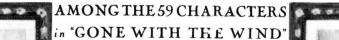

THOMAS MITCHELL
as Gerald O'Hara

EVELYN KEYES
as Suellen O'Hara

BARBARA O'NEIL
as Ellen O'Hara

ONA MUNSON
as Belle Watling

ANN RUTHERFORD
as Carreen O'Hara

LAURA HOPE CREWS
as Aunt "Pittypat"

CARROL NYE
as Frank Kennedy

This booklet, edited by Howard Dietz, is sold
in theatres showing "Gone With The Wind"
and may be purchased from Ellison B.
Greenstone, 145 W. 45th St., New York City.
25c per copy

ALICIA RHETT
as India Wilkes

Charles Chaplin

with

PAULETTE GODDARD

in

The GREAT DICTATOR

written and directed by

CHARLES CHAPLIN

Released thru United Artists

Credits

Musical direction by *Meredith Willson*

Assistant Directors

Dan James, Wheeler Dryden, Bob Meltzer

Directors of Photography

Karl Struss   *Roland Totheroh*
A.S.C.   I.A.T.S.E.

Art Director   *J. Russell Spencer*

Film Editor   *Willard Nico*

Sound

Percy Townsend, Glenn Rominger

Cast

PEOPLE OF THE PALACE

Hynkel, Dictator of Tomania   *Charles Chaplin*

Napaloni, Dictator of Bacteria   *Jack Oakie*

Schultz   *Reginald Gardiner*

Garbitsch   *Henry Daniell*

Herring   *Billy Gilbert*

Madame Napaloni   *Grace Hayle*

Bacterian Ambassador   *Carter de Haven*

PEOPLE OF THE GHETTO

A Jewish Barber   *Charles Chaplin*

Hannah   *Paulette Goddard*

Mr. Jaeckel   *Maurice Moscovich*

Mrs. Jaeckel   *Emma Dunn*

Mr. Mann   *Bernard Gorcey*

Mr. Agar   *Paul Weigel*

AND

Chester Conklin, Esther Michelson

Hank Mann, Florence Wright

Eddie Gribbon, Robert O. Davis

Eddie Dunn, Peter Lynn

Nita Pike

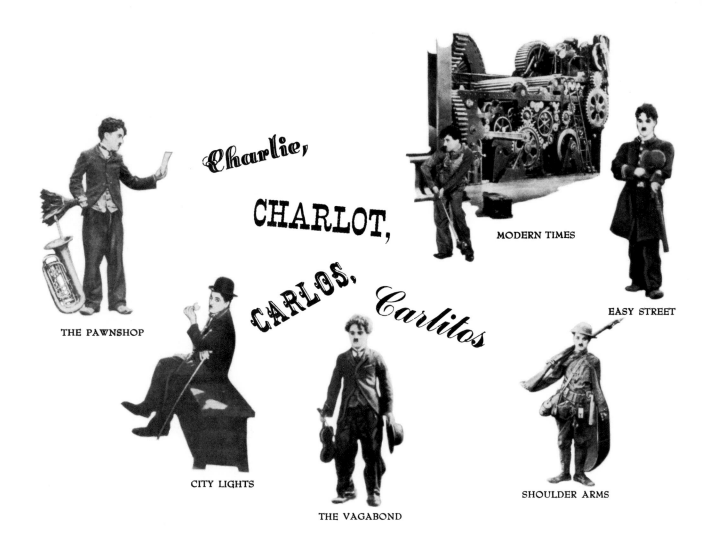

Charlie, CHARLOT, CARLOS, Carlitos

THE PAWNSHOP

MODERN TIMES

EASY STREET

CITY LIGHTS

THE VAGABOND

SHOULDER ARMS

CHARLES SPENCER CHAPLIN, whose name has been translated into almost every language there is and whose cane and derby and over-sized shoes have become the most familiar symbols of laughter the world has ever known, was born in London on April 16, 1889, less than a hundred hours before the birth, across the Channel in Austria, of one Adolf Hitler. It is somehow significant that it was on the fiftieth anniversary of this coincidence that Chaplin began production on "The Great Dictator," his most ambitious comedy to date, and the first all-talking motion picture he has ever made.

In the period between his birth in a back street rooming-house and the release of his latest and probably greatest film, Charlie Chaplin has experienced the extremes of both human poverty and the fame and fortune he enjoys today. His father was a music hall singer; his mother, a gypsy, died when he was a child, and the young Charlie lived a life of almost Dickensian destitution in the slums and dingy shops of London. When his father came to town he used to stand in the wings and watch him, fascinated, and finally picked up enough of the music hall routine to find occasional employment on the stage. One of his first parts was that of the page-boy in a production of "Sherlock Holmes," but before long he was in vaudeville with an act called "A Night with an English Music Hall." When the company came to America, as eventually it did, the little man with the moustache who didn't say a word throughout the performance instantly stole the show. In 1913, after he had completed his second vaudeville tour of the United States, Charlie Chaplin signed his first motion picture contract with Mack Sennett and the Keystone Film Company of Los Angeles.

That contract called for a salary of one hundred and fifty dollars a week. But almost the moment the American movie public saw his figure on the screen they expressed their pleasure so unmistakably that other studios hastened to sign him up. Within the next two years he made dozens of two-reel comedies and in 1917 put his signature to the only motion picture contract specifying a salary of a million dollars a year.

After producing "A Dog's Life" in 1918, Chaplin, along with Mary Pickford and Douglas Fairbanks, made his historic tour of the U.S. for the Third Liberty Loan drive. He followed this trip with the production of "Shoulder Arms," his hilarious war comedy which, contrary to all established notions, was a tremendous hit in a country still at war. By this time Chaplin was producing his own pictures, as well as doing the directing, writing, and most of the acting. This policy he has followed ever since, and with the advent of sound has added to his chores that of composing the musical score. In 1921 Chaplin topped all previous successes with his production of "The Kid," which introduced Jackie Coogan to the world. After making "The Idle Class," in which he played a dual role (as he does in "The Great Dictator") Chaplin made a triumphal grand tour of Europe, where he was received with wild adulation.

When he returned to America in 1919, he formed United Artists together with Douglas Fairbanks, Mary Pickford and D. W. Griffith, and it has been under that banner that he has since released his motion pictures. "A Woman of Paris," starring Adolphe Menjou, was the last of his productions in which he himself did not appear; it was an experimental film and one of the most popular and influential of its time. Charlie's later hits—"The Gold Rush," "The Circus," "City Lights" and "Modern Times"—are all classics of cinematic comedy, the acknowledged masterpieces of the man whom George Bernard Shaw called "the only genius in motion pictures."

But Charlie Chaplin is more than a genius. He is an institution, the idol of millions of all races and creeds, the champion of the pathetic and oppressed. And, at a time when the world is sore and sick at heart, the little man with the funny moustache is something of a savior, bringing with him at a time we need it most the invaluable therapy of laughter.

THE COUNT

CHAPLIN IS CHAPLIN
EVEN AS DICTATOR

Charlie Chaplin is back! To old-timers who can remember the two-reelers he made more than a quarter of a century ago . . to kids who weren't alive when his last picture was released . . to almost everybody, young and old, rich and poor, American or European or Asiatic, the return of Charlie to the screen is an event of major importance. That it is in "The Great Dictator," moreover, that he is making his reappearance after an absence of five years, makes the occasion even more newsworthy. For this is the film that for two long years has been surrounded in mystery, that was reported shelved time and time again, that gave birth to more rumors and whispers than any other Hollywood production.

Now that the truth can be told, the story behind "The Great Dictator" is a very simple one. Chaplin wrote the story and the dialogue, directed the picture, produced it, played the starring dual roles, edited the film and wrote the musical score. But even for someone with the inexhaustible energy of Chaplin this takes time, and "The Great Dictator" was in production for 177 days. This is the time during which the cameras turned; actually it took two years to make the picture.

It also took two million dollars. This, too, is not hard to understand when one remembers that "The Great Dictator," being Chaplin's first all-talking picture, necessitated a complete revamping of the Chaplin studios, the addition of expensive sound equipment, and the multiplication of the daily budget. When Charlie's films were silent, he was accustomed to make them up, more or less, as he went along, often reshooting entire sequences many times before hitting on what he wanted. Such a system is of course impossible in the production of talking pictures, where every minute costs a tidy fortune, and so Chaplin prepared a complete shooting-script of "The Great Dictator" before a single scene was shot.

It was back in September of 1938 that the idea of doing a picture on totalitarian countries and the men who rule their destinies first began to take definite shape in Chaplin's mind. By the middle of the next summer casting was started and by the next September the cameras had commenced to roll. Production was technically over last March, but from that date on almost to the moment of its release, "The Great Dictator" has undergone the rigorous routine of retakes, cutting, editing and, finally, scoring, this last accomplished by Chaplin himself on an old upright piano, which he plays by ear while a corps of arrangers at his elbow transcribe his improvisations to paper.

Chaplin's decision to talk created more problems than merely the physical ones of studio equipment. To begin with, he was faced with a hazardous undertaking of giving a voice to a character that up until now he remained silent (with the exception of the song in gibberish sung in "Modern Times") and also of inventing one for his portrayal in the picture, that of the dictator himself. For the little familiar tramp—in this case a barber—Chaplin kept dialogue at a minimum, and mostly monosyllabic, while as Hynkel, the Dictator of Tomainia, he speaks in a rich and reminiscent guttural, his English interspersed with inspired passages of jargon. The two characters even move differently in the film; the sequence in which the barber appears were filmed at 16 frames a second, the dictator sequences at 25.

"The Great Dictator" represents still more technical advances than the addition of sound. In it for the first time Chaplin has discarded the makeshift backdrops and two-dimensional perspectives which appeared in his earlier films. For this new production he had constructed some of the most lavish and spectacular sets ever seen in a motion picture, some of the most elaborate props. One cannon, built for the war scenes, is 100 feet long, took two months to build, and cost $15,000. That is merely an example of Chaplin's readiness to spend his own money for a single effect that he desires; the sequence in which the cannon appears takes only a few minutes on the screen.

Chaplin's new picture represents great technical advances over his previous productions. But he remains the same Charlie that the world has grown to know and love. The moustache is still there, and the cane and the big shoes and the hat. He has learned to talk, but his message—a message of laughter which the world can understand—is still the same.

CHARLIE CHAPLIN

Admiration for the little tramp with the derby hat, the trick shoes and the expressive cane is confined to no race, class or creed. Essentially, Charlie Chaplin belongs to the "little guy"—the men, the women and the children who make up the overwhelming portion of the population of all the countries of the world.

Charlie Chaplin has long since passed the stage of being a "cult." The adulation he receives from people of all sorts and degrees is no longer clouded with phony high-brow appraisals. Even the intellectuals—notable die-hards —have surrendered to the innate charm and simplicity of the little tramp, and they no longer attempt to explain his genius in terms of their own genius!

Chaplin has been called—by actors—"the greatest living actor—not only of today, but of all time." This may sound like extravagant praise, but its tone is no more extravagant than the opinions of Chaplin expressed by world-famous figures.

George Bernard Shaw, the white-bearded iconoclast, has referred to Chaplin as ". . . the only genius in motion

pictures . . ." and, adding the proverbial Shavian touch, ". . . the only man living . . . who knows as much about filming as I do!"

Alexander Woollcott, famous author and critic, bestows this tribute: "His like has not passed this way before, and we shall not see his like again."

The late Will Rogers observed, "Chaplin is the only genius developed in the films since they started."

The most unstinted praise of all, perhaps, comes from Chaplin's own countryman, Thomas Burke, author of the famous "Limehouse Nights." Burke wrote: "He is the man who has brought the whole civilized and uncivilized world together in warm laughter and delight." Burke's is a summation which might well apply to the message "The Great Dictator" will convey to a storm-tossed world!

But, while not unmindful of the tribute of the great, Chaplin himself prefers the form of praise he gets from the little man — laughter!

JACK OAKIE

as the "other dictator" in the Chaplin film, has one of the richest parts in his long career as a comedian. Born Lewis Offield in Sedalia, Mo. in 1903, Oakie has been acting since he was sixteen, with only a brief intermission from the screen in 1938 when he deserted Holly-wood to head a nation-wide radio program.

PAULETTE GODDARD

playing Hannah, the daughter of the Ghetto, is at home in a Chaplin picture. Her first big break came in "Modern Times" when Charlie advanced her to the position of star after seeing her do a "bit" in Eddie Cantor's "Kid From Spain." Since then she has appeared in "The Young in Heart," "Dramatic School," "The Cat and the Canary," "The Women," and "The Ghost Breakers," to mention only a few of her recent pictures.

MAURICE MOSCOVICH

playing the role of the kindly old Jaeckel in "The Great Dictator," died only a few months after completion of the picture. Much mourned by drama lovers everywhere, the late Mr. Moscovich began his career in the last century, appearing first in his native Russia and later on the principal stages of Europe and America.

REGINALD GARDINER

as the sympathetic Schultz, reached fame overnight on Broadway by imitating wallpaper, train-whistles and furniture. Since his first appearance on the New York stage his services have been constantly in demand both there and in Hollywood, where he has lent his talents to several motion pictures.

EMMA DUNN

Mrs. Jaeckel in "The Great Dictator," has been playing mothers ever since she was twenty and Richard Mansfield played her son. As "Old Lady 31," a part created especially for her by Rachel Crothers, she scored a phenomenal success on Broadway, and has since appeared in dozens of Hollywood films.

BILLY GILBERT

who has literally sneezed his way to success, plays Herring in "The Great Dictator." Gilbert was born in Louisville, Ky. in 1894, and has spent practically his entire lifetime on the stage or before the motion picture cameras.

PRICE 25c per copy

216 THE GREAT DICTATOR

SOUVENIR PROGRAM

ORSON WELLES

Citizen Kane

AN RKO-RADIO PICTURE

THE

ORSON WELLES reached Hollywood in August, 1939, with a much-photographed beard, a radio reputation and a four-way contract as author, producer, director and star with Mr. George Schaefer, president of RKO Radio Pictures. Hollywood scoffed at the idea of anyone without motion picture experience presuming to attempt the production of a film of the magnitude of "Citizen Kane". It refused to take Welles seriously—and even now can't get over the marvel of it all.

Now Hollywood is neither a savage nor a primitive place, yet the analogy to a Ulysses sent on Homeric wanderings in a cockleshell, or a Crusoe or Swiss watchmaker tackling a wilderness single-handed, holds true in Orson's case for all that.

A full-length feature film, such as "Citizen Kane," has come to be the most intricate form of all the arts, and a group, not an individual, production. But Welles, with no previous experience whatsoever except in the related media of the stage and radio, undertook to be a one-man orchestra.

He was to write the piece, star in it, direct it, produce it. No wonder a Hollywood, accustomed to seeing pictures born only through the co-operative effort of many minds and talents, kept its fingers crossed as the erstwhile "boy wonder" of Broadway and the air waves took up his task.

Some player-downers said, "Why, shucks, there's Chaplin. He's a one-man band, too." But that overlooked the fact that Chaplin's genius is the flowering of many years of cultivation, that he didn't spring full-fledged upon the screen.

Others declared, "It's a stunt. He'll find out it can't be done and go home." Each new delay — and Orson encountered plenty of them — was greeted with, "Well, that's the end. He's through."

1 Orson as he directed that internationally sensational Martian broadcast—'til now the most widely known exploit of an amazing career.

2 Classical dramatists gasped when Orson staged his famed Shakespeare in modern dress. Here he is in the role of Brutus.

3 First American triumph for Orson was his enactment of the title role in a New York Federal Theatre production of Marlowe's "Dr. Faustus".

4 That famous beard! Here's Orson as he left for Hollywood to sign his four-way pact with RKO Radio. A genius at twenty-four —with or without the beard.

1AZING MR. WELLES

Six-feet-two Orson, however, strangely stuck along. Like Swiss Robinson on his island, he was learning how to do things as he progressed. He was in Hollywood, but not of it. Parties of the stars knew him not. Where you could find him, however, was on the RKO Radio lot, often at night, nosing into every department, learning how movies are made.

No Cook's tour this, and no Hollywood-in-ten-easy-lessons. It went on month upon month, more than a year, before Welles was ready to launch into production. That prolonged delay itself drew criticism from Doubting Thomases, "Aw, he'll never get started."

But Welles went right along, learning how to put Sound into pictures, how to cut 'em to eliminate dud footage and point up the drama, how to make the camera as fluid in its observations as the eyes of another party in the room. He studied lighting, set designing, special effects — those tricks with which movie wizards make things seem what they aren't.

Finally he went to work producing "Citizen Kane" from his own story of an American colossus striding across sixty years of living history. He directed it, starred in it, learned to dance for it, put all his recently acquired knowledge at work, picked up more as he went along. When it was finished, he supervised the scoring, too.

Sure, he was new to the movies. But the young Welles who stirred Broadway with his gangster-dictator version of "Julius Caesar," his All-Negro production of "Macbeth," was pretty new then to the stage, too. The Welles who scared the pants off the country with drama of an invasion by Martian monsters couched in terms of a newscast, was no ancient in Radio. You have to be pretty new to everything when you're still in the middle twenties.

MAN OF ENDLESS SURPRISES –

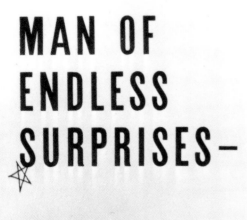

THIS is the story of Orson Welles, or the case history of one of America's most amazing young geniuses.

Genius is definitely the word for Mr. Welles, who at the ripe old age of twenty-five can look back upon a successful career as an author, playwright, actor, broadway director and producer, radio star and painter.

Born in Kenosha, Wis., Orson was the son of Richard Head Welles, a well-known inventor and manufacturer. His mother was Beatrice Ives Welles, a concert pianist from whom he drew much of his artistic perception and sensitivity.

Orson at an early age exhibited the amazing precociousness that has characterized his entire career. At eleven, for example, he made a solitary walking tour of Europe. At an even younger age he staged his first theatrical venture —a backyard puppet show of Shakespeare!

Until the death of his mother, when he was eight years old, Orson's schooling had consisted largely of home tutoring, with a few months of formalistic training in a Madison, Wis., school.

His father, however, was resolved to make the process of education more systematic than it had been, so he enrolled young Orson at the Todd School in Woodstock, Ill.

There the future stage, screen and radio star first played at the drama for public consumption. Participating in the dramatic activities of the school, he staged an original version of Shakespeare's "Julius Caesar," enacting vigorously the parts of both Cassius and Marc Antony.

During this period, also, he exhibited a surprising proclivity for painting. He was so good, as a matter of fact, that his instructor predicted he would become America's greatest painter.

It was with this prediction in mind that, at the age of sixteen, Orson began a walking trip through Ireland to paint the sights he encountered.

And while in Dublin, he found his true vocation. He decided to become an actor. So he went to the manager of the famed Gate Theater and announced that he was Orson Welles, star of the New York Guild Theater.

The ruse worked—and Orson found himself starring in the next production of the theater. He remained there a full season, drawing universal acclaim for his superb work. During the period, also, he set a record by becoming the first American ever to act as a guest star with the world-famous Abbey Players of Dublin. His career was definitely launched!

RKO RADIO STUDIOS
Hollywood, California

1

Returning to New York in 1932, he found the producers there less susceptible to his blandishments than their colleagues in Ireland.

So, not daunted, he set sail for Africa to see what the dark continent was like. His explorations, however, were side-tracked in Morocco, when he decided to write a book.

The volume, "Mercury Shakespeare", is still a best-seller in its class.

A year later, Orson again found himself in New York. This time he managed to secure an introduction to Katharine Cornell, who thought so much of his ability that she gave him a place in a company she was then organizing to tour the hinterlands.

From the noted actress, Welles received a thorough grounding in the theatre. He appeared with her in such plays as "Candida," "Romeo and Juliet," and "The Barretts of Wimpole Street."

Then, in rapid succession, he became a Broadway Star, got himself a job impersonating The Shadow in the radio thriller serial, became commentator for the March of Time program on the air and was appointed producer for the Federal Theater in New York.

His success here led to the formation of the Mercury Theatre, which he organized with John Houseman. And from this group stemmed the Mercury Theater of the Air, under whose auspices Welles staged Radio's most sensational broadcast — The Martian Invasion.

This was the broadcast which frightened millions of listeners throughout the country into outright panic so widespread that a Congressional investigation was threatened!

When Welles signed his now-famous contract with RKO Radio Pictures, he insisted on a clause permitting him to continue his work with the Mercury Players.

Many of the actors of the company make their screen debuts with Orson in "Citizen Kane." Among the cast are such well-known stage and radio figures as Dorothy Comingore, Ruth Warrick, George Coulouris, Joseph Cotten, Paul Stewart and Harry Shannon.

As a matter of fact, you won't find a single familiar movie name in the group. Orson, with his customary disregard of tradition, has introduced fifteen new actors in this film — an unprecedented figure in Hollywood productions!

But then, setting new precedents has always been a Welles forte. And, from all indications, it will continue to be so.

1 The still-bearded Orson learns the intricacies of cutting and editing via the Moviola and technician, Fred Maguire.

2 Producer-Director Welles confers with himself and decides "they" don't quite like the way the turban designed for Dorothy Comingore looks.

3 Actor Welles and Director Welles slightly mixed up as he takes a look at a scene from the other end of the camera.

4 Author Orson dictating some bits of new business to be incorporated into the script before the cameras start turning. Only a day or two more left for that beard!

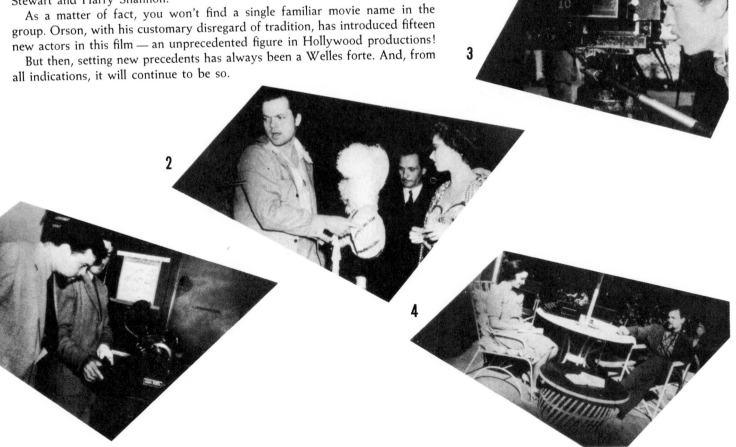

HIGHLIGHTS IN THE LIFE OF *Citizen* KANE

Orson Welles as he appears in the title role at one stage of the story, in which he portrays a fictional newspaper tycoon. The following photo sequence presents the highlights in the life of "Citizen Kane."

1 The boyhood of Charles Foster Kane is the only portion of his life which, for obvious reasons, Orson Welles does not enact in RKO Radio's "Citizen Kane." To make up for his absence, he cast in this part a seven-year-old actor whose resemblance to himself is astounding. The youthful double is Buddy Swan. Buddy in this scene is being introduced by his mother, Agnes Moorhead, to George Coulouris, who has just informed her that property she owns has been found to be worth millions of dollars. In the background is Harry Shannon, who is seen as Kane, Sr.

2 Three young men begin newspaper careers. They are Joseph Cotten, noted Broadway actor, Orson Welles and Everett Sloane. In this scene, Charles Foster Kane is manifestly young, enthusiastic, handsome. Welles' characterization from this youthful stage to that of an old man is an outstanding example of dramatic interpretation.

3 Spectacular highlight in the life of "Citizen Kane" is sequence depicting him as playboy. In this scene, Orson Welles proves that he can dance as well as act, write, produce and direct. He's chorus boy above!

4 Social peak in career of "Citizen Kane" was his marriage to niece of prominent statesman. Here Welles is shown with bride, Ruth Warrick, and wedding party on White House lawn. Depicted marriage is failure, ends in divorce.

5 Citizen Kane's second wife is a singer, portrayed by Dorothy Comingore. Here she is shown as she appears in opera Welles finances for her. Sequence is typical of colorful and elaborate settings in picture. For opera episode, Welles ordered original score written for mythical musical play.

6 Dramatic highpoint is the meeting between wife No. 1 and wife No. 2 in this scene. The actors are Ray Collins, Dorothy Comingore, Orson Welles and Ruth Warrick.

7 Excitement-packed chapter in life of "Citizen Kane" is his race for Governorship. Here Orson Welles is shown delivering oration in course of campaign. Note careful staging, unusual camera angle of this scene, in which Welles displays fiery qualities as political spieler.

8 Old age is darkened by rift between Kane and second wife. Here Orson Welles and Dorothy Comingore, are shown in tense moment. Welles is famed for his enactment of aged parts, such as that he played in his Broadway version of G. B. Shaw's "Heartbreak House."

9 End of trail. In this scene his earthly belongings are being auctioned off. It's a powerful dramatic presentation. Shown in scene are Paul Stewart and William Alland, both well-known New York actors. Stewart portrays Kane's butler, Alland a reporter.

"CITIZEN KANE"

A MERCURY PRODUCTION   By ORSON WELLES

The Mercury Theatre is proud to introduce:

JOSEPH COTTEN ....as......*Jedediah Leland*
DOROTHY COMINGORE ....as......*Susan Alexander*
EVERETT SLOANE ....as......*Mr. Bernstein*
RAY COLLINS ....as......*James W. Gettys*
GEORGE COULOURIS ....as......*Walter Parks Thatcher*
AGNES MOOREHEAD ....as......*Mrs. Kane (mother)*
PAUL STEWART ....as......*Raymond*
RUTH WARRICK ....as......*Emily Norton*
ERSKINE SANFORD ....as......*Herbert Carter*
WILLIAM ALLAND ....as......*Thompson*

AND

Fortunio Bonanova ....*Matiste*
Gus Schilling ....*Headwaiter*
Philip Van Zandt ....*Mr. Rawlston*
Georgia Backus ....*Miss Anderson*
Harry Shannon ....*Kane's father*
Sonny Bupp ....*Kane III*
Buddy Swan ....*Kane (age 8)*
Orson Welles ....*Kane*

Direction-Production
ORSON WELLES

Photography   *Original Screen Play*
GREGG TOLAND   HERMAN J. MANKIEWICZ
                                                    ORSON WELLES

Music Composed and Conducted by   *Editing*..........Robert Wise
    Bernard Herrmann   *Recording*...{ Bailey Fesler
Special Effects..Vernon L. Walker, A.S.C.   { James G. Stewart
Art Director........Van Nest Polglase   *Set Decorations*..Darrell Silvera
Associate ....Perry Ferguson   *Costumes*....Edward Stevenson

QUICK-STEPPING THROUGH A FEW OF THE OUTSTANDING SCENES OF "CITIZEN KANE

IN HIS FIRST PRODUCTION AN UNUSUAL, COMPELLING, DRAMATIC ENTERTAINMENT—

NOW IT'S
ORSON WELLES
OF
Hollywood

SCENES FROM HIS FIRST MOTION PICTURE PRODUCTION,
"CITIZEN KANE"

THAT UNPREDICTABLE PERSONALITY, ORSON WELLES, WHO BRINGS TO THE SCREEN

DISTINCT NEW MOTION PICTURE TECHNIQUE THAT IS YEARS AHEAD OF ITS TIME!

★ ORSON WELLES ★

AUTHOR

THE "FOUR-MOST" PERSONALITY

PRODUCER

★ ORSON WELLES ★ ...

DIRECTOR

OF MOTION PICTURES!

STAR ★

★ ORSON WELLES ★

AGNES MOOREHEAD (Mrs. Kane, the mother) first met Orson Welles when he was a very grown-up young man of five years. He had just returned to the Waldorf Hotel from a concert and delivered a dramatic and rather rhetorical description of the evening's music. Only when Miss Moorehead joined the Mercury Players in Hollywood did she associate the precocious child with the man who was playing the title role in "Citizen Kane."

RAY COLLINS (James W. Gettys) has played upwards of 900 roles in the theatre and on radio. Even since he ran away from home when seventeen years of age, he has been one of the busiest of actors. He averages 20 to 25 radio shows each week, exclusive of theatrical engagements. After joining Welles' Mercury Theatre group at its start, he also played roles in Welles' phonographic recordings of Shakespearean plays.

PAUL STEWART (Raymond) currently in the cast of Orson Welles' Broadway production of "Native Son", seventh in his list of stage appearances, can look back upon the day when he recommended the giant Orson to radio director Homer Fickett as the ideal voice for the air version of "The March of Time". "Citizen Kane", Paul's film debut, finds the pair still together.

GEORGE COULOURIS (Walter Parks Thatcher) appeared in London as Sir Thomas Grey in "Henry IV," as Tybalt in "Romeo and Juliet," and in Noel Coward's "Sirocco." In New York he played in "The Apple Cart," with Pauline Lord in "The Late Christopher Bean," with Helen Hayes in "Mary of Scotland," with Philip Merivale in "Valley Forge," with Katharine Cornell in "Saint Joan," with Barry Fitzgerald in "The White Steed" and with Orson Welles as Marc Anthony in "Julius Caesar."

WILLIAM ALLAND (Thompson) makes his debut as a film actor in "Citizen Kane." At eighteen, with a semi-professional troupe of Baltimore, he edited, acted, directed and stage-managed the whole repertory. A scholarship at the New York Neighborhood Playhouse brought him to New York. To come to Welles' notice, he secured a humble part as one of the mob in Welles' modern-dress "Julius Caesar," intrigued with the stage manager till he was promoted to errand runner. In this capacity he marched into Welles' dressing room with a lunch tray, locked the door and read him the part of Marullus. He won the role.

MOST OF THE PRINCIPAL PLAYERS IN "CITIZEN KANE" ARE NEW TO MOTION PICTURES .. THE MERCURY THEATRE IS PROUD TO INTRODUCE

THE MERCURY ACTORS

...H WARRICK (Emily ...n) reached New York ... as custodian of a live ... which she carted up ...teps of City Hall and ...ted to His Honor the ...r, as part of some civic ...ation which chose her ... Jubilesta." She re-...d in New York, where ...radio work commended ... Welles. A screen test ...rmed his opinion. She ... her film debut as the ...Mrs. Kane in "Citizen ..."

JOSEPH COTTON (Jedediah Leland) was leading man to Katharine Hepburn in the Broadway run of "The Philadelphia Story." His thespic talents were developed by understudying Lynn Overman in "Dancing Partner" and Melvyn Douglas in "Tonight Or Never." In his association with Welles he played the lead in "Shoemaker's Holiday" and appeared in "Julius Caesar," "Horse Eats Hat" and "Dr. Faustus." His performance in "Citizen Kane" brought him a long-term contract with RKO Radio.

DOROTHY COMINGORE (Susan Alexander) took two screen tests to attain a Hollywood foothold. Discovered by Charlie Chaplin at the Carmel Little Theatre, his praise won her a contract with a studio which terminated three months after without benefit of screen test. A second studio, more foresighted, gave her a screen test and then relegated her to crowd scenes. She smashed a Hollywood tradition by breaking her contract, refusing to appear unless permitted to act. Welles was introduced to her at a party. Her second screen test was rewarding. With her first big part as the second Mrs. Kane she embarks on her second Hollywood career.

EVERETT SLOANE (Mr. Bernstein) entered the theatre, after graduating from University of Pennsylvania, via Jasper Deeter's Hedgerow Theatre. Unable to find a Broadway engagement, he tried his hand in a Wall Street brokerage house, which collapsed in 1929. He next turned to radio acting and has been at it since, with the exception of some time out for plays, among them "Three Men on a Horse" and "Boy Meets Girl." He has taken part in every one of the Welles weekly radio broadcasts, including the famous "The War of the Worlds." He played Sammy Goldberg in the Goldberg family radio show for nine years, leaving when signed by Welles for "Citizen Kane."

ERSKINE SANFORD (Herbert Carter) was playing the title role in "Mr. Pim Passes By" nineteen years ago at Kenosha, Wis. Backstage he was introduced to a seven-year-old lad who startled him with the remark "an admirable performance, Mr. Sanford." It was Welles, who had just been taken to his first play! When Welles began his series of Broadway productions, Sanford left the Theatre Guild, with which he was associated for fifteen years, to join the Mercury Theatre players.

MASTER OF MAKE-UP

Remarkable photo sequence shows evolution of Citizen Kane from his young, wealthy, devil-may-care dandy days through middle-age success, retirement and tired old age. Compare these last photos with the enthusiastic youth of earlier days.

Chiefly responsible for the remarkable make-up feat of aging Citizen Kane, was Maurice Seiderman who has worked with Orson Welles throughout latter's sensational career.

Orson Welles, according to reputation, is wont to do things in the grand manner. And judging by the coldly scientific statistics gathered during the production of "Citizen Kane", the reputation is well deserved, indeed.

Now take the matter of illuminating gas. Some obscure genius has figured out that a set on "Citizen Kane", used more illuminating gas than any set of its size or kind in history. It's a fireplace 25 feet wide and 18 feet deep — statistics! — presumably burning logs, but actually consuming 2240 cubic feet of gas per hour. This is enough to warm the average home for at least three months in sub-zero weather.

Did you know that 215, 555 linear feet of raw 35-mm negative rolled through the cameras in the shooting of "Citizen Kane?" If shown continuously, this would take 2395.55 minutes, or 39.925 hours. No one looks at it that way, of course, but a statistician. It is not at all unusual in the movies, in fact, to use this much film.

Figures Unbelievable

Then there is the matter of the makeup man — always a sound source of strange information. According to Maurice Seiderman, who concocted the makeups that transform "Kane" players from young folks to venerable antiques of 75 during the course of the story, his initial outlay was for fourteen 300-pound barrels of casting plaster.

From there, Seiderman went on to make plaster casts of the players' heads, faces, noses, cheekbones, chins and what other anatomical tid bits would need working over as the characters aged. From these came latex moulds, which were glued on under the makeup. Just imagine — it took 75 gallons of the liquid latex (otherwise, and less scientifically, rubber) to make the makeup. Seiderman assures everyone that this amount of rubber would make seven or eight complete sets of auto tires.

Welles' Costumes Good for Statistics

Orson's costumes are always good for statistics. He wears 37 different ones in the film. This line could be pursued to the point where the number of needles dulled by frenzied tailors could be determined. What tossed the tailors into the sartorial dither was the fact that Orson ages from 25 to 75 in the film, and his figure alters along with the makeup (Sly Seiderman is in again with 20 sponge rubber gadgets for the figure alterations.) The tailors were particularly proud of a nifty little evening number in bright purple serge. Three of them saw spots before their eyes for seven days afterward.

The art director had his day of contributing statistics. His name is Perry Ferguson, and as he crawled out from under a six-foot pile of sketches, he announced that there were either 106 or 116 different sets for "Citizen Kane." His inaccuracy was due to the fact that his best previous score on a movie was around 65.

Great Days for the "Swing Gang"

It was the property department that really acquired a statistical wing-ding, though. Set Dresser Al Fields had to get furnishings for the biggest interior of a home ever seen in a movie. Twenty men—known to the trade as a "swing gang"—lugged stuff into the set, said stuff consisting of items ranging from antique snuff boxes to stray hunks of a 15th Century Shinto shrine from Japan. The man Kane, you'll gather, gathered antiques. You bet he did.

The prop boys were really proudest though about their packing cases. It seems that the new-fangled paper carton has made packing cases almost a collector's item. But never let it be said a prop man fell down—the RKO Radio boys dug up 72, count 'em, 72, and even six dozen assorted crates.

Lurching around in his numerical Sargasso, the statistician apparently overlooked one minor detail. There are also actors in the picture.

In fact, there are also 796 extras, 19 dancing girls, 84 bit players, 28 stand-ins (you won't see them), and 28 players of parts.

Among the players of parts is Orson Welles. He appears in the title role—and for the sake of statistics, he is also the producer, the director—and the guy who started off all the statistics.

STAR ORSON WELLES MAKES FLUID CAMERA THE STAR OF "CITIZEN KANE"

The camera boom loomed above the movie set, vaguely reminiscent of some prehistoric monster's articulated skeleton. It was a structure of steel lattice, anchored at one end, tilted sideward and ground up and down by a winch. At the end, sticking up in the air, was a movie camera, a saddle seat, and a bald-headed man occupying it. He kept squinting downward at the set through the camera range finder.

"Okay," he finally called. "Let me down now."

So the winch operator lowered him to stage level and he leaped out of the saddle — not only bald but gray-mustached. He was a large man. He was in his shirt sleeves. He leaped around very spryly at variance with his seeming age.

Well, that was as it should be, for the man was Orson Welles, who is only 25. So he had to apply makeup, for he was about to step into the picture and play the part of a man of 70.

Welles, who plays all ages of his titular hero over a range of fifty-odd years, in "Citizen Kane," had been busy figuring out camera angles for a scene. Now he turned the camera over to its legitimate operator, the famed Gregg Toland, and went about something else.

Startles Hollywood

It was like that all the time on the sets. If it wasn't like that it was something else. For Welles is the daring young man on the flying trapeze, if ever Hollywood saw one. What with being producer, director, writer and star of his first picture venture, he managed to keep pretty well occupied.

But he doesn't let it get him down. Perhaps back in New York, where on the stage he produced "Macbeth" with an all-Negro cast and "Julius Caesar" in modern dress, where in the radio world he played "The Shadow" and also the invader from Mars, scaring the life out of the populace in the hinterlands with that broadcast — perhaps back there they became used to his ebullience.

Hollywood, however, never saw any man float through the air with that greatest of ease which young Welles displays, violating just about all traditions of movie-making as he does so, and having a grand time for himself besides.

Unhampered by Precedent

Welles in dealing with his script is by Hollywood standards fantastic. He had never made a movie. So, despite a year's intensive study of all processes involved before he turned a wheel on production, he still wasn't hampered by facts.

That became apparent immediately he went to work. He started out with a script, but kept it carefully guarded. It is known, however, that he had slashed that script almost beyond recognition in the weeks he was at work on actual production. He revised, amended, augmented, deleted, as he went along.

Take, for instance, a notable sequence in which Welles, as publisher of a newspaper, hosts the staff. As originally written, the scene lasted just long enough to establish that Citizen Kane's best friend, played by Joseph Cotten, didn't want to take a certain job.

But when Welles came to shoot in actuality what earlier he had devised on paper, he decided a few items were lacking. He wanted to include things which would add both to delineation of his principal characters and to the entertainment values of his picture. Result: for a week they went on shooting, adding this and tossing in that, in the old "shooting off the cuff" style — a style which, incidentally, produced "Intolerance" and "Birth of a Nation."

It's Revolution!

Upshot was the scene as finally filmed included a lot of guests with lines to speak, a special song with a hoofer (type of the Nineties) to sing it, a chorus of can-can girls and Welles dancing with them. He even painstakingly learned the dance routine.

In the matter of lighting his sets, too, Welles has worked a revolution. Hollywood for years has been accustomed to light its sets from the top. That means, of course, no ceilings. But Welles blandly said a room wasn't a room without ceilings, and he wanted ceilings.

So something new in lighting effects can be looked for in "Citizen Kane."

Incidentally, of course, the use of ceilings necessitated new ways of recording sound. Not to become technical, sound engineers have been accustomed to poke the recording mike on the end of a long arm above the heads of actors. But how to do it with a ceiling in the room — a ceiling which would stop the mike, and also would record its shadow cast by the lights?

No wonder Hollywood was talking months in advance about "Citizen Kane" with a curiosity all but unparalleled. Only Selznick's "Gone With the Wind" when in the making, and Chaplin's "The Great Dictator," aroused comparable speculation.

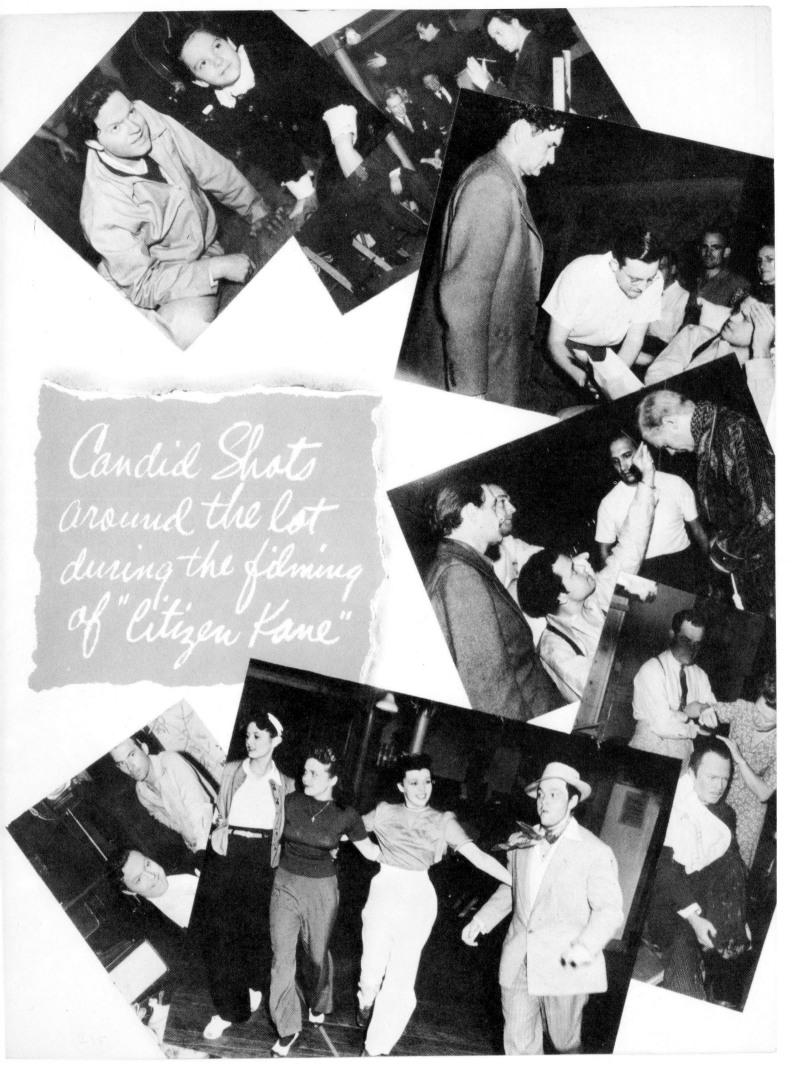

Candid Shots around the lot during the filming of "Citizen Kane"

236   CITIZEN KANE